FICTION CATALOG

2003 SUPPLEMENT
TO THE
FOURTEENTH EDITION

EDITED BY

JOHN GREENFIELDT

NEW YORK AND DUBLIN
THE H.W. WILSON COMPANY
2004

Library of Congress Control number 00-054645

ISBN 0-8242-1005-0

Printed in the United States of America

PREFACE

This 2003 Supplement to the Fourteenth Edition of *Fiction Catalog* lists 526 works of English-language adult fiction. Included among these are 13 analytic entries for novelettes and composite works, some of which may have previously been published separately. Although out-of-print titles are eligible for inclusion in the belief that good fiction is not obsolete simply because it goes out of print, no out-of-print titles are listed in this Supplement.

The titles listed in the Supplement were selected on the basis of reviews and the advice of experts in an attempt to include not only the most popular fiction but also a representative collection of literary and genre titles.

Prices quoted have been obtained from the publishers and are as current as possible. The Direction for Use should be consulted for further information about the content and arrangement of the Supplement.

The H. W. Wilson Company sincerely thanks those publishers who have supplied copies of their books and provided information about prices and editions.

DIRECTIONS FOR USE

Fiction Catalog is arranged in two parts as described below.

Part 1 lists works of fiction in alphabetical order by the last name of the author or by title if that is the main entry. Bibliographical data provided include author, title, publisher, date of publication, paging, price, ISBN designation, and Library of Congress control number. A descriptive summary and, in most instances, an excerpt from a reviewing source follow.

References are made from variant forms of authors' names and from names of joint authors. Analytical entries, which are introduced by the word "*In*," are made for parts of composite works.

Part 2 is a Title and Subject Index. Each book is listed under title, which is followed by the name of the author under which the entry of the book will be found in Part 1. Books are also listed under their main subjects or themes, as well as under headings for genre, form, and literary technique if appropriate. Subject headings and subject cross references are printed in capital letters.

FICTION CATALOG

2003 SUPPLEMENT

A

Abrahams, Peter, 1947-

Their wildest dreams. Ballantine Bks. 2003 291p $24.95

ISBN 0-345-43939-2   LC 2002-43655

"Nicholas is slowly losing his zest for writing as the sales of his last crime novel plummet. . . . To spice up his life, Nick heads to a small town on the Mexican border, where he stumbles into a strip club patronized by Clay, a crooked detective. Stripping for the house is Mackey, who has troubles of her own. Stuck with an IRS bill from her ex-husband, she scrubs toilets and bares almost all to pay the mortgage. To top it off, she is raising her teenage daughter alone. When Mackey meets Nick, their lives are never the same again." Libr J

"The author's up-to-the-minute pop-culture references lend an easygoing immediacy, and his wry humor is spot on." Publ Wkly

Abu-Jaber, Diana

Crescent. Norton 2003 349p $24.95

ISBN 0-393-05747-X   LC 2002-152907

"Sirine's now-deceased missionary parents were Iraqi and American; she's been raised since she was nine by her beloved Iraqi uncle. Her world is his house, the café where she is chef, and the air of Los Angeles. She's nearly 40, and inside her pale skin and green eyes she feels the rhythms of her uncle's Arabic stories and the scent of Eastern spices. Hanif ('Han'), a professor of Arabic literature at the local university comes to the café for the tastes of home, and he and Sirine fall into an affair of wild, sweet tenderness. . . . Abu-Jaber's language is miraculous, whether describing the texture of Han's skin or Sirine's way with an onion. It is not possible to stop reading." Booklist

Adam, Christina

Love and country. Little, Brown 2003 276p $23.95

ISBN 0-316-73500-0   LC 2003-40148

"In a small Idaho town, new arrival Kenny Swanson is still off-balance from his parents' divorce. A highschool freshmen, he is not allowed to pursue his passion for bronc riding because his mother, Lenna, can't afford insurance. Lenna fears her life is becoming the stuff of country songs and struggles to balance her mothering instinct with her own need for love. On the other side of the tracks, Cynthia Dustin, a highschool senior and an aspiring pianist, has yet to find a single foothold in her relationship with her hard-edged father. Linking them all is Roddy Moyers, a handsome, free-spirited rodeo hero." Booklist

"Adam's loving portrayal of Idaho ranch country . . .

and her strong supporting cast of hardscrabble cowboys and local eccentrics gives depth and texture to her tale." Publ Wkly

Alexie, Sherman, 1966-

Ten little Indians; stories. Grove Press 2003 243p $24

ISBN 0-8021-1744-9   LC 2003-44832

Analyzed in Short story index

Contents: The search engine; Lawyer's league; Can I get a witness?; Do not go gentle; Flight patterns; The life and times of Estelle Walks Above; Do you know where I am?; What you pawn I will redeem; What ever happened to Frank Snake Church?

"These short stories feature Spokane Indians from many urban walks of life. Alexie's characters include a student, a lawyer, a basketball player, and a feminist mother; their stories might be angry, tragic, humorous, or ironic—but they are all believable, and irresistibly engaging." SLJ

Ali, Monica

Brick lane; a novel. Scribner 2003 369p $25

ISBN 0-7432-4330-7   LC 2003-42795

"Nazeen, a young Bangladeshi woman, moves to London's Bangla Town (around the street of the title) in the mid-nineteen eighties after an arranged marriage with an older man. Seen through Nazeen's eyes, England is at first utterly baffling, but over the seventeen years of the narrative (which takes us into the post-September 11th era), she gradually finds her way, bringing up two daughters and eventually starting an all-female tailoring business. . . . In Ali's subtle narration, Nazeen's mixture of traditionalism, and adaptability, of acceptence and restlessness, emerges as a quiet strength." New Yorker

Alison, Jane

The marriage of the sea. Farrar, Straus & Giroux 2003 262p $24

ISBN 0-374-19941-8   LC 2002-33887

"The fulcrum of this novel is Oswaldo, a frail, elderly, and very rich Venetian. He funds a foundation that gives grants to artists. One recipient, Anton, a struggling architect nearing 40, reluctantly leaves his wife in New Orleans and goes to Venice on a grant to teach architecture. In Manhattan, artist Lach abandons his lover, Vera, and flees to Venice for a romantic rendezvous. But Vera has won a prize from Oswaldo's foundation, so she also embarks for Italy. Meanwhile, Max quits London for New Orleans, ostensibly to accept a chair in the History of Food, but primarily to woo Lucinde, an events planner. As soon as Max arrives, however, Lucinde flies to Venice to stay with Oswaldo, an old mentor of hers." Publ Wkly

The author "wonderfully captures the romantically stymied antics of smart people who lack the emotional grit needed to figure out the relationship they are in before drifting on to the next." Libr J

Allan, John B.

For works written by this author under other names see Stark, Richard; Westlake, Donald E.

Ammaniti, Niccolò, 1966-

I'm not scared; translated from the Italian by Jonathan Hunt. Canongate 2003 200p $23

ISBN 1-84195-297-4

"During a piercingly hot summer, a few kilometres from a bone-dry hamlet in rural Tuscany, a shy, nervy, nine-year-old boy called Michele explores a derelict house and discovers, under moldering leaves, a horrifying secret. The novel is saved from sensationalism by Ammaniti's almost cinematic ability to conjure detail." New Yorker

Andrews, Colin *See* Wilson, F. Paul (Francis Paul)

Antunes, António Lobo, 1942-

The inquisitors' manual; translated by Richard Zenith. Grove Press 2003 435p $25

ISBN 0-8021-1732-5   LC 2002-33858

Original Portuguese edition, 1997

"Antonio de Oliveira Salazar is not the best known of 20th-century dictators, but he was as cruel and ruthless as any of them in his rule over Portugal from 1932 to 1968 . . . . [The author] recreates the harrowing story of Salazar's regime, building gradually from the petty problems and thoughts of a host of characters, related in stream of consciousness, to blunt exposition of the inhuman inner workings and brutal violence of authoritarianism." Publ Wkly

"Lobo Antunes, one of the most skillfull psychological portraitists writing anywhere, renders the turpitude of an entire society through an impasto of intensely individual voices." New Yorker

Armitage, G. E. *See* Edric, Robert, 1956-

Ashley, Renée

Someplace like this. Permanent Press (Sag Harbor) 2003 192p $26

ISBN 1-57962-090-6   LC 2002-38188

A "novel about a couple who move from New York City to their island summer home in an attempt to repair their fractured marriage. The story is told from the point of view of 37-year-old Dore, a thoughtful, withdrawn woman whose discontent with her husband, Evan, is so profound that she declares on the eve of her anniversary, 'Tommorow we've been married at least a thousand years.'" Publ Wkly

Atherton, Nancy

Aunt Dimity takes a holiday. Viking 2003 199p $22.95

ISBN 0-670-03200-X   LC 2002-28095

"After the reading of an earl's will results in a destructive family feud involving her own husband, Lori Shepherd requests her ghostly aunt's help. This delightful title takes place in a beautiful home fraught with danger and intrigue." Libr J

Atkinson, Kate

Not the end of the world; stories. Little, Brown 2002 244p il $23.95

ISBN 0-316-61430-0   LC 2003-40117

Analyzed in Short story index

Contents: Charlene and Trudi go shopping; Tunnel of fish; Transparent fiction; Dissonance; Sheer big waste of love; Unseen translation; Evil dopplegangers; The cat lover; The bodies vest; Temporal anomaly; Wedding favors; Pleasureland

"While not as intense or unified as Atkinson's full-length work, this is a sharp and wholly original collection." Publ Wkly

Atwood, Margaret, 1939-

Oryx and Crake; novel. Talese 2003 376p $26

ISBN 0-385-50385-7   LC 2002-73290

"Having once led a life of comfort and self-indulgence, Jimmy, now known as Snowman, has survived an ecological disaster that has destroyed the world as we know it. As he struggles to function without everythinghe once knew, including time, Snowman reflects on the past, on his relationships with two characters named Oryx and Crake, and on the role of each individual in the destruction of the natural world." Libr J

"Rigorous in its chilling insights and riveting in its fast-paced 'what if' dramatization, Atwood's superb novel is as brillantly provocative as it is profoundly engaging." Booklist

Axton, David, 1945-

For works written by this author under other names see Koontz, Dean R. (Dean Ray), 1945-

B

Bahal, Aniruddha, 1967-

Bunker 13. Farrar, Straus & Giroux 2003 345p $24

ISBN 0-374-11730-6   LC 2002-192521

This novel's "protagonist, MM, is a tough-as-nails ex-army officer turned investigative journalist with a penchant for risk, drugs and rough sex. Covering the army, MM learns that a small band of corrupt officer s in Kashmir are engaged in smuggling drugs and weapons, and he soon becomes involved in an intricate web of guerrilla fighting, espionage, Russian mobsters and nuclear missles." Publ Wkly

"The story proceeds with tremendous energy and in a whirl of gaudy literary effects from Delhi to Kashmir to Moscow and back again." N Y Times Book Rev

Baker, Kage

The anvil of the world. TOR Bks. 2003 350p $25.95

ISBN 0-7653-0818-5   LC 2003-42649

"A Tom Doherty Associates book."

"Smith agrees to lead a small caravan from desert-bound Troon to Salesh by the sea and, although inexperienced as well as incognito, gets most clients and cargo safely across the intervening, bandit-and-demon-infested wasteland. . . . Imagine an Errol Flynn classic ebulliently re-imagined by Monty Python director Terry Gilliam: that's this wacky romp whose pace never flags." Booklist

Baker, Nicholson

A box of matches. Random House 2003 178p $19.95

ISBN 0-375-50287-4   LC 2002-69704

This novel is a "comic monolog in 33 chapters written on a series of winter mornings in Maine. Emmett, the middle-aged narrator, lights a fire in the fireplace using just one wooden match, drinks his coffee, and jots down his thoughts before the rest of the family wakes. The novel ends when the match box is empty." Libr J

"Baker offers a celebration of all things mundane, such that even the most common things take on the aura of the heroic." Booklist

Baldwin, Alex

For works written by this author under other names see Griffin, W. E. B.

Baldwin, Margaret *See* Weis, Margaret, 1948-

Bannister, Jo

True witness. St. Martin's Minotaur 2002 263p $23.95

ISBN 0-312-30817-5   LC 2002-24508

"Quiet, unassuming, and harmless Daniel Hood . . . witnesses a brutal murder and then tries unsuccessfully to help police. The detective in charge, however, has his own agenda: this murder has strong connections to three ten-year-old rape/murders, and he thinks that he knows the culprit. Locals scapegoat Daniel for not identifying the bad guy until his friend Brodie—who finds things for people—acts on her own theory. This well-done British police procedural features psychological interaction, small-town insecurities, and parental fears." Libr J

Barker, Nicola, 1966-

Behindlings; a novel. Ecco Press 2002 535p $27.95

ISBN 0-06-018569-4   LC 2002-69731

In this novel, " a wily practical joker named Wesley is continually glancing behind him. The creator of the Loiter, a nationwide treasure hunt devised for a confectionary company, he is followed by a motley collection of fans as he tramps around Great Britain. The Behindlings, as Wesley calls them, spend the book debating elaborate riddles, found in candy-bar wrappers, that lead them to Canvey Island, a dreary spot in the Thames estuary. Barker is a talented writer whose verbal acuity can be exhilarating." New Yorker

Barker, Pat, 1943-

Double vision. Farrar, Straus & Giroux 2003 258p $23

ISBN 0-374-20905-7   LC 2003-54736

"Kate Frobisher, a sculptor working on a monumental figure of Jesus, is recovering from a car accident and grieving for her husband, Ben, a war photographer killed in Afghanistan. Stephen Sharkey, a journalist (and friend of Ben's) suffering from post-traumatic stress syndrome after covering Bosnia, Rwanda and other conflicts, has left London and a failed marriage to write a book about 'the way wars are represented.' An ensemble cast gathers around these two haunted figures: Stephen's brother Rob-ert and his family; Alec Braithewaite, the friendly vicar, and his Cambridge-bound daughter Justine; and Peter Wingrave, Kate's studio assistant and Justine's ex." Publ Wkly

Barker "writes superbly, with economy and a lovely talent for darting images. The subject matter is dark, and much is left unsaid, but the reader is drawn on, from page to page." Economist

Barnard, Robert

The mistress of Alderley. Scribner 2003 281p $24

ISBN 0-7432-3688-2   LC 2002-30461

"Caroline Fawley, the weekend mistress of a married tycoon named Marius Fleetwood, glories in her unorthodox status. She lives on a gracious Yorkshire estate, accepted by all the nice people in the village. Her younger children get on swimmingly with her lover's son, and everyone admires her grown daughter, who is poised to make a brillant debut as an opera singer. It's all so very civilized—until Marius is murdered and these perfectly lovely people turn perfectly hateful." N Y Times Book Rev

Barr, Nevada

Flashback. Putnam 2003 387p il $24.95

ISBN 0-399-14975-9   LC 2002-68264

This Anna Pigeon mystery is "set in little-known Dry Tortugas National Park, 70 miles off Key West in the Gulf of Mexico. Anna takes up her post on Garden Key, home to Fort Jefferson, a notorious Union prison during the Civil War, after fleeing a marriage proposal from just-divorced Sheriff Paul Davidson. As she goes about her duties, Anna quickly becomes ensnared in one life-threatening situation after another." Publ Wkly

"Barr's technique of flashing between the past and present in intervening chapters works magically, weaving the two together into an exciting climax." Booklist

Barry, Max

Jennifer Government; a novel. Doubleday 2003 321p $19.95

ISBN 0-385-50759-3   LC 2002-19436

"Free enterprise runs amok in Barry's satirical near-future nightmare: the American government has been privatized and now runs most of the world, including 'the Australian territories of the U.S.A.,' where the book is set. American corporations sponsor everything from schools to their employee's identities, and literally go to war with one another. By taking a drink at the wrong water cooler, Hack Nike, a merchandising officer at the athletic shoe company whose name he bears, is coerced into a nefarious marketing plot to raise demand for Nike's new $2,500 sneakers by shooting teenagers." Publ Wkly

"Though pensive readers may extract political commentary from it, Barry's latest novel has more value as entertainment. A refreshingly creative and unique read." Booklist

Basch, Rachel

The passion of Reverend Nash. Norton 2003 330p $23.95

ISBN 0-393-05768-2   LC 2003-1045

Basch, Rachel—*Continued*

This novel revolves around " Rev. Jordanna Nash, the new minister at Hutchinson Congregational Church. Jordanna has the support of her sister, who helped her get the job, and her dynamic personality and massive presence—she's over six feet tall—to win over her congregation. But just as things seem to be going well, her professional and personal lives begin to unravel." Libr J

"Only after humbly assessing and forgiving her own shortcomings is Jordanna able to figuratively rise again in this uplifting—but never saccharine—tale of faith, doubt, and redemption." Booklist

Bastable, Bernard

See also Barnard, Robert

Baxter, Charles

Saul and Patsy. Pantheon Bks. 2003 317p $24
ISBN 0-375-41029-5   LC 2003-42027

"Young-marrieds Saul and Patsy move to Five Oaks from Evanston, Ill., when Saul is hired to teach at the local high school. They rent a farmhouse, where they make love in every room and even in the backyard, settling into the rhythms of domestic life. Patsy, a former modern dancer who finds work as a bank teller, gives birth to a daughter, and with infinite patience tolerates her 'professional worrier' of a husband. The narrative is dense with quotidian detail, precisely charted shifts of consciousness and pitch-perfect moments of emotional truth." Publ Wkly

Baxter, Stephen

Evolution; a novel. Del Rey/Ballantine Bks. 2003 578p $25.95
ISBN 0-345-45782-X   LC 2002-31422

"As a group scientists gathers in the South Pacific for a conference to save the human race from extinction, their actions represent the culmination of millions of years of struggle by their primate ancestors to survive in an ever-changing world. . . . [Baxter] uses a modern-day story as a frame within which he relates a series of vignettes tracing the history of the evolution of intelligent life on Earth, from its mammalian beginnings in the Cretaceous era to the present. Spanning more than 165 million years and encompassing the entire planet, Baxter's ambitious saga provides both an exercise in painless paleontology and superb storytelling." Libr J

Beaton, M. C.

Death of a village; a Hamish Macbeth mystery. Mysterious Press 2003 245p
ISBN 0-89296-677-7   LC 2002-75360

"Macbeth knows something is amiss in the village of Stoyre, because the residents have become even more religious and closemouthed than usual. Discovering and rooting out the cause will cost him dearly. All Macbeth's talents are on display as he performs a heroic rescue, outwits some crooks and meets violence with violence. For all his nonchalance, the laconic Macbeth does his best to protect his people and preserve his way of life among them." Publ Wkly

Bellows, Nathaniel

On this day; a novel. HarperCollins Pubs. 2003 265p $24.95
ISBN 0-06-051211-3   LC 2002-27272

"Narrator Warren is 18 and his sister Joan is 20 when their father dies of cancer and their mother falls apart and eventually commits suicide. Soon afterward, their father's business partner seizes the opportunity to take over their nursery business and cut Joan and Warren off. Focusing on small family moments, the eloquent yet down-to-earth narrative balances gut-wrenching scenes of grief with some funny, ironic passages." Publ Wkly

Berger, Thomas, 1924-

Best friends; a novel. Simon & Schuster 2003 209p $24
ISBN 0-7432-4183-5   LC 2002-42617

"Roy Courtright is a bit of an ascetic, a wealthy vintage auto dealerwho stays fit, and something of a womanizer, although more romantic than rake. Sam Grandy is a vastly overweight spendthrift with a sleek banker wife named Kristin. Their lifelong friendship is tested when Sam's heart attack throws together Roy and Kristin, who asks Roy to stop bailing out Sam (he now wants $50,000). The relationship between this formerly standoffish pair heats up, and Sam's games and tricks cause the situation to deteriorate further." Libr J

"The motor of the novel's intellectual ingenuity, its comedy and its considerable suspense is the transformation of the indicative into the conditional. Three-way betrayal is not only the plot but a theme inherent in the title." N Y Times Book Rev

Bing, Stanley

You look nice today; a novel. Bloomsbury Press 2003 291p $24.95
ISBN 1-58234-280-6   LC 2003-60092

This "novel concerns one Robert (Harb) Harbert, who seems too human to last at the Global Fiduciary Trust Company. . . . In fact, Harb's undoing is his compassion for his secretary, an apparently vulnerable creature named CarolAnne. She repays his cloying kindnesses (generous raises, a car, an apartment) with a harassment suit." New Yorker

"The density of detail makes for slow going early in the novel, but the account of the civil trial that follows is a riveting and often hilarious account of CaroleAnne's fabrications and the corporate legal response." Publ Wkly

Birdwell, Cleo *See* DeLillo, Don

Blake, James Carlos

Under the skin; a novel. Morrow 2003 292p $25.95
ISBN 0-380-97751-6   LC 2002-23892

"Set in Galveston, with forays into west Texas and Mexico during Prohibition, this is the story of Jimmy Youngblood, bastard son of a Pancho Villa lieutenant, who grows up to be bodyguard and hit man for Galveston gangsters Rose and Sam Maceo. . . .A love affair with the young wife of an elderly Mexican warlord adds still other dimensions to this tough and tender story of lawlessness and retribution, exposing the human frailties of the hardest of criminals." Libr J

Blanchard, Alice

The breathtaker. Warner Bks. 2003 391p $24.95
ISBN 0-446-53139-1   LC 2003-45059

Blanchard, Alice—*Continued*

"Promise, Oklahoma, may not be much, but it is ground zero for storm chasers, an eccentric mix of meteorologists, amateur scientists, and plain-old crazies who stalk tornadoes like kids stalk ice-cream trucks. Police chief Charlie Grover is assessing the damage from a recent storm when he discovers the Pepper family. Husband, wife, and teenage daughter all killed—presumably storm victims, but Grover suspects a serial killer among the storm chasers." Booklist

"Blanchard makes a bold move by linking her villain to tornadoes—each such powerful forces of destruction and chaos—and while it's a little far-fetched, it pays off in this dark depiction of environmental and human turmoil." Publ Wkly

Blanchard, Keith

The deed; a novel. Simon & Schuster 2003 304p $23

ISBN 0-7432-2387-X   LC 2002-29435

"A missing 17th-century deed to the island of Manhattan has a young advertising executive, a petty law student and a couple of mobsters in a tailspin in Blanchard's. . .novel." Publ Wkly

"There is a winning sentimentality and a lot of fun to be found in Blanchard's urban fantasy." N Y Times Book Rev

Blevins, Meredith

The hummingbird wizard. Forge 2003 400p $24.95

ISBN 0-7653-0769-3   LC 2003-46849

"A Tom Doherty Associates book"

"Ever since she lost her husband in a motorcycle accident, Annie Szabo has tried to steer clear of his unconventional Gypsy family—especially Mina, her disapproving mother-in-law, who also happens to be a fortune-teller, and the alcoholic, free-wheeling sister-in-law who has botched her marriage to Jerry, Annie's oldest friend. When Jerry dies under suspicious circumstances, Annie joins Mina in tracking down a murderer. . . .Blevins flavors her lively prose with frequent humor and unexpected twists." Libr J

Block, Lawrence, 1938-

Small town. Morrow 2003 448p $24.95

ISBN 0-06-001190-4   LC 2002-31536

The novel's "cast includes a novelist whose next book becomes a hot property after police suspect him of murdering a real-estate agent, a beautiful folk-art dealer whose string of sexual adventures are triggered by the killing, a gay housecleaner who keeps finding his clients dead, and a serial killer who lost his family in the collapse of the World Trade Center." Libr J

"This is a novel at once profoundly disturbing, graphically erotic, satiric, and above all, entertaining." Booklist

Blunt, Giles

The delicate storm. Putnam 2003 301p

ISBN 0-399-14865-5   LC 2002-36817

"A Marian Wood book"

"The freakish weather casts a spooky fog around Algonquin Bay, melts the ice on Lake Nipissing and rouses hibernating bears from their caves. When human body parts are found in the woods, Detective John Cardinal and his partner, Lise Delorme, are quick to recognize them as the leftover meal of hungry bears. But their macabre case turns uglier once the Canadian Security Intelligence Service. . .steps in and tries to pass the victim off as an anonymous American tourist." N Y Times Book Rev

"In a genre where writers often compete to create vile, loathsome villains perpetrating outrageous crimes, Blunt stands as a master craftsman who shows us not only darkness, but also decency." Publ Wkly

Bourdain, Anthony

The Bobby Gold stories. Bloomsbury Pub. 2003 165p $19.95

ISBN 1-582-34233-4   LC 2003-41882

First published 2002 in the United Kingdom with title: Bobby Gold

The author "tells the story of Bobby Gold, probably the world's most unlikely gangster. A nice Jewish premed student implicated in a drug deal gone bad. Bobby goes to prison for 10 years and emerges with an entirely different set of uses for his knowledge of anatomy. Once released, he goes to work for his old friend Eddie Fish, a mobster turned nightclub owner, and falls in love with Nikki, a boisterous sous-chef with dangerous ambitions. Bobby and Nikki get involved in a botched robbery, forcing both to run for their loves. . . .Readers will. . .be delighted by Bourdain's charming, rugged sensibility, like a modern-day Damon Runyon, and his gourmet blend of wit, suspense and style." Publ Wkly

Bova, Ben, 1932-

Saturn. TOR Bks. 2003 412p $24.95

ISBN 0-312-87218-6   LC 2003-40216

"A Tom Doherty Associates book"

"When Earth's leadership decides to 'encourage' its dissidents to leave the planet aboard an interstellar habitat destined for Saturn, Susan Lane joins the expedition, eager to begin a new life. Attracted to Malcolm Eberly, the charismatic director of the habitat, Susan (now calling herself Holly) dedicates herself to the task of helping Malcolm organize life aboard the habitat, remaining blissfully unaware of the sinister politics going on among the habitat's leaders and blinding herself to Malcolm's real agenda." Libr J

"Bova is definitely the man to do justice to the astronomical marvels of the Saturnian system with its enormous potential as a second home for humanity, especially in the complex environments of its moons. Loud, prolonged applause, then, for the strengths of this book." Booklist

Bowen, Peter, 1945-

Badlands. St. Martin's Minotaur 2003 250p $23.95

ISBN 0-312-26252-3   LC 2002-37196

Montana sheriff Gabriel Du Pré's "suspicions are aroused when the Host of Yahweh immediately destroys the ranch buildings, sells the livestock and erects a makeshift metal chapel for secret rites. Soon, reportsof mass murders and suicides bring in cautious FBI agents ever mindful of the Waco debacle. Du Pré's blunt speech and sometimes opaque thought patterns can be hard to follow, but his pursuits of wrongdoers over cliffs, canyons and arid river beds are truly riveting." Publ Wkly

Box, C. J.

Winterkill; a novel. Putnam 2003 372p $23.95

ISBN 0-399-15045-5   LC 2002-37120

As the story begins, "Joe Pickett, game warden of Wyoming's Twelve Sleep County, is caught in a mountain blizzard with a dead body beside him in his pick-up truck. The body belongs to a much-hated federal bureaucrat, who may have been killed by a group of survivalists calling themselves the Sovereigns. . . .Box handles this controversial material superbly, showing vividly how government rigidity causes human tragedy in the name of patriotism. Pickett remains an utterly sympathetic, Gary Cooperish hero, but as the series developes he has begun to darken to darken noticeably." Booklist

Boyd, William, 1952-

Any human heart; a novel. Knopf 2003 498p $26

ISBN 0-375-41493-2   LC 2002-27451

"At 17, Logan Mountstuart starts a journal. He faithfully keeps it, except when he can't bear to, until his death at 85. It records, mostly at a cool panoramic distance but with plunges into close-up shattering, his life as a minor British writer, art dealer, spy, chance aquaintance of dozens of the famous, repeatedly ill-fated husband and lover, and broken-compass navigator through the mild pleasures and harsh poisons of English life over most of the 20th century." N Y Times Book Rev

"This flawed yet immensely appealing protagonist is one of Boyd's most distinctive creations, and his voice—articulate, introspective, urbane, stoically philosophical in the face of countless disappointments—engages the readers empathy." Publ Wkly

Boyle, T. Coraghessan

Drop City. Viking 2003 443p $25.95

ISBN 0-670-03172-0   LC 2002-66371

"After riding cross-country together, Star and Ronnie join Norm Sender's California commune and quickly move in different directions. Ronnie attempts to take as many drugs and make it with as many women as possible, while Star gets involved with the draft-dodging Marco. Meanwhile, Norm finds out that the board of health is going to condemn the buildings and, in a classic evocation of 1960s romanticism and naïveté, informs the group that they are moving to his uncle's cabin in Alaska." Libr J

"But for all its glorious physicality and riveting action, this is a frank and penetrating critique of a naïïve but courageous time, a stinging indictment of machismo and a paean to womanhood and an unabashed celebration of true love and liberty." Booklist

Bradbury, Ray, 1920-

Bradbury stories; 100 of his most celebrated tales. Morrow 2003 893p $29.95

ISBN 0-06-054242-X   LC 2003-42189

Analyzed in Short story index

Contents: The whole town's sleeping; The rocket; Season of disbelief; And the rock cried out; The drummer boy of Shiloh; The beggar on O'Connell Bridge; The flying machine; Heavy-set; The first night of Lent; Lafayette, farewell; Remember Sascha?; Junior; That woman on the lawn; February 1999: Ylla; Banshee; One for his lordship, and one for the road!; The Laurel and Hardy love affair; Unterderseaboat doktor; Another fine mess; The dwarf; A wild night in Galway; The wind; No news, or what killed the dog?; A little journey; Any friend of Nicholas Nickleby's is a friend of mine; The garbage collector; The visitor; The man; Henry the ninth; The messiah; Bang! you're dead!; Darling Adolf; The beautiful shave; Colonel Stonesteel's genuine home-made truly Egyptian mummy; I see you never; The exiles; At midnight, in the month of June; The witch door; The watchers; 2004-05: the naming of names; Hopscotch; The illustrated man; The dead man; June 2001: and the moon be still as bright; The burning man; G.B.S.—Mark V; A blade of grass; The sound of summer running; And the sailor, home from the sea; The lonely ones; The Finnegan; On the Orient, North; The smiling people; The fruit at the bottom of t

he bowl; Bug; Downwind from Gettysburg; Time in thy flight; Changeling; The dragon; Let's play "poison"; The cold wind and the warm; The meadow; The Kilimanjaro device; The man in the Rorschach shirt; Bless me, father, for I have sinned; The pedestrian; Trapdoor; The swan; The sea shell; Once more, Legato; June 2003: way in the middle of the air; The wonderful death of Dudley Stone; By the numbers!; April 2005: Usher II; The square pegs; The trolley; The smile; The miracles of Jamie; A far-away guitar; The cistern; The machineries of joy; Bright phoenix; The wish; The lifework of Juan Diaz; Time intervening/interim; Almost the end of the world; The great collision of Monday last; The poems; April 2026: the long years; Icarus Montgolfier Wright; Death and the maiden; Zero hour; The Toynbee convector; Forever and the earth; The handler; Getting through Sunday somehow; The pumpernickel; Last rites; The watchful poker chip of H. Matisse; All on a summer's night

"This massive retrospective of self-selected Bradbury stories offers a compendium of his eccentrics, misfits, losers, and small-town dreamers, who typically inhabit an uncanny setting or confront a strange, unsettling situation." Libr J

Bragg, Melvyn, 1939-

A son of war; a novel. Arcade Pub. 2003 426p $25.95

ISBN 1-559-70686-4   LC 2002-44058

This sequel to A soldier's return "finds Sam and Ellen Richardson and their son, Joe, still in the dreary slums of Wigton, waiting for their chance for a new council house in a developing outskirt. Times are tough, and they are barely scraping by." Libr J

"A hauntingly evocative slice of postwar life." Booklist

Bram, Christopher, 1952-

Lives of the circus animals; a novel. HarperCollins Pubs. 2003 341p $24.95

ISBN 0-06-054253-5   LC 2002-192195

"Henry Lewse is a British actor starring in a Broadway musical. Jessie Doyle is his much-needed personal assistant. Her brother, Caleb, is a playwright whose latest play was shredded by theater critic Kenneth Prager. Frank, Jessie's new boyfriend, is directing a reality play in Apartment 2B. Toby, Caleb's former lover, is trying hard to break into show biz." Libr J

Bram, Christopher, 1952-—*Continued*

"Bram has a sophisticated understanding of celebrity and the intersection of gay and straight worlds. His savvy—and his easy familiarity with the New York theater scene—gives edge and nuance to this witty entertainment." Publ Wkly

Braun, Lilian Jackson

The cat who brought down the house. Putnam 2003 p. cmp

ISBN 0-399-14942-2   LC 2002-68138

"Thelma Thackery, in her 80s, comes back to Pickax after a long Hollywood career in food. She's turning the old opera house into a revival movie theater, sparks a few other local delights, but can't seem to get her ne'er-do-well nephew to do well at all. Qwill plugs away at old lies and a death in Thelma's family. We learn stuff through his newspaper column and his journal entries, and through the responses of his Siamese cat, KoKo. All the murders are offstage: the fun part is in food, clothing, and the quotidian joys of small-town life." Booklist

Brett, Simon, 1945-

Murder in the museum; a Fethering mystery. Berkley Prime Crime 2003 341p $22.95

ISBN 0-425-19043-9   LC 2003-45329

In this episode "Carole Seddon finds herself a member of the Bracketts Trust, which is responsible for the upkeep of Bracketts, former home of West Sussex litterateur Esmond Chadleigh. Tension arises between the Trust's new director, Gina Locke, who represents the new world of 'management structures,' and former trustee Sheila Cartwright, who's from the old school volunteers. While they wrangle over Bracket's future, a skeleton turns up in the garden." Publ Wkly

"Another marvelous mix of social satire and traditional cozy." Booklist

Brink, André Philippus, 1935-

The other side of silence; [by] André Brink. Harcourt 2003 c2002 311p

ISBN 0-15-100770-5   LC 2002-32748

First published 2002 in the United Kingdom

This novel "takes as its point of departure a German program at the turn of the twentieth century whereby women were shipped out to Germany's colonies in South-West Africa (now Namibia) to be wives—or, failing that, sexual fodder—for the colonizers. Brink's protagonist, Hannah X., an abused orphan from Bremen, is eager for the imagined romance of the desert, but life in the colonies turns out to be even worse than what she has known before. . . .Brink's powerful and brutal story is an effective response to those who suspected that the end of apartheid would leave him without a subject, and a shrewd meditation on the dehumanizing power of hatred." New Yorker

Brockmeier, Kevin

The truth about Celia. Pantheon Bks. 2003 216p $22

ISBN 0-375-42135-1   LC 2002-35513

This novel is "presented as if written by one Christopher Brooks, a science-fiction writer. In 1997, Christopher lives happily with his wife, Janet, and seven-year-

old daughter, Celia, in a beautifully preserved 19th-century house in a peaceful small town. One morning, while Celia and her father are home alone, Celia vanishes from the backyard. There are no clues, no suspects. . . .The fragmented narration may deflect some readers, but others will cherish Brockmeier's seductive turns of phrase and sharp imagination." Publ Wkly

Brookner, Anita

Making things better; a novel. Random House 2003 275p $23.95

ISBN 0-375-50888-0   LC 2002-69860

This novel "describes the daily routines and musings of Julius Herz, who at 73 has been forced into retirement when his shop is sold. He has been a passive player in his own life, not so much making decisions as accepting the anxieties and responsibilities thrust upon him by his inept family." Libr J

Brookner "never steps out from behind the curtain, never indulges in jazzy little riffs to show you how clever she is. All she does is tell her stories. N Y Times Book Rev

Brown, Dale, 1956-

Air Battle Force. Morrow 2003 xx, 426p $25.95

ISBN 0-06-009409-5   LC 2002-41092

In this thriller, the "Taliban have plans to take over oil-rich Turkmenistan, thus causing a global crisis. Maj. Gen Patrick McLanahan and the Air Battle Force are tasked to stop them." Libr J

"This absorbing techno-thriller follows the author's established pattern of fast action in the air and on the ground, its hard-driving protagonists equipped with an arsenal of futuristic hardware." Publ Wkly

Brown, Dan, 1964-

The Da Vinci code; a novel. Doubleday 2003 454p $24.95

ISBN 0-385-50420-9   LC 2002-40918

"In a two-day span, American symbologist Robert Langdon finds himself accused of murdering the curator of the Louvre, on the run through the streets of Paris and London, and teamed up with French-cryptologist Sophie Neveu to uncover nothing less than the secret location of the Holy Grail. It appears that a conservative Catholic bishop might be on the verge of destroying the Grail, which includes an alternate history of Christ that could bring down the church. . . .The story is full of brain-teasing puzzles and fascinating insights into religious history and art." Booklist

Brown, Fredric, 1906-1972

Bloody moonlight

 In Brown, F. Hunter and hunted p309-457

Compliments of a fiend

 In Brown, F. Hunter and hunted p459-620

Dead ringer

 In Brown, F. Hunter and hunted p147-308

Fabulous clipjoint

 In Brown, F. Hunter and hunted p1-145

Hunter and hunted; the Ed and Am Hunter novels. Stewart Masters Pub. 2002 620p (Frederic Brown mystery library, pt. 1) $29.99

ISBN 0-9718185-0-9   LC 2002-8826

Brown, Fredric, 1906-1972—*Continued*

First title in the projected seven volume set of the author's mystery fiction

"The Ed an Am Hunter novels star a nephew (Ed) and uncle (Am) who begin as amateur sleuths but eventually become professional detectives. Of the four novels collected here—The Fabulous Clipjoint(1947), The Dead Ringer (1948), The Bloody Moonlight (1949), and Compliments of a Fiend (1950)—the best s the first, in which 18-year-old Ed helps his uncle solve the murder of Ed's father. The setting is a beautifully realized postwar Chicago. Like Hammett, Brown relishes specificity of place as he tracks Ed and Am's peregrinations across the city's North Side slum. . . . The streets are mean, but the characters are amiable, and the prose is almost jaunty." Booklist

Brown, Larry, 1951-

The rabbit factory. Free Press 2003 339p $25
ISBN 0-7432-4523-7   LC 2002-45591

Set in or near Memphis, this novel focuses on "hooker Anjalee; older man Arthur along with his younger, sexually dissatisfied wife, Helen; 'gunslinger' Frankie and his just desserts; ex-prisoner Domino and his sordid attempts to make a go of it outside the big house, and other equally 'attractive' men and women working out their own destinies even when love, sex and money (or the lack of any or all of the three) get in their way. . . . You definitely can't go wrong with a novel that has dogs as fully developed characters in their own right." Booklist

Browne, Marshall, 1935-

Eye of the abyss. Thomas Dunne Bks. 2003 c2002 290p $23.95
ISBN 0-312-31156-7   LC 2003-47297

"Franz Schmidt, chief auditor for a family-owned bank in an unnamed south German city, loses his eye defending a Jew attacked by Nazi thugs in 1935. A quiet and meticulous man, he apparently bears no grudges, though his wife and best friend aren't so sure. Three years later, when his bank is chosen as a repository for large amounts of Nazi Party cash, the other shoe drops, and Schmidt becomes a man of action. First, he takes great risks trying to help a female bank employee whose mother was Jewish. Then he dreams up a plan to punish Dietrich, the sleek and seductive party operative placed inside the bank." Publ Wkly

"Like the shifting reality of Schmidt's life, the changes in his character are as subtle as they are harrowing, a triumph of Browne's clean, exacting style." N Y Times Book Rev

Bruen, Ken

The guards. St. Martin's Minotaur 2003 291p $23.95
ISBN 0-312-30355-6   LC 2002-35855

"Ousted from Ireland's police force, the Garda Siochana (or Guards), Jack Taylor ekes out a living on the unmodernized margins of Galway. . . .When Ann Henderson walks into the pub that serves as Taylor's office, asking him to prove that her daughter Sarah was not a suicide but a murder victim, Taylor finds himself investigating a sex-and-murder tangle—and in love." Booklist

"Bruen's astringent prose and death's-head humor keep this quest for redemption from getting maudlin, just as his 'tapestry of talk' makes somber poetry of the barstool laments that serve as dialogue." N Y Times Book Rev

Bryan, Mike

The afterword. Pantheon Bks. 2003 195p $16
ISBN 0-375-42212-9   LC 2002-30710

In this "novel, Mike Bryan poses as an author writing a follow-up explanation of a wildly successful first novel. 'The Deity Next Door' supposedly described an ordinary man's discovery that he was 'a new and unexpected divinity' and the modest ways he put his powers to the test. . . . Supposedly hounded by readers for information about the book's genesis, the narrator of 'The Afterword' laces his thoughts on religion, contemporary society and the nature of fiction with various outtakes." N Y Times Book Rev

"Bryan brings a very human dimension to the spiritual crisis facing his protagonist by eschewing the hollow literary tricks of most postmodern fiction." Libr J

Buckley, William F. (William Frank), 1925-

Getting it right; a novel; by William F. Buckley Jr. Regnery Pub. 2002 311p $24.95
ISBN 0-89526-138-3   LC 2002-151632

"Woodroe (Woody) Raynor witnesses (and is shot in) the 1956 Hungarian Revolution while doing Mormon missionary work across the border in Austria. He returns to attend Princeton and becomes a Birch Society operative on graduation. At the founding meeting of the Young Americans for Freedom. . .Woody meets Leonora Goldstein, an acolyte in 'the Collective' surrounding Ayn Rand." Booklist

"Gussying up the epic struggle with a hearts-and-flowers romance between a Bircher and an Objectivist, Buckley has a lot of fun with the period. And if any reader doubts the truth of the story, there are footnotes aplenty." Libr J

Burdett, John

Bangkok 8. Knopf 2003 317p $24
ISBN 1-400-04044-2   LC 2002-40658

"The narrator, a Buddhist cop named Sonchai Jitplecheep, finds himself plunged into a dangerous investigation of the deaths of his partner Pichai Apiradee and U. S. Embassy Sgt. William Bradley. Sonchai is an unusual character on several levels, from the mysteries of his violent past to his conversations with the ghost of Pichai. His ambiguous feelings toward Kimberley Jones, an American FBI agent brought in to work the case, reflect his upbringing as the child of a Thai mother and an unknown American father. . . .The mix of detective work, Bangkok street life, the Thai sex trade and drug smuggling forms a powerful mélange of images and insight." Publ Wkly

Burke, James Lee, 1936-

Last car to Elysian Fields; a Dave Robicheaux novel. Simon & Schuster 2003 335p $25
ISBN 0-7432-4542-3   LC 2003-54386

Burke, James Lee, 1936-—*Continued*

"Dave Robicheaux, an Iberia Parish homicide detective with an 'abiding anger' for the corrupters of innocence and the despoilers of beauty, is roped into investigating [legendary R & B guitarist Junior] Crudup's fate by Jimmie Dolan, a priest whose moral crusades cause mobsters to put out a hit on him. Burke's heavies make great showpieces, but Max Coll, a stone killer who repents of his sins and causes all kinds of mayhem trying to do penance, knocks them all off the shelf. In the absence of plagues of locusts, a good hit man can really clean up a dirty town." N Y Times Book Rev

Busch, Frederick, 1941-

A memory of war. Norton 2003 352p $25.95

ISBN 0-393-04978-7   LC 2002-32668

"In the opening pages of Frederick Busch's. . .novel, a Manhattan psychologist named Alex Lescziak is confronted by a firts-time patient with a remarkable assertion: that he is Alex's half-brother. The patient, William Kessler, tells this story: during World War II, after Alex's late parents, Januscz and Sylvia, had escaped from Poland to England, and William's father, Otto Kessler, a German SS interpreter, was a prisoner of war there, Sylvia and Otto had an affair." N Y Times Book Rev

"While the novel's emotional landscape is bleak, Busch's portrait of a man trying to surmount his demons is masterful." Publ Wkly

Butler, Gwendoline

Coffin knows the answer. Thomas Dunne Bks. 2003 187p $22.95

ISBN 0-312-29033-0   LC 2002-41568

"Chief Commander of Police John Coffin. . .has been investigating a serial murderer in London, ultimately finding tie-ins to the 'stalker with a paedophile slant' who sent pictures to Coffin's wife. Fascinating British procedural intricacies from a talented hand." Libr J

Butterworth, W. E. (William Edmund), 1929-

For works written by this author under other names see Griffin, W. E. B.

Byatt, A. S. (Antonia Susan), 1936-

A whistling woman. Knopf 2003 429p $26

ISBN 0-375-41534-3   LC 2002-72957

A "study of England in the Swinging Sixties. . . . Having abandoned university teaching, Frederica Potter finds herself the host of a cutting-edge TV show called Through the Looking-Glass that is bringing her some unwanted fame. She's a single mom struggling with young son Leo, who is having trouble learning how to read, and in addition can't commit to lover John, whose twin, Paul, heads up a rock band called Zag and the Syzgy Zy-goats. Events conspire to draw these characters to a Body-Mind conference at a northern university plagued by an Anti-University, even as a religious cult is getting started at a farm across the way." Libr J

"There is no other writer alive who is as interested as Byatt in creating characters who are thinking women and men while at the same time recognizing the limits of cognition in the face of unreason, or love." N Y Times Book Rev

Byatt, Antonia Susan *See* Byatt, A. S. (Antonia Susan), 1936-

C

Camilleri, Andrea, 1925-

The snack thief; translated by Stephen Sartarelli. Viking 2003 $21.95p $21.95

ISBN 0-670-03223-9   LC 2003-41090

Original Italian edition, 1998

In this mystery, Sicilian Inspector Salvo Montaldo "suspects a link between the stabbing of a businessman in an apartment-house elevator and the shooting of a crewman on a fishing boat. Connecting the two are an enterprising Tunisian prostitute, now vanished, and her young son, who has been surviving by stealing lunches from schoolchildren. Montalbano fits the pieces together gradually, taking time, as always, for plenty of leisurely lunches but eventually exposing a wide-ranging plot fuelled by high-level corruption." Booklist

Camp, John, 1944-

See also Sandford, John, 1944-

Cannell, Stephen J.

Hollywood tough. St. Martin's Press 2003 346p $24.95

ISBN 0-312-29102-7   LC 2002-31878

"LAPD investigator Shane Scully agrees to return a favor to former snitch Nicky Marcella, a street hustler turned shady movie producer. He wants Shane to find Carol White, his former New Jersey high school classmate and an aspiring actress. What Shane finds is that she's abandoned her dreams for an abyss of drugs and prostitution, but her core of inherent decency touches him. When she's murdered he refuses to allow her to be dismissed as just another dead whore. . . . This is an entertaining mix of thrills, humor, and street justice." Booklist

Cantor, Jay

Great Neck; a novel. Knopf 2002 703p $29.95

ISBN 0-375-41394-4   LC 2002-67123

This novel "starts in 1960 with a group of largely Jewish grade schoolers on Long Island learning the lessons of the Holocaust, then takes them through the radical decades of Freedom Summer, Weathermen, Black Power, bombs, and courts—as both defenders and defended. Meanwhile, the group is immortalized through comic-book characters drawn in their image by another member of the group (Billy Bad Ears, in the comic), a genius and best-selling cult favorite." Libr J

A novel "so rich in character and incident that you can't help wishing it a long shelf life and many devoted readers. Overflowing with brainpower—as though all the minds Cantor investigates were somehow networked and engaged in furious serial processing—it finds room for heart, too. It is, after all, a novel about friends." N Y Times Book Rev

Carey, Edward, 1970-

Alva & Irva; the twins who saved a city. Harcourt 2003 207p il map $24

ISBN 0-15-100782-9   LC 2002-13701

Carey, Edward, 1970-—_Continued_

"Entralia, the fictitious metropolis at the heart of Edward Carey's. . . novel, exists not only in our imagination and in the pages of 'Alva & Irva' (which serves as Entralia's one and only guidebook) but in the form of tiny plasticine models of its streets and houses, seen in the appealingly smudgy photographs that punctuate the novel. A re-creation of Entralia also appears in the story of 'Alva & Irva,' since the twins of the book's title are the designer and sculptor, respectively, of their native city in miniature." N Y Times Book Rev

This novel is "mock epical in its consequential-ridiculous tone. . .and comedically symphonic in the precision and daffy chasteness of its diction. For all its ludicrousness, it is honorably pathetic, too—a genuine human comedy," Booklist

Carey, Jacqueline

The Crossley baby. Ballantine Bks. 2003 287p $23.95

ISBN 0-345-45990-3   LC 2003-545383

"Having a baby changes everything. But when your're congenitally competitive sisters, like Jean and Sunny Crossley, each vying for the right to raise their deceased sister's daughter, the more things change, the more they stay the same. A free-spirited single mom, Bridget dies during a routine operation, leaving custody of baby Jade in question. As a hotshot headhunter married more to her career than to her husband, Jean is childless by choice, but when Jade is orphaned, Jean surprises everyone by filing for adoption and surprises no one by simultaneously filing a malpractice suit. Meanwhile, Sunny, an overachieving soccer mom with two kids of her own, stays true to her nature, blithely assuming that Jade will live with her." Booklist

"If the book is a little too cluttered with interior monologues, Carey is nonetheless an engaging and often funny writer. . . . Her sharp descriptions of the sisters' various milieus give the novel its piquancy." Publ Wkly

Carey, Peter

My life as a fake. Knopf 2003 266p $24

ISBN 0-375-41498-3   LC 2003-52746

A novel told through the "eyes of Lady Sarah Wode-Douglass, editor of a struggling but prestigious London poetry journal, who one day in the early 1970s finds herself accompanying an old family friend, poet and novelist John Slater, out to Malaysia. There they encounter an eccentric Australian expatriate, Christopher Chubb, who concocted, Slater says, a huge literary hoax in Australia just after the war, creating an imaginary genius poet, Bob McCorkle, whose publication by a litle magazine led to the suicide of the magazine's editor. Now Chubb offers Lady Sarah a page of poetry that shows undoubted genius and claims it is from a book in his possession. Lady Sarah's every acquisitive instinct is inflamed, but to get her hands on the book she has to listen, as Chubb inflicts on her, Ancient Mariner-like, the amazing story of his own epic struggle with McCorkle." Publ Wkly

This work "is so confidently brilliant, so economical yet lively in its writing, so tightly fitted and continuously startling in its plot that something, we feel, must be wrong with it. It ends in a bit of a rush, and left several questions dangling in this reader's mind. Unfortunately, to spell out those questions would be to betray too much

of an intricate fictional construct where little is as it first seems and fantastic developments unfold like scenes on a fragile paper fan." New Yorker

Carroll, James

Secret father. Houghton Mifflin 2003 344p $25

ISBN 0-618-15284-9   LC 2003-41725

This work "focuses on a single weekend in 1961, just before the Berlin Wall created an impenetrable barrier between East and West. On an idealistic lark, three American high school students travel to the Communistic side of Berlin for the May Day parade. Ensnared by the East Germans for alleged currency violations, they are clapped in jail. Meanwhile, their frantic parents mobilize, with two of them traveling to Berlin to pluck the kids loose. Surprisingly, this generic plot supports a beautifully textured exploration of relationships between husbands and wives, parents and sons, friends and lovers." Libr J

Carson, Tom, 1956-

Gilligan's wake. Picador 2003 342p $25

ISBN 0-312-29123-X   LC 2002-29256

Carson "uses characters from the Gilligan's Island TV series to explore 20th-century political, literary, and pop culture. Each character is allotted a chapter, starting with Gilligan, who thinks that he's hanging out with Lawrence Ferlinghetti in San Francisco when, in fact, he is in a mental institution in Minnesota. The skipper meets John Kennedy in the Pacific. Thurston Howell III helps Alger Hiss get a government job, and Howell's wife uses opium with Gatsby's love, Daisy Buchanan. Then there's Ginger, who explores Hollywood's low-budget film industry, as the Professor works with Oppenheimer on the bomb and Mary Anne moves from Kansas to Paris and has an affair with filmmaker Jean-Luc something or other." Libr J

"The pastiche is surprisingly smart and entertaining; it offers some genuinely inspired sketches for those who know their television—and their Cold War history." Publ Wkly

Carter, Vincent O., 1924-1983

Such sweet thunder; foreword by Herbert R. Lottman. Steerforth Press 2003 537p $25.95

ISBN 1-58642-058-5   LC 2002-154280

"Written in 1963 and shelved, this hefty, astonishing novel by a black American expatriate who died in 1983 tells—in electric modernist vernacular prose—the story of a black child's life in Jim Crow America.In France during WWII, soldier Amerigo Jones thinks back on his youth in the 1920s and '30s in a black community resembling the author's native Kansas City." Publ Wkly

Cassirer, Nadine Gordimer _See_ Gordimer, Nadine, 1923-

Cavell, Benjamin

Rumble, young man, rumble. Knopf 2003 191p $22

ISBN 0-375-41464-9   LC 2002-27525

Analyzed in Short Story index

Contents: Balls, balls, balls; All the nights of the world; Killing time; Evolution; The art of the possible; Blue yonder; The death of cool; Highway; The ropes

Cavell, Benjamin—*Continued*

"Though Cavell occasionally comes on too strong, the collection is filled with dead-on, often hilarious dialogue and offers a thoughtful meditation on masculinity and class." Publ Wkly

Chalmers, Robert

Who's who in hell. Grove Press 2002 360p $13

ISBN 0-8021-3924-8 (pa)   LC 2002-21470

"Daniel, a former layabout, failed therapist and habitué of bars, writes rapier-witted obituaries for a large and unnamed London daily newspaper. His girlfriend, Laura, is an amateur sky diver who was born in America; the couple live together, eventually with their son, above the cafe she manages in London's Crouch End. . . . There are missteps, particularly in Chalmer's inept sketching of parenthood and in his largely impersonal relationship with novel's female characters, especially Laura, but these are probably to be expected—the book, to steal a title of Hornby's, is about a boy. And for that, it makes for fine and highly pleasurable reading." N Y Times Book Rev

Chappell, Helen

A whole world of trouble; a novel. Simon & Schuster 2003 213p $23

ISBN 0-7432-1529-X   LC 2003-42512

Carrie Hudson "comes home to Oysterback, Maryland, after her mother dies. Carrie, who scours estate sales and sells her treasures to antique dealers, doesn't get along with her sister Earlene on her bland husband, but the two are forced together to plan the burial of their mother, who died travellng to meet her latest boyfriend, and ex-con." Booklist

"Chappell sometimes lays on the folksy charm a little thick. . .but for the most part Carrie's sympathetic, wry voice gives some depth to what would otherwise be a predictable gallery of smalltown oddballs." Publ Wkly

Chesney, Marion

Snobbery with violence. St. Martin's Minotaur 2003 226p $22.95

ISBN 0-312-30451-X   LC 2003-41351

"Capt. Harry Cathcart, youngest son of a baron, 'fixes' ackward situations for members of the British aristocracy. When he investigates the background of a potential suitor for an earl's daughter, Cathcart proves the suitor to be a cad. In the process, though, the daughter suffers the social consequences of scandal—ostracism. Her parents send her to a 'second chance' country-house party, where she's entangled in a murder mystery, which she and Cathcart solve together. This is a delightful costume melodrama, featuring wry humor and sleuthing protagonists with a pesky love/hate relationship." Libr J

Chesnutt, Charles Waddell, 1858-1932

The conjure woman

In Chesnutt, C. W. Stories, novels & essays p1-96

The house behind the cedars

In Chesnutt, C. W. Stories, novels & essays p267-461

The marrow of tradition

In Chesnutt, C. W. Stories, novels & essays p463-718

Stories, novels & essays; [by] Charles W. Chesnutt. Library of Am. 2002 939p $35

ISBN 1-931082-06-5   LC 2001-38120

Analyzed in Short story index

Contents: The conjure woman; The wife of his youth and other stories of the color line; The house behind the cedars; The marrow of tradition; Uncollected stories; Selected essays

The conjure woman (1899): Contents: The goophered grapevine; Po' Sandy; Mars Jeem's nightmare; The conjurer's revenge; Sis' Becky's pickaninny; The gray wolf's ha'nt; Hot-foot Hannibal

The wife of his youth and other stories of the color line (1899): Contents: The wife of his youth; Her Virginia mammy; The sheriff's children; A matter of principle; Cicely's dream; The passing of Grandison; Uncle Wellington's wives; The bouquet; The web of circumstance

Includes the following uncollected stories: Dave's neckliss; A deep sleeper; Lonesome Ben; The dumb witness; The march of progress; Baxter's Procrustes; The doll; White weeds; The kiss

The house behind the cedars (1900) is " concerned with a light-complexioned black woman who is undecided whether to enjoy comfort as a white man's mistress or the sincere love of a black man." Oxford Companion to Am Lit. 6th edition

The marrow of tradition (1901) explores the struggles of black and white half-sisters. Based on the 1898 massacre in Wilmington, North Carolina, the novel explores the emerging segregationist status quo

The wife of his youth and other stories of the color line

In Chesnutt, C. W. Stories, novels & essays p97-266

Child, Lee

Persuader; a Jack Reacher novel. Delacorte Press 2003 342p $24.95

ISBN 0-385-33666-7   LC 2002-34965

"Beginning with a stunning set-piece involving the apparent kidnapping of a college student, the novel offers the brooding Reacher, a former military policeman, the chance to settle a score with an old nemesis, renegade army intelligence officer Quinn, whom Reacher believed was dead until a chance encounter on a Boston street." Booklist

"What makes the novel really zing, though, is Reacher's narration—aunique mix of the brainy and the brutal, of strategic thinking and explosive action, moral rumination and ruthless force, marking him as one of the most memorable heroes in contemporary thrillerdom." Publ Wkly

Child, Lincoln, 1957-

(jt. auth) Preston, D. Still life with crows

Chisholm, P. F., 1958-

See also Finney, Patricia, 1958-

Clark, Curt

For works written by this author under other names see Stark, Richard; Westlake, Donald E.

Clark, Nancy, 1952-

The Hills at home. Pantheon Bks. 2003 481p $25

ISBN 0-375-42203-X   LC 2002-72314

"In the summer of 1989, septuagenarian Lily Hill's serenely solitary life in her ramshackle family home in Towne, MA, comes to a screeching halt. A torrent of Hill relatives with a richly diverse menu of dysfunctional quirks pours into her life, and they forget to leave." Libr J

"The plot is mild and ambling, and the darker emotions are kept strictly offstage, but plot and angst are not the point. The point is the revelation of a particular kind of life, and at that the book succeeds brilliantly." N Y Times Book Rev

Clement, Hal, 1922-2003

Noise. TOR Bks. 2003 252p $23.95

ISBN 0-7653-0857-6   LC 2003-55987

A Tom Doherty Associates book.

"Linguist Mike Hoani arrives on the water planet Kainui to study the evolution of the language of its original Polynesian colonists. His travels on a planet with no fixed land except for floating artificial cities plunge him into a maritime adventure that tests his knowledge of both language and human nature." Libr J

"Clement skillfully weaves together challenging science, a unique familial society, and an encounter with a 'lost' city in a narrative that allows the reader to puzzle out Mike's questions along with him." Booklist

Clements, Marcelle

Midsummer. Harcourt 2003 291p $24

ISBN 0-15-100836-1   LC 2002-153525

"Taking place over eight summer weekends at a rented mansion in the Hudson River Valley, [this novel] is a portrait of a group of old friends—witty, middle-aged, neurotic, bourgeois-bohemian Manhattanites—who anticipate an idyll of leisure and gossip, only to find all their dissatisfaction and regret surfacing as they sift through past mistakes and missed opportunities." New Yorker

Clynes, Michael

For works written by this author under other names see Doherty, P. C.

Coben, Harlan, 1962-

No second chance. Dutton 2003 338p $24.95

ISBN 0-525-94729-9   LC 2002-192530

"Marc Seidman, a plastic surgeon near New York City, wakes up in a hospital to learn that he has been gravely wounded, his wife shot dead and his infant daughter, Tara, snatched. The ensuing narrative, which shuttles between third person and Marc's first person, covers more than a year in Marc's hunt for Tara." Publ Wkly

"The novel, spanning 18 months and jumping between the father and the kidnappers, sets off depth charges of meets, double-crosses, near-misses, and vengful acts. Coben holds it together with his hero's determination and smarts." Booklist

Cockey, Tim

Murder in the hearse degree. Hyperion 2003 324p $22.95

ISBN 0-7868-6712-4   LC 2002-27458

Wisecracking undertaker Hitchcock Sewell "finds out that his former squeeze, Libby Gellman, is back in town with her two children but sans husband and nanny. The nanny, surprisingly pregnant, is more than geographically distant: she's fallen from a very high bridge and drowned. Or was she pushed? The police support a knee-jerk suicide theory. The nanny's loyal mother doesn't. So Hitch sets off to see exactly what happened. . . . Brimming with humor—much of it dark—this book is perfect for the reader who has finished all the books by Janet Evanovich or Sue Grafton and doesn't know what to read next." Libr J

Coe, Tucker

For works written by this author under other names see Stark, Richard; Westlake, Donald E.

Coetzee, J. M., 1940-

Elizabeth Costello. Viking 2003 230p S21.95

ISBN 0-670-03130-5   LC 2003-60849

"Elizabeth Costello, a fictional aging Australian novelist who gained fame for a Ulysses-inspired novel in the 1960s, reveals the workings of her still-formidable mind in a series of formal addresses she either attends or delivers herself (an award acceptance speech, a lecture on a cruise ship, a graduation speech)." Publ Wkly

"There is no justice in the ability of youth to shame age, and yet it's a fundamental fact of the embodied life. Coetzee's unflinching exploration of this desolate and strangely beautiful terrain represents the cruelest and best use to which literature can be put." N Y Times Book Rev

Coffey, Brian, 1945-

For works written by this author under other names see Koontz, Dean R. (Dean Ray), 1945-

Coghlan, Peggie, 1920-

See also Stirling, Jessica

Cohen, Leah Hager

Heart, you bully, you punk. Viking 2003 $23.95p $23.95

ISBN 0-670-03167-4   LC 2002-69191

"Cohen offers a bittersweet love story involving a 31-year-old math teacher at a Brooklyn private school, her star pupil, and the student's father. Ann James, the star student, breaks both heels when she slips (or jumps?) from the top of the bleachers. Her injuries render her immobile for a time; to help her keep up in math, Ann's teacher, Esker, volunteers to tutor her at home. After meeting Ann's father, Wally, Esker begins, despite herself, to fall in love with him. . . . Cohen demonstrates that there can be beauty even in sadness." Booklist

Connelly, Joe, 1963-

Crumbtown. Knopf 2003 259p $23

ISBN 0-375-41364-2   LC 2002-72930

"Set in a phantasmagoric dreamscape that is part New York City slum and part absurd parallel universe, Crumbtown is a place in which little is as it appears. The story centers on Don Reedy, in prison for a Robin Hood-style bank robbery, who is freed from jail to act as a

Connelly, Joe, 1963——*Continued*

consultant on a TV show based on his life. Once out, he quickly falls for Rita, a Russian émigré bartender, and teams up with half twins Tim and Tom, his former partners-in-crime, who sold him out to the police 15 years earlier. With them, he plots a new robbery set to take place during the filming of the bank robbery scene of the TV show. The result is a wildly inventive and darkly satiric take on a world constantly shifting and media image." Libr J

Connelly, Michael, 1956-

Lost light; a novel. Little, Brown 2003 360p $25.95

ISBN 0-316-15460-1   LC 2002-36848

"The cop who failed to collar the person who strangled Angela Benton on her 24th birthday can't do much about it now; having taken a bullet in the spine, he's paralyzed from the neck down. But the man can talk, and he talks Harry Bosch into taking the cold case. . . . Despite some shockingly sunny developments in his personal life, Bosch wears his depression like armour, making him the perfect hero for our paranoid age." N Y Times Book Rev

Cook, Robin, 1940-

Seizure. Putnam 2003 464p $24.95

ISBN 0-399-14876-0   LC 2003-43225

This "medical thriller centers around two men—Daniel Lowell, a brillant researcher and Ashely Butler, a powerful southern senator. Daniel and his girlfriend, Stephanie D'Agostino, are the cofounders of CURE, a medical research company, the existence of which relies heavily on biotechnology legislation that Butler is trying to block. . . . Cook is at his best when focusing on fascinating cutting-edge biotechnology procedures." Booklist

Cornwell, Bernard

Sharpe's havoc; Richard Sharpe and the campaign in northern Portugal, spring 1809. HarperCollins Pubs. 2003 306p $25.95

ISBN 0-06-053046-4   LC 2002-191284

"It is 1809, and Napoleon has plans to annex the Iberian Peninsula; British troops are sent to help the Portugese in their battle against the French. Sharpe and his small regiment of riflemen are separated from the main body of British troops, and once again find themselves in the thick of the action, which centers in and around the city of Oporto. Complicating matters is Kate Savage, the daughter of a British wine mechant in Oporto, whom Sharpe must find and escort to to safety. Meanwhile, a French spy marries Kate solely to get his hands on her fortune. The action shifts between battle scenes and the spy, whom Sharpe unmasks. Although the outcome is never in doubt, this nevertheless makes for a rousing story." Libr J

Vagabond. HarperCollins Pubs. 2002 405p $25.95

ISBN 0-06-621080-1   LC 2002-68884

"In this sequel to The Archer's Tale, gifted archer Thomas of Hookton continues his quest to avenge his father's murder and to find the Holy Grail, which King Edward III believes will help England defeat the French. Thomas finds himself embroiled in a series of events beginning with the Battle of Neville's Cross (October 1346) and ending with the English victory at La Roche—Derrien (spring 1347)." Libr J

"Cornwell is meticulous about historical facts and period detail, and his descriptions of butchery with arrow, mace and battleaxe are nothing if not convincing. As expected, the book culminates with battlefieldslaughter on an epic scale." Publ Wkly

Cornwell, Patricia Daniels

Blow fly; [by] Patricia Cornwell. Putnam 2003 465p $26.95

ISBN 0-399-15089-7   LC 2003-62314

"Booted out of her position as the chief medical examiner of Virginia, Scarpetta is reduced to living in a cottage in Delray Beach and hiring herself out as a consultant. But nothing lights her fire until she receives a message from Jean-Baptiste Chandonne, the monstrous killer she put on death row in an earlier novel, promising to fill her in on the atrocities currently being committed in Baton Rouge by his equally insane twin brother." N Y Times Book Rev

Craig, Amanda, 1959-

Love in idleness; a novel. Talese 2003 340p $23.95

ISBN 0-385-50776-3   LC 2002-43570

"When eight adults and three children vacation together in a rented Italian villa, the children discover fairies, and the adults discover truths about themselves as they reunite with old lovers or find themselves changed and ready for new relationships." Libr J

"The novel reprises Shakespeare's mercurial farce about Athenian lovers and fairy royalty wandering around a forest at night, falling in and out of besottedness at the instigation of the mischievous Puck." N Y Times Book Rev

Craig, Philip R., 1933-

A vineyard killing; a Martha's Vineyard mystery. Scribner 2003 229p $24

ISBN 0-7432-0524-3   LC 2002-42878

This installment "begins with a bang: an unknown assailant shoots someone outside the delicatessen where series private investigator J. W. Jackson is eating with his wife. Jackson is soon embroiled in a murder case involving grabby real estate developers and recalcitrant islanders. Off-season atmosphere and the usual high-caliber sleuthing." Libr J

Crais, Robert, 1953-

The last detective; a novel. Doubleday 2003 302p $24.95

ISBN 0-385-50426-8   LC 2002-41507

This Elvis Cole thriller finds the "Los Angeles P. I. racing the clock to rescue his girlfriend's 10-year-old son, Ben, from a team of kidnappers who claim to be paying Cole back for atrocities they say he committed in Vietnam." N Y Times Book Rev

"Fast action, though guys, vivid Los Angeles details, and snappy dialog are Craig's trademarks, and this tale has them all." Libr J

Crichton, Michael, 1942-

Prey; novel. HarperCollins Pubs. 2002 376p $26.95

ISBN 0-06-621412-2   LC 2002-32338

Crichton, Michael, 1942-—*Continued*

"Jack Forman has been laid off from his Silicon Valley job as a senior software programmer and has become a househusband, while his wife continues her career with a biotech firm involved in defense contracting. Jack is called in as a consultant to debug one of their products, and finds himself confronting a full-blown emergency, about which his wife and others in the organization have been suspiciously deceptive." SLJ

"Despite its absurd moments, 'Prey' is irresistibly suspenseful. You're entertained on one level and you learn something on another, even if the two levels do ultimately diverge." N Y Times Book Rev

Cullin, Mitch, 1968-

Undersurface; a novel; art by Peter I. Chang. Permanent Press (Sag Harbor) 2002 166p il $24

ISBN 1-57962-077-9   LC 2001-36621

An "account of a Tucson teacher's descent into the lurid, furtive world of illicit gay sex, which lands him in the wrong place at the wrong time when a murder is committed. John Connor is the ordinary, sensitive narrator whose descent begins when he finds himself frequenting adult video stores after his sex life with his wife sours. . . . As a crime narrative based on a true story, the book is a chilling if somewhat dated tale of a misstep morphing into free fall; as a literary character study, Connor's attempt to come to terms with his situation is both haunting and compelling." Publ Wkly

Culver, Timothy J.

For works written by this author under other names see Stark, Richard; Westlake, Donald E.

Cumyn, Alan, 1960-

Losing it. St. Martin's Press 2003 365p $24.95

ISBN 0-312-30691-1   LC 2002-31882

"The Sterlings are ordinary members of the educated middle class living in Ottawa, but turmoil lurks beneath their surface calm. Bob Sterling, a professor of literature specializing in Edgar Allan Poe, is secretly obsessed with women's underthings; Julia, Bob's much younger wife and former student, is quietly losing her mind from the exhaustion of caring for Matthew, their two-year-old, and her mother, Lenore, who is tormented by Alzheimer's." Publ Wkly

"The nuanced persuasive characterization propels the story forward and provides depth and texture. . . . A bonus is that Cumyn spices up this essentially sad story with some horrifyingly funny scenes." Booklist

Cussler, Clive

White death; a novel from the NUMA files; [by] Clive Cussler with Paul Kemprecos. Putnam 2003 419p $26.95

ISBN 0-399-15041-2   LC 2003-46501

This thriller "chronicles the exploits of Kurt Austin, leader and hero of NUMA's Special Assignment Team. The plot involves Austin and his partner Zavala, who are investigating a feud between a radical environmentalist group and a Danish cruiser. Austin and Zavala must come to the rescue of men trapped on the ship. They find that a giant multinational corporation is seeking to kill anyone who attempts to stop its efforts to control the seas." Booklist

D

Daniel, Margaret Truman *See* Truman, Margaret, 1924-

Dann, Jack

Jubilee. TOR Bks. 2003 441p $27.95

ISBN 0-7653-0676-X   LC 2002-73275

Analyzed in Short story index

Contents: The diamond pit; Going under; Voices; Fairy tale; Marilyn; The black horn; Bad medicine; Tattoos; Camps; Da Vinci rising; Kaddish; The extra; A quiet revolution for death; Jumping the road; Blind shemmy; Tea; Jubilee

"The 17 stories in this collection illustrate the varied talents of one of the genre's most flexible and enduring writers." Libr J

Davis, Amanda

Wonder when you'll miss me. HarperCollins Pubs. 2003 259p $24.95

ISBN 0-688-16781-0   LC 2002-24118

The ironically named 16-year-old Faith Duckie is "running from a brutal assault that led to a suicide attempt and a stay in rehab, where she shed 48 pounds but not her despair. When she returns to school, nobody seems to notice, except her imaginary 'fat girl' alter ego who convinces her to exact bloody vengeance on the boy who was a key participant in the violence. Fleeing the aftermath of her angry attack, she joins the small travelling Fartlesworth Circus, where she cleans up after elephants and horses and gradually detaches herself from the haunting fat girl who delights in dogging her every move." Publ Wkly

"This is an astonishing debut: dark, disturbing, and fiercely openhearted." Booklist

De Lint, Charles, 1951-

Spirits in the wires. TOR Bks. 2003 448p $27.95

ISBN 0-312-87398-0   LC 2003-41410

A Tom Doherty Associates book

"Claiming that she was born in the web site known as the Wordwood, Saskia Madding strikes up a friendship with Christiana Tree, who believes herself to be the shadow twin of writer Christy Riddell, a resident of the Canadian town of Newford. When a sudden disruption of the Internet results in Saskia's abrupt disappearance, her friends search for her and other vanished site visitors in the otherworld that exists beyond the nomal reality of Newford. . . . [This] work combines world mythologies with cyberculture to produce an new vision of interwoven realities." Libr J

De Loo, Tessa *See* Loo, Tessa de

Deaver, Jeff

The vanished man; a Lincoln Rhyme novel; (by) Jeffrey Deaver. Simon & Schuster 2003 399p $25.95

ISBN 0-7432-2200-8   LC 2002-42826

Deaver, Jeff—*Continued*

In this thriller the "killer is a master magician who murders his victims in the style of classic magic acts. He is also able to change his appearance at will and plants evidence at the murder scenes to mislead the police. It is up to Rhyme and his paramour, cop Amelia Sachs, to sort out the few clues from manufactured ones." Libr J

"Among the crimes rendered with Deaver's customary grace and wit are sadistic variations on Houdini's Water Torture Cell, P. T. Selbit's neat trick of sawing a woman in half and one of Howard Thurston's animal acts, in which he brought a dead bird back to life." N Y Times Book Rev

Deaver, Jeffery *See* Deaver, Jeff

Deb, Siddhartha, 1970-

The point of return. Ecco Press 2003 304p $24.95

ISBN 0-06-050151-0   LC 2002-35300

This novel explores "what it was like to come of age in a provincial town during the nationalistic fervor in the time of Indira Gandhi's rule. Babu, the inquisitive son of a Bengali civil servant, grows up in a remote northeastern Indian state. His father, Dr. Dam, the director of the veterinary and dairy department of the state, was a principled, devoted government official who grew up in the time of India's partition and fled with his family from East Pakistan, which became Bangladesh." Booklist

"To allow Dr. Dam to evolve through most of the book in a self-generated fog of benevolence and to shatter it in the last pages is a brilliant stroke. . . . Storytelling of the kind Deb lavishes, for most of his book, on Dr. Dam is rare and precious and uplifting." N Y Times Book Rev

DeLillo, Don

Cosmopolis; a novel. Scribner 2003 209p $25

ISBN 0-7432-4424-9   LC 2002-30540

"Most of the action takes place inside a 'prousted' (cork-lined) stretch limo, as the reclusive financial wizard Eric Packer is chauffeured across Manhattan for a haircut. Thanks to a presidential visit, antiglobalization demonstrations, and a celebrity funeral, this journey takes up most of the day." Libr J

"DeLillo, master novelist and seer, tells the surreal, electrifying story of this dehumanized moneyman in English scrubbed so clean and assembled so exquisitely it seems like a new language." Booklist

Delinsky, Barbara, 1945-

Flirting with Pete; a novel. Scribner 2003 355p $26

ISBN 0-7432-4642-X   LC 2003-42721

"Therapist Casy Ellis knew she was a product of a one-night stand between her mother (now comatose) and her renowned psychologist father. But she never met him, and he never acknowledged her until after his death, when he left her his mortgage-free townhouse in Boston's upscale Beacon Hill. Casey has every intention of selling it and reaping a sizable nest egg, but circumstances cause her to linger. When she discovers writings about a young woman named Jenny Clyde among her father's belongings, she is determined to find out more

about Jenny and to understand the father she never knew." Libr J

"Seamlessly and compassionately weaving Jenny's unsettling past with Casey's uncertain future, Delinsky delivers a scintillating study of each woman's search for answers and absolution." Booklist

Deutermann, Peter T., 1941-

Darkside. St. Martin's Press 2002 406p maps $24.95

ISBN 0-312-28120-X   LC 2002-68393

An "account of some creepy goings-on at the U.S. Naval Academy in Annapolis. As the book opens, the school is buzzing with the news that a plebe has plummeted from a sixth-story window and died. Amid questions of suicide, a new twist emerges; the plebe was wearing a pair of panties belonging to Midshipman First Class Julie Markham, a perky senior at the academy and an acquaintance of the dead plebe, who then gets drawn into the investigation. Her father, a retired former fighter pilot and academy history professor, hires crack defense lawyer Liz DeWinter, fearing that Markham will somehow be scapegoated by the Navy Criminal Investigation Service." Publ Wkly

Dexter, Pete, 1943-

Train; a novel. Doubleday 2003 280p $26

ISBN 0-385-50591-4   LC 2003-51946

Lionel "Train" Walk is a "young black caddy at an exclusive L.A. country club in 1953. Train is a self-taught golfer, too, and his natural ability catches the eye of an enigmatic cop, Miller Packard (or 'Mile-Away-Man,' as Train dubs him). As the stories of Train, Packard, and Norah Still, the survivor of a yacht hijacking (and eventually, Packard's wife), interject and ultimately implode, Dexter painstakingly reminds us that noir is all about disappointment, too." Booklist

Dickinson, Charles, 1951-

A shortcut in time. Forge 2003 288p $24.95

ISBN 0-7653-0579-8   LC 2002-34688

"A Tom Doherty Associates book"

"Josh Winkler's settled life changes when he chooses a shortcut to town and ends up 15 minutes in the past. On the same path, he meets Constance, another bewildered time traveler from the year 1908. No one believes them, especialy Josh's doctor wife, who orders neurological tests. To validate their experiences, Josh researches Constance's disappearance in the local library's newspaper archives and discovers that Constance's boyfriend, a suspect in her disappearance, was hanged by an angry mob; Constance needs to find her way back to 1908 to prevent his death." Libr J

"Dickinson conjures a notably mundane environment, then makes it extraordinary" Booklist

Dierbeck, Lisa, 1963-

One pill makes you smaller. Farrar, Straus & Giroux 2003 312p $24

ISBN 0-374-22649-0   LC 2002-44675

This novel revolves around "11-year-old Alice Duncan, a Manhattan girl of declining privilege who has been left in the slipshod care of her 16-year-old half sister. Her young mother, Rain, has long since disappeared; her fa-

Dierbeck, Lisa, 1963-—*Continued*
ther, a 60-year-old failed artist, is in a mental institution. It's 1976. Alice and her sister, known as Aunt Esmé, rattle around a tattered Upper East Side brownstone in a haze of nonsupervision, drugs, rock music and Esmes hippie boyfriends." N Y Times Book Rev

"This unsettling and disorienting—but also deliciously pop—account of deplorable actions and shattered innocence is a tour de force, a meshing of the myths of the counterculture with the fantastic universe of Lewis Carroll. It's a genuinely original, compulsively readable first novel, sure to stir up controversy. Publ Wkly

Diliberto, Gioia, 1950-

I am Madame X; a novel. Scribner 2003 261p il $25

ISBN 0-7432-1155-3 LC 2002-26802

"A Lisa Drew book"

"John Singer Sargent's provocative portrait of aloof and alluring Virginie Gautreau scandalized the Paris Salon in 1884. In it, the artist offset his subject's luminous white skin with a revealing black evening gown. . . . Diliberto's writing brings Virginie to life in a way that Sargent's portrait does not, creating a complex woman who recognizes that her beauty is her most precious commodity. The author uses evocative images and sharp descriptions of both people and places to crete a wordpicture of Parisian society at the turn of the century." Libr J

Doctorow, Cory

Down and out in the Magic Kindgom. TOR Bks. 2003 208p $22.95

ISBN 0-7653-0436-8 LC 2002-73277

"A Tom Doherty Associates book"

"Jules, a relative youngster at more than a century old, is a contented citizen of the Bitchun Society that has filled Earth and near-space since shortage and death were overcome. . . . What Jules wants to do is move to Disney World, join the ad-hoc crew that runs the park and fine-tune the Haunted Mansion ride to make it even more wonderful. When his prudently stored consciousness abruptly awakens in a cloned body, he learns that he was murdered; evidently he's in the way of somebody else's dreams. . . . Doctorow has served up a nicely understated dish: meringue laced with caffeine." Publ Wkly

Docx, Edward

The calligrapher. Houghton Mifflin 2003 360p $24

ISBN 0-618-34397-0 LC 2003-51149

The novel's "protagonist, Jasper Jackson, is a Londoner whose current job is to transcribe the Songs and Sonnets of John Donne for a wealthy client. Like Donne, Jasper is also a relentless womanizer, a charming cad who lives for love affairs. When the woman of his dreams appears in his own garden, Jasper succumbs to real love for the first time and slowly begins to realize what it feels like to be the pursuer rather than the pursued." Publ Wkly

Doherty, P. C.

The gates of hell; a mystery of Alexander the Great; [by] Paul Doherty. Carroll & Graf Pubs. 2003 292p il $24

ISBN 0-7867-1157-4

This mystery revolves "around the military exploits of Alexander the Great and the behind-the-scenes adventures of Telamon, his boyhood friend and personal physician. When Alexander's determination to invade and conquer Halicarnassus, a city inextricably linked to his infamous father, is threatened by an unsettling series of murders within his own inner circle, Telamon must use his considerable powers of detection in order to uncover a treasonous plot linked to the legendary Pythian manuscript. Booklist

Donohue, John J., 1956-

Sensei. Thomas Dunne Bks. 2003 258p $23.95

ISBN 0-312-28812-3 LC 2002-32507

"Someone who calls himself Ronin—masterless Samurai—is apparently killing off martial-arts masters across the U.S., and Connor Burke, a university professor and martial-arts student, is brought into the investigation by his brother, a New York detective assigned to the case. Connor recruits his own sensei, Yamshita, and this unusual pair uncover the facts with a combination of mental skill and good, old-fashioned (amateur) detective work." Booklist

Dorrestein, Renate

Without mercy; translated by Hester Velmans. Viking 2003 v2002 223p $23.95

ISBN 0-670-03188-7 LC 2002-44900

This translation first published 2002 in the United Kingdom

"First published in Holland, this work follows the grieving process of Franka and Phinus Vemeer as they attempt to deal with the senseless murder of their 15-year-old son. Dorrestein's novel. . . seems at first to be a straightforward exploration of parental grief but slowly transforms into a much darker story in which disturbing memories and relationship-destroying secrets are revealed in bits and pieces. The slow-building and well-crafted plot accurately illustrates the process by which guilt and denial become pathological." Libr J

Douglas, Carole Nelson

Cat in a neon nightmare; a Midnight Louie mystery. Forge 2003 365p $24.95

ISBN 0-7653-0680-8 LC 2002-45491

"A Tom Doherty Associates book"

In this episode sleuth and supercat Midnight Louie "and his human associates, Temple Barr and Max Kinsella, tangle with the Synth, a gang of outlaw magicians up to no good. Tracking down the elusive renegades takes Louie to a private magic club called Nightmare—imagine the bar in Star Wars but not quite as friendly." Booklist

Douglass, Billie, 1945-

For works by this author see Delinsky, Barbara, 1945-

Drake, Bonnie, 1945-

For works by this author see Delinsky, Barbara, 1945-

Drake, David, 1945-

Grimmer than hell. Baen Bks. 2003 373p $24

ISBN 0-7434-3590-7 LC 2002-34194

Drake, David, 1945-—*Continued*

Analyzed in Short Story index

Contents: Rescue mission; When the devil drives; Team effort; The end; Smash and grab; Mission accomplished; Facing the enemy; Failure mode; The tradesmen; Coming up against it; With the sword he must be slain; Nation without walls; The predators; Underground

"Fourteen short stories and an introduction make up the latest, highly recommended collection from a leading light of military sf. . . . The intoduction puts everything in perspective with a minimum of apologetics, compressing Drake's psychological history since the Vietnam War into a short essay valuable to new and old fans alike." Booklist

Ducornet, Rikki

Gazelle. Knopf 2003 189p $21

ISBN 0-375-41124-0   LC 2002-34000

"Recounts the sexual awakening of Elizabeth, a 13-year-old American girl in 1950's Cairo. While her father, an academic, plays war games with tiny toy soldiers and her mother moves out to satisfy her extramarital appetites, Elizabeth devours—and is awakened by—a provocatively illustrated edition of 'The Arabian Nights." N Y Times Book Rev

"Lushly detailed yet swiftly paced, this mythic coming-of-age novel archly traces the plexus of sensuality, intelligence, and imagination that defines the human soul." Booklist

Due, Tananarive, 1966-

The good house. Atria 2003 482p $25

ISBN 0-7434-4900-2

"After her 15-year-old son Corey's suicide, Angela Toussaint spent several months in a mental hospital. Now, divorced and focused on her work, she receives word of potential buyers of her grandmother's house in Sacajawea, Washington, in which Corey died. Realizing that she must put the tragedy to rest, Angela decides to go to the house to try to understand exactly what happened. Sacajawea is, however, a town beset by evil." Booklist

"Due handles the potentially unwieldy elements of her novel with confidence, cross-cutting smoothly from past to present, introducing revelatory facts that alter the interpretation of earlier scenes and interjecting powerfully orchestrated moments of supernatural horror that sustain the tale's momentum." Publ Wkly

Duisberg, Kristin Waterfield

The good patient; a novel. St. Martin's Press 2003 328p $23.95

ISBN 0-312-30039-5   LC 2002-36877

"Darien Gilbertson is a 28-year-old Manhattan advertising executive known for her biting sarcasm, morbid humor and party-girl tendencies. But beneath the sleek facade, she hides the scars, bumps and bruises of her secret life—she enjoys violently hurting herself. Her husband, Robert, knows of her penchant for pain, but Darien can't seem to stop and refuses to get help. Then she goes too far and breaks her hand. . . . Robert forces her to see a psychiatrist, and despite herself, Darien begins to trust cool Dr. Rachel Lindholm." Publ Wkly

"From the facile duplicity of Darien's counseling sessions to the innocence of her interior dialogues,

Duisberg's first-person narrative is electrifying in its unfeigned candor, harrowing in its unnerving vulnerability." Booklist

Dukthas, Ann

For works written by this author under other names see Doherty, P. C.

Dwyer, K. R., 1945-

For works written by this author under other names see Koontz, Dean R. (Dean Ray), 1945-

E

Eagles, Cynthia Harrod- *See* Harrod-Eagles, Cynthia

Eco, Umberto

Baudolino; translated from the Italian by William Weaver. Harcourt 2002 522p $27

ISBN 0-15-100690-3   LC 2002-2345

Original Italian edition, 2000

An "adventure about a 12th-century Italian peasant gifted in learning languages, telling lies and putting himself in the middle of genuine historical situations." N Y Times Book Rev

"In this whimsical yet deadly earnest tale, Eco puts forth the question that perpetually beguiles him and with which he beguiles the rest of us: If a teller of tales tells us he's telling the truth, how can we know for sure what really happened?." New Yorker

Edric, Robert, 1956-

The book of the heathen. Thomas Dunne Bks. 2002 351p $24.95

ISBN 0-312-28888-3   LC 2002-75447

"At a declining British outpost in the Congo, a man stands accused of murdering a young native girl. The prisoner, Nicholas Frere, an intelligent and once-respected employee, denies none of the charges. His sole remaining friend, James Frasier (the narrator), is the only one who has not already judged and condemned Frere." Booklist

"There are no pretty characters or easy lessons here, but the book paints a memorable picture of this ravaged stretch of jungle and the misery of the people—both European and African—who inhabited it at the height of the European empires." Publ Wkly

Edwards, Louis, 1962-

Oscar Wilde discovers America; a novel. Scribner 2003 287p $24

ISBN 0-7432-3689-0   LC 2002-30879

The protagonist of this novel is "22-year-old William Traquair, who travels as valet to Oscar Wilde throughout his U.S. lecture tour. African American, Bowdoin-educated, and son of the butler to a wealthy abolitionist family, Traquair has had a relatively sheltered and privileged childhood. Already a follower of Wilde's aesthetic philosophy, he overlooks his distaste for servitude to learn at Wilde's elbow. Libr J

"An entertaining and thought-provoking narrative grounded in social and literary history." Booklist

Ellis, David

Life sentence. Putnam 2003 390p $24.95

ISBN 0-399-14979-1   LC 2002-68137

"Jon Soliday and Grant Tully share a dirty secret from their teenage years: after a night of drinking and drugs, Soliday climbed through the bedroom window of a beautiful young woman and then blacked out. Consequently, he doesn't remember anything after that—not even how she ended up dead. Via family connections, Soliday eludes prosecution, and 20 years later he is chief legal counsel to Senator Tully, who is running a fierce campaign for governor. . . . Elegant prose skillfully impels Soliday through a haze of deadly deceit, where no one is who he appears to be." Libr J

Emmons, Cai

His mother's son. Harcourt 2003 366p $25

ISBN 0-15-100734-9   LC 2002-2990

"Dr. Jana Thomas has a secret that no one knows—not even her husband. Fifteen years before, she had a different life and a different name, which she abandoned when her younger brother murdered their parents and went on a killing spree at his school. Now Jana has a young son, and she begins to panic when she sees the warning signs that no one noticed in her brother." Libr J

"Those looking for domestic drama and hidden lives will enjoy Emmons' book and find the anxious and troubled character of Jana interesting." Booklist

Epstein, Joseph, 1937-

Fabulous small Jews; stories. Houghton Mifflin 2003 339p $23

ISBN 0-395-94402-3   LC 2002-27621

Analyzed in Short story index

Contents: Felix emeritus; Artie Glick in a family way; The third Mrs. Kessler; Moe; Love and The Guinness book of records; Family values; The executor; Saturday afternoon at the zoo with dad; Freddy Duchamp in action; Don Juan Zimmerman; Dubinsky on the loose; Coming in with their hands up; The master's ring; Howie's gift; A loss for words; My little Marjie; Postcards; Uncle Jack

"Like his emotionally candid, low-key protagonists, Epstein is intrinsically honest. Gratifying and genuine, this collection examines all sorts of respones to the encroachment of old age on human dignity." Publ Wkly

Epstein, Leslie

San Remo Drive; a novel from memory. Handsel Press 2003 238p il $26

ISBN 1-59051-066-6   LC 2002-35547

This novel "portrays one talented but troubled Hollywood family through the eyes of the elder son, Richard, who becomes a famous artist. His director father, Norman Jacobi, wittily mocks the HUAC during his televised hearing, his mother, Lotte, is beautiful and a bit of a loose cannon; and his strange little brother, Barton, is given to fits and visions, serving as a trickster figure, the fool who reveals the truth." Booklist

"There is something of 'The Winter's Tale' in the way Epstein pulls it all together, something of the miraculous second chance. Losing and finding, he shows us love between fathers and sons as the most powerful and enduring in life. . . . In doing so he has given us, along with

F. Scott Fitzgerald's 'Last Tycoon,' Budd Schulberg's 'What Makes Sammy Run?' and his own 'Pandaemonium,' one of the four best Hollywood novels ever written." N Y Times Book Rev

Erdrich, Louise

The Master Butchers Singing Club. HarperCollins Pubs. 2002 289p $25.95

ISBN 0-06-620977-3   LC 2002-68501

"Erdrich tells the story of Fidelis Waldvogel, a WWI sniper and master butcher with a 'talent for stillness' and for singing. After marrying Eva, the pregnant fianceé of his best friend, who was killed in the war, he emigrates to America. Settling in Argus, N. Dak., he and Eva establish a butcher shop known for its Old World expertise and for housing Fidelis's beloved singing club." Publ Wkly

"Erdrich is demonstrably capable of pursuing a potent image or theme throughout a narrative. And although this novel's leitmotif of violent, gruesome death is a bit too obvious, its smaller symbols succeed better, perhaps because they're accompanied by less fanfare." N Y Times Book Rev

Estleman, Loren D.

Black powder, white smoke. Forge 2002 318p $24.95

ISBN 0-7653-0189-X   LC 2002-69266

"A Tom Doherty Associates book"

Honey Boutrille is a "freed slave who kills a white man to save a working girl in the New Orleans brothel he owns. 'Twice' Emerson is a career criminal on the run after a botched train robbery. Most of the time, Honey travels in Texas, while Twice hides out in the West. We know that they will eventually cross paths, but part of this story's charm is how it will happen." Libr J

Poison blonde; an Amos Walker novel. Forge 2003 269p $24.95

ISBN 0-7653-0447-3   LC 2002-35242

"Latin singer Gilia Cristobal, the hottest commodity in show business, hires Detroit private eye Amos Walker to get to the botom of a scam involving the singer's designer gowns, but her real problem is blackmail. It turns out she's not really who she claims to be. . . . Walker is a classic hard-boiled private eye. He breathes air heavy with smoke and cordite, he delivers his dialogue through clenched teeth, and he operates by a murky moral code only he understands." Booklist

Evanovich, Janet

To the nines; a Stephanie Plum novel. St. Martin's Press 2003 312p il $25.95

ISBN 0-312-26586-7

"Bounty hunter Stephanie Plum is at it again. Singh has jumped ship, abandoning his fianceé, stealing her dog, and owing his landlord back rent. Through their sleuthing, Stephanie and Ranger track him down in Vegas. Unfortunately, owing to a previous problem with the law, Ranger isn't allowed to go to Vegas. This leaves Stephanie with Lulu and Connie as her traveling companions." Libr J

F

Fairstein, Linda

The bone vault; a novel. Scribner 2003 386p $25

ISBN 0-7432-2354-3   LC 2002-26686

A thriller starring Alexandra Cooper, "a Manhattan assistant district attorney. This time out, she and her sidekick, cop Mike Chapman, are drawn into a particularly mysterious case: a Metropolitan Museum of Art intern is found dead in a sarcophagus, and though she's been dead for months, her body is perfectly preserved. When it is discovered that she died of arsenic poisoning, the plot thickens. This is fun reading." Libr J

Falconer, Colin, 1953-

Feathered serpent; a novel of the Mexican conquest. Crown 2002 374p $22.95

ISBN 0-609-61029-5   LC 2002-24711

"Born an Aztec princess and sold into slavery after her father's death, Malinali was at 15 given to conquistador Herman Cortes. A highly intelligent woman gifted in several languages, she made herself indispensable as an interpreter to the Spaniards. Her desire for revenge against Montezuma II, whom she held responsible for the murder of her father, and her belief that Cortes was actually the god Feathered Serpent, coupled with the Spaniards' overwhelming greed for gold, initiated a disastrous sequence of events that led to the fall of the Aztec empire." Libr J

"This enthralling reconstruction of the birth of modern Mexico is rooted in both genuine history and cultural myth." Booklist

Fallon, Martin, 1929- *See* Higgins, Jack, 1929-

Fforde, Jasper

Thursday Next in Lost in a good book; a novel. Viking 2003 399p il $24.95

ISBN 0-670-03190-9   LC 2002-71304

Companion volume to: The Eyre affair

First published 2002 in the United Kingdom with title: Lost in a good book

"Thursday Next, who literally jumps into books to do her detective work, must locate a surprise enemy in Poe's 'The Raven' to save her beloved." Libr J

"Time flies—and leaps and zigzags—while reading this wickedly funny and clever fantasy. Would-be wordsmiths and mystery fans will find the surreal genre-buster irresistible." Publ Wkly

Finney, Patricia, 1958-

Gloriana's torch. St. Martin's Press 2003 452p $24.95

ISBN 0-312-31285-7   LC 2003-58454

This "tale is set on the eve of the sailing of the Spanish Armada in 1588. David Becket, clerk of the ordnance and sometime spy for Elizabeth I, is ordered by the queen to discover the details of a top-secret Spanish plot dubbed the 'Miracle of Beauty.' In addition, Becket is commanded to rescue his fellow English spy and friend, Simon Ames, who has been condemned by the Spanish Inquisition as a heretic. . . . The various threads of this wide-ranging tale of intrigue do not come together neatly, but Finney's vivid prose and the high level of historical imagination on display make for a satisfying read." Publ Wkly

Fitzhugh, Bill

Heart seizure. Morrow 2003 438p $21.95

ISBN 0-380-97758-3   LC 2002-26420

"Rose Tailor, in her late sixties and suffering from a bad ticker, is next in line for a heart transplant. Unfortunately for her, the president of the U.S. suffers a massive coronary, and his devious chief of staff, Martin Brooks, bumps Rose and puts the president at the top of the transplant list. This doesn't sit well with her son, Spence—the proverbial lawyer with a heart of gold—who steals the donor heart and kidnaps novice surgeon Dr. Debbie Robbins. What then follows is a hilarious road trip from L.A. to Salt Lake City." Booklist

Foley, Mick, 1965-

Tietam Brown; a novel. Knopf 2003 243p $23.95

ISBN 0-375-41550-5   LC 2002-29856

"Andy Brown is an archetypal high school underdog, a misshapen, motherless misfit tormented by the football coach and tantalized by the minister's daughter. At home, dad Tietam is an alcoholic bodybuilding enthusiast who does nude calisthenics in the living room in between noisy bedroom sessions with a parade of three-night-stand women; he parents Andy by offering him beer, condoms and crude sexual pointers. . . . Readers in the mood of for vigorous pulp may enjoy this steroid-fueled brawl." Publ Wkly

Follett, Ken, 1949-

Hornet flight. Dutton 2002 420p $26.95

ISBN 0-525-94689-6   LC 2002-37903

"Tale of amateur spies pursued by Nazi collaborators in occupied Denmark in 1941. Harald Olufsen is an 18-year-old physics student who stumbles into espionage when he accidentally discovers a secret German radar installation on the island where he lives. . . . Follett starts out fast and keeps up the pace, revealing how ordinary people who want to do the right thing are undone by their own enthusiasm and inexperience. He also paints a vivid and convincing picture of life in occupied Denmark, of easy collaboration with the Nazis and of the insidious, creeping persecution of the Jews. Publ Wkly

Ford, Robert

The student conductor. Putnam 2003 289p $24.95

ISBN 0-399-15037-4   LC 2003-46514

"Eight years after dropping out of Juilliard, 30-year-old Cooper Barrow makes a bid to restart his career, going to work with Karlheinz Ziegler, a legendary conductor from prewar days who now teaches at a provincial music school. A strongly antagonistic relationship develops between them, exacerbated by Barrow's continuing anxiety, Ziegler's brusquely authoritarian manner and the young American's romantic interest in Petra Vogel, a young oboist in the student orchestra, a refugee from East Germany." Publ Wkly

"This is finally a novel about power—the power of a

Ford, Robert—*Continued*

great conductor driving a well-trained orchestra, the power of the past to enslave us, the power of the future to free us, and the power of the individual to love and to forgive. There is hardly a wrong note, from the moment Ford lifts his baton to the final refrain." Booklist

Forstchen, William R.

(jt. auth) Gingrich, N. Gettysburg

Forsyth, Frederick, 1938-

Avenger. Thomas Dunne Bks. 2003 370p $24.95

ISBN 0-312-31951-7   LC 2003-53163

"World War II, Vietnam, Bosnia, and Cambodia take turns commanding center stage, held together by two protagonists: a middle-age lawyer and an aging business tycoon, who have both suffered devastating losses. The tycoon's loss, that of his grandson on a relief mission in Bosnia, becomes subsumed in the mission of attorney Calvin Dexter, grieving father and former 'Nam tunnel rat, whose mission in life is to bring justice to those who have gotten away with murder. . . . Forsyth's extraordinary care with detail, his solid voice, and his exquisite pacing make this a totally engrossing thriller." Booklist

Franklin, Tom

Hell at the breech; a novel. Morrow 2003 520p $23.95

ISBN 0-688-16741-1   LC 2002-40982

"When a storekeeper campaigning for the state legislature is assassinated, Mitcham Beat is swept by a wave of violence that includes lynchings and shootings, barn burnings, and robberies. A gang of hooded men known as the Hell-at-the-Breech gang is terrorizing the community, and the only man to stop them is an aging sheriff ready to retire with his whiskey bottle. It sounds like the wild, wild West, but Franklin. . . has taken a little-known event in Alabama history, the Mitcham Beat War, and transformed it into a Faulknerian tale of bloody revenge and vigilante justice." Libr J

Freda, Joseph, 1951-

The patience of rivers; a novel. Norton 2003 351p $24.95

ISBN 0-393-05176-5   LC 2002-13330

"It is 1969, and Nick Lauria is spending his final summer before college hanging out with his best friend, Charlie Miles, while working at his family's campgrounds in Delaware Ford, a small New York town just up the road from the farm where Woodstock is to be held. Nick spends his spare time trying to bed Darlene Van Vooren, the youngest of the three gorgeous Van Vooren sisters. But beneath the surface of Nick's idyllic existence, his family is in trouble." Publ Wkly

"This is an appealing coming-of-age tale set to a classic rock soundtrack." Libr J

French, Nicci

Land of the living. Warner Bks. 2003 341p $23.95

ISBN 0-446-53151-0   LC 2002-33149

In the "opening scenes, 25-year-old Abbie Devereaux finds herself blindfolded and shackled in some filthy hole, the victim of a kidnapping she can't recall. Through sheer luck Abbie escapes her prison, only to realize that no one in authority believes her story. . . . Although the thwarted killer who is still stalking Abbie is too real for us to share her terror of going mad, we're with her all the way in her gritty quest to forge a new identity and discover what went wrong with the old one." N Y Times Book Rev

Freudenberger, Nell

Lucky girls; stories. HarperCollins Pubs. 2003 225p $22.95

ISBN 0-06-008879-6   LC 2003-44875

Analyzed in Short story index

Contents: Lucky girls; The orphan; Outside the Eastern gate; The tutor; Letter from the last bastion

"A remarkably poised collection of stories about Americans abroad." N Y Times Book Rev

Fromm, Pete, 1958-

As cool as I am. Picador 2003 388p $24

ISBN 0-312-30775-6   LC 2003-49869

This "coming-of-age story follows Lucy Diamond of Great Falls, Mont., for two years, from 14 o 16. They're turbulent years, but more so for Lucy because her parents, themselves married as teenagers, are both self-centered, trying to recapture the youth they feel they missed. Chuck, her father, appears only for a few days every few months; he is a charmer, and Lucy has inherited his humor and smart mouth. Though he claims to be a logger, it becomes clear that there must be other reasons for his long disappearances. Lucy's mother, Lainee, frustrated by her absent husband, has a long string of boyfriends, all of whom, like her husband, eventually disappear. Lucy, meanwhile, drifts into an affair with her best friend, scrawny, funny Kenny, whose divorced mother is an alcoholic." Publ Wkly

"Fromm explores the sexual evolution of a cynical teenage girl who has the spunk and wit to survive two flaky parents and the urges of unbridled adolescence." Booklist

G

Galloway, Janice

Clara. Simon & Schuster 2003 425p $25

ISBN 0-684-84449-4   LC 2002-26800

First published 2002 in the United Kingdom

This work focuses on the life of "18th century composer and piano virtuoso, Clara Schumann. Schumann, better known as the wife of Robert Schmann, and the musical associate of such greats as Brahms and Mendelssohn, was a true artist in her own right. She was also the mostly submissive daughter of an egomaniacal and manipulative father and the long-suffering spouse to a mentally disturbed genius." Libr J

"The Schumanns' marriage was forged of perfectly dissonant material, and Galloway allows the collisions to speak for themselves." N Y Times Book Rev

García, Cristina

Monkey hunting. Knopf 2003 251p $23

ISBN 0-375-41056-2   LC 2002-35916

García, Cristina—*Continued*

This novel "chronicles the fortunes of Chen Pan, a Chinese who is enslaved in the Cuban sugar fields in 1857 and later becomes a prosperous businessman in Havana; the mulata slave Lucrecia, whose relationship with Chen Pan is poignantly rendered; and their descendants: Lorenzo, a doctor of herbal medicine in Havana; lesbian Chen Fang, a teacher imprisoned for counter-revolutionary activities in Mao's China; and Domingo Chen, an immigrant to New York City who serves in the U.S. Army in Vietnam." Libr J

"For all the ground Garcia covers, the most beautiful and moving parts of her novel are the chapters on Chen Pan's youthful sufferings. Here, horror and wonder alternate unblinkingly, as if they are random occurrences in a dark once-upon-a-time." N Y Times Book Rev

García-Roza, Luiz Alfredo, 1936-

December heat; translated by Benjamin Moser. Holt & Co. 2003 273p $23

ISBN 0-8050-6890-2   LC 2002-38825

Original Portuguese edition published 1998 in Brazil

Second title in the author's trilogy featuring Inspector Espinosa from Rio de Janeiro

"This time the plot concerns Espinosa's friend, a retired policeman who appears to be the likely suspect when his hooker girlfriend is murdered. Confusing the issue, though, is a series of subsequent murders whose tenuous links to the first are fading as precious time passes." Booklist

"An exciting procedural, infused with exotic ambience, sympathetic detectives, and a little romance." Libr J

Gay, William

I hate to see that evening sun go down; collected stories. Free Press 2002 303p $24

ISBN 0-7432-4088-X   LC 2002-73945

Analyzed in Short story index

Contents: I hate to see that evening sun go down; A death in the woods; Bonedaddy, Quincy Nell, and the fifteen thousand BTU electric chair; The paperhanger; The man who knew Dylan; Those Deep Elm Brown's Ferry Blues; Crossroads Blues; Closure and roadkill on the life's highway; Sugarbaby; Standing by peaceful waters; Good 'til now; The lightpainter; My hand is just fine where it is

"Gay is richly gifted: a seemingly effortless storyteller, a writer of prose that's fiercely wrought, pungent in detail, yet poetic in the most welcome sense." N Y Times Book Rev

Gear, Kathleen O'Neal

People of the owl; a novel of prehistoric North America; [by] Kathleen O'Neal Gear and W. Michael Gear. Forge 2003 560p il maps $25.95

ISBN 0-312-87741-2   LC 2003-40019

"A Tom Doherty Associates book"

An "account of six prehistoric Native American clans living in the Lower Mississippi Valley. Salamander, the protagonist, is an unlikely leader of the Owl clan and struggles to maintain peace among the fractious clans. Even though many of his family, friends, and enemies believe him to be a naïve young fool, a certain mystique surrounds him when his shamanistic visions empower

him to keep violence at bay." Libr J

"Propelled by the Gears' spry storytelling, this sturdy epic skillfully navigates the ancient swamplands of Louisiana, with their lapping brown waters, hanging vines and brooding skies." Publ Wkly

Gear, W. Michael

(jt. auth) Gear, K. O. People of the owl

Geary, Joseph M.

Spiral. Pantheon Bks. 2003 355p $24.95

ISBN 0-375-42223-4   LC 2002-35679

"Biographer Nick Greer learns that a crucial missing source, Jacob Grossman, is alive and in Manhattan, but Grossman is killed shortly after Greer visits him and tapes his final interview. Grossman's untimely death hinders Greer in his efforts to track down a lost painting called the Incarnation that was the penultimate work of his subject, a controversial artist named Frank Spira who was romantically linked to Grossman." Publ Wkly

Lynch "has breathed life into a increasingly familiar mystery milieu—the art world—with assured detail and peopled it with a crowd of fascinating characters. He plants clues like a master and ratchets up the suspense so subtly we're lightheaded before we notice we haven't been breathing." Booklist

Gerritsen, Tess

The apprentice; a novel. Ballantine Bks. 2002 344p $24.95

ISBN 0-345-44785-9   LC 2002-23185

Boston "detective Jane Rizzoli is called to a crime scene out of her jurisdiction. The victim is a wealthy doctor, found with his throat slashed, sitting on the floor of his living room in his pajamas, with a teacup in his lap. His wife is missing, but her nightgown is found folded neatly on a chair in the bedroom. There are unmistakable similarities to the work of serial killer Warren Hoyt, nicknamed 'the Surgeon,' but he is in prison, which leads Rizzoli to suspect a copcat killer." Libr J

The sinner. Ballantine Bks. 2003 342p $24.95

ISBN 0-345-45891-5   LC 2003-59151

"When two Boston nuns are found brutally beaten—one fatally and one with a scintilla of life left in her—it's up to homicide detective Jane Rizzoli to find the perpetrator. Medical examiner Dr. Maura Isles, nicknamed the Queen of the Dead, has the unlucky fortune to discover that the murdered nun, a young woman about to make her final vows, hid untold secrets from the rest of the aging convent. . . . Woven within the horror of this gruesome story is the old allegory of good versus evil, but relating it through these two fascinating individuals, Gerritsen avoids cliches." Booklist

Gibson, William, 1948-

Pattern recognition. Putnam 2003 356p $25.95

ISBN 0-399-14986-4   LC 2002-67955

"Cayce Pollard is a brand consultant whose father disappeared on September 11th. She becomes fascinated by mysterious scraps of film footage—seemingly random scenes, luminously shot—that are disseminated on the Web and have spawned cults of viewers. Gibson wisely avoids addressing the import of 9/11 head on, but he somehow establishes a powerful correlative for it in

Gibson, William, 1948-—_Continued_

Cayce's strange quest—through the Tokyo red-light district and the Moscow underworld—to find the anonymous filmmaker. In Gibson's eerie vision of our time, the future has come crashing upon us, fragmentary and undecipherable." New Yorker

Gill, Bartholomew, 1943-2002

Death in Dublin; a novel of suspense. Morrow 2003 294p $24.95

ISBN 0-06-000849-0   LC 2002-32582

"Gill's final novel pits Police Chief Peter McGarr against a thief and murderer: a night watchman at Dublin's Trinity College has been killed and the irreplaceable Book of Kells stolen. McGarr suspects an infamous and most dangerous band of IRA zealots. Excellent work from a tried-and-true hand." Libr J

Gilling, Tom

The adventures of Miles and Isabel. Atlantic Monthly Press 2002 198p $23

ISBN 0-87113-861-1   LC 2002-16414

First published 2001 in Australia with title: Miles McGinty

"The story of two headstrong people born under unusual circumstances on the same day in Sydney in 1856. One (Miles) becomes a 'vehicle' for a traveling levitator, while the other (Isabel) is accidentally launched into the air owing to the error of a passing drunkard balloonist, whose notebooks Miles inherits after the balloonist's bizarre death. Synchronicities abound." Libr J

Gingrich, Newt

Gettysburg; a novel of the Civil War; [by] Newt Gingrich and William Forstchen; and Albert S. Hanser, contributing editor. St. Martin's Press 2003 463p il $24.95

ISBN 0-312-30935-X   LC 2003-41381

"On July 1, 1863, the Army of Virginia, under the command of Gen. Robert E. Lee, and the Army of the Potomac, under Gen. George G. Meade, clashed in deadly combat near Gettysburg, PA. Of course, Union forces won, but Gingrich and Forstchen imagine a different outcome in which Confederate forces do a surprise march around Union lines to flank and cut off the Union troops from their supply and information routes. In the course of their narrative, the authors depict the gallantry and heroism of Lee, Longstreet, Chamberlain, Hancock, Hunt, and many other officers and enlisted men on both sides of the conflict." Libr J

Glancy, Diane

Stone heart; a novel of Sacajawea. Overlook Press 2002 156p $21.95

ISBN 1-58567-365-X   LC 2002-30820

"Sacajawea, the Shoshone native who accompanied Lewis and Clark on their famed expedition, narrates this fictional version of the magnificent, yet harrowing, journey. As told through the heart of a woman and through the spirit of a Native American, the Lewis and Clark expedition takes on entirely new contours." Booklist

Glendinning, Victoria

Flight. St. Martin's Press 2003 260p $23.95

ISBN 0-312-31498-1   LC 2003-43125

The "protagonist is an aloof English structural engineer whose specialty is glass and whose innovations have made him a celebrity on the international design circuit. But his capacity to bear emotional loads has never been tested until he meets a French socialite whose ancestral chateau is to become the hotel for an airport he is designing. Glendinning has researched her architecture, and her glass, and she ingeniously explores the theme of responsibility in both work and love, managing to fashion her apparently airy material into a satisfying whole." New Yorker

Gordimer, Nadine, 1923-

Nobel Prize in literature, 1991

Karma

In Gordimer, N. Loot, and other stories p151-237

Loot, and other stories. Farrar, Straus & Giroux 2003 240p $23

ISBN 0-374-19090-9   LC 2002-42601

Analyzed in Short story index

Includes the novellas Karma and Mission statement and the following short stories: Loot; Visiting George; The generation gap; L,U,C,I,E.; Look-alikes; The diamond mine; Homage; An emissary

In Karma a deceased insurance executive's spirit makes successive returns to earth in various guises. Mission statement is about a middle-aged Englishwoman who has a sexual relationship with a native while working for an international aid agency in an impoverished African country

"This compelling collection presents a bleak view of human existence in general and of Africa's colonial past in particular. Written with a sharp sense of irony, it should be a part of every fiction collection." Libr J

Mission statement

In Gordimer, N. Loot, and other stories p7-66

Gordon, Neil, 1958-

The company you keep. Viking 2003 406p $24.95

ISBN 0-670-03218-2   LC 2002-44905

"When limousine-leftist lawyer and single dad Jim Grant is unmasked as Jason Sinai, an ex-Weather Underground militant wanted for a deadly bank robbery, he abandons his daughter and goes on the lam. As he evades a manhunt and seeks out old comrades, the author introduces a sprawling cast of drug dealers, bomb-planting radicals turned leftist academics, Vietnam vets, FBI agents and Republicans who collectively ponder the legacy of the '60s." Publ Wkly

"If the book has a political stance, it might be called the radical center, training equal skepticism, even humorous contempt, on the excesses of both left and right." N Y Times Book Rev

Gowdy, Barbara

The romantic; a novel. Metropolitan Bks. 2003 305p $24

ISBN 0-8050-7190-3   LC 2002-29904

"At 10, a year after Louise's own mother left her and her father, the Richters, an older couple with an adopted son, move in next door. . . . Louise befriends Abel in

Gowdy, Barbara—*Continued*

order to get to Mrs. Richter, but her love soon transfers to the solitary, sensitive boy. The connection between the two flourishes, and Louise never stops thinking about Abel, even when he moves away. It is his return, when they meet at a high-school party, that marks the beginning of their adult relationship." Booklist

"Each of the characters, even minor ones, has a unique voice and a vivid, quirky personality. Louise's need to have Abel create the world for her resonates with unfulfilled passion." Publ Wkly

Grace, C. L.

For works written by this author under other names see Doherty, P. C.

Graham, James, 1929- *See* Higgins, Jack, 1929-

Grass, Günter, 1927-

Crabwalk; translated from the German by Krishna Winston. Harcourt 2002 234p $25

ISBN 0-15-100764-0   LC 2002-13205

"The plot centers on the fate of the vessel Wilhelm Gustloff, which was built as a cruise ship in the Third Reich, was fitted out as a troop carrier in World War II and was turned into a refugee ship for German civilians fleeing the Russian Army. On Jan. 30, 1945, 12 years after the Nazis rose to power, it was torpedoed in the Baltic Sea by a Soviet submarine and, in what was apparently the biggest recorded disaster in maritime history, sank with the loss of some 9,000 souls." N Y Times Book Rev

"A writer who refuses to avert his eyes from unpleasant truths, Grassremains an eloquent explorer of his country's troubled 20th-century history." Publ Wkly

Greeley, Andrew M., 1928-

Second spring; a love story. Forge 2003 347p $24.95

ISBN 0-7653-0236-5   LC 2002-32549

Fifth installment in the author's O'Malley Family saga; previous titles A midwinter's tale (1998); Younger than springtime; Christmas wedding (2000); September song

"In this installment, Charles 'Chucky' O'Malley and his spirited family face the 1970s. Here we find Chucky approaching 50 and stuck in a vicious midlife and spiritual crisis. While O'Malley can count his blessings—an adoring wife, an amazing sex life, a prestigious career, and a large, happy family—he still feels unfulfilled. In addition, he is no longer able to take comfort in his faith. As a photographer of some importance, O'Malley travels the world snapping historical photos and searching for his own happiness." Booklist

Green, Norman, 1954-

The angel of Montague Street. HarperCollins Pubs. 2003 293p $24.95

ISBN 0-06-018819-7   LC 2002-32885

Silvano Iurata "should never be in Brooklyn in the first place. It's 1973, the city is broke and mean, and he's ben bumming around since he got out of Vietnam, avoiding his Mafia-employed family and keeping clear of his loco cousin, Domenic, who wants to settle and old family

quarrel by killing him with his bare hands. But Iurata is on some private redemptive mission, and he figures that if he can find out what happened to his sweet, mildly retarded brother, last seen in Brooklyn Heights, he might be able to give up the dead and rejoin the living. . . . Green writes about mobster families with a knowledge that is unnerving in its intimacy." N Y Times Book Rev

Griesemer, John

Signal & noise. Picador 2003 593p $26

ISBN 0-312-30082-4   LC 2003-42938

"Brilliant engineer Chester Ludlow is soon transformed into a mesmerizing showman when he becomes involved in the laying of the trans-Atlantic cable. Attempting to raise the cash needed to launch the initiative, Ludlow travels with a musical 'Phantasmagorium Show,' which bowls over willing investors with its complex scene-shifting and inspiring narration. Soon the money is pouring in, and Chester becomes a celebrity and begins a passionate affair with the beautiful piano player. Meanwhile, his wife, Lily, still grieving the death of their child some years before, embarks on an intense spiritual quest in an attempt to communicate with her dead daughter." Booklist

Griesemer "has created some fine set pieces of disaster: the failed launch of the Great Eastern, two spectacular fires, a train crash that wrecks Ludlow's invention of a great Civil War cannon and, best of all, a breathtaking storm at sea. At the other end of the scale, the detail that fleshes out the novel's world is equally convincing." N Y Times Book Rev

Griffin, W. E. B.

Final justice. Putnam 2003 466p $26.95

ISBN 0-399-14926-0   LC 2002-68266

Philadelphia police "detective Sergeant Matthew Payne is working on three cases. In the first, a kitchen supervisor and a cop are murdered at a fast-food r staurant. The second is a case of rape and murder, and the third concerns a suspect who has fled the country, leaving behind a trunk containing the mummified body of his girfriend." Booklist

"What holds it all together is Griffin's infectious respect for and fascination with police work." Publ Wkly

Grimes, Martha, 1931-

Foul matter. Viking 2003 372p $25.95

ISBN 0-670-03259-X   LC 2003-50153

"Best-selling author Paul Giverney will sign with publisher Mackenzie-Haack only if it drops literary author Ned Isaly and assigns Isaly's talented editor to Paul. Ambitious editor Clive Esterhaus wants Giverney for himself but isn't comfortable with the solution proposed by Bobby Mackenzie, owner of MackenzieHaack—hiring hit men." Libr J

"The serpentine plot is fun to follow, once Giverney realizes the extent of the mischief he has set in motion. But it's the nasty inside stuff—from the Dickensian names for authors and their publishing houses to the barbaric rituals of a power lunch—that incites rolling in the aisles." N Y Times Book Rev

Grøndahl, Jens Christian, 1959-

Lucca; translated from the Danish by Anne Born. Harcourt 2003 c2002 332p $26

ISBN 0-15-100594-X   LC 2002-154301

Grøndahl, Jens Christian, 1959-—_Continued_

Original Danish edition, 1998

"The title character is an actress who has renounced her career (for love) and then blinded herself in a drunken car crash after being dumped by her husband. Her doctor has become an emotional recluse since, or possibly before, being dumped by his wife. Over the course of many pages we get their back stories." N Y Times Book Rev

The author "proves himself to be master of the poetry of small moments that can lead to shattering discoveries." Libr J

Gruber, Michael

Tropic of night. HarperCollins Pubs. 2003 419p $24.95

ISBN 0-06-050954-6　　　　LC 2002-24385

"The protagonist, who bears the real but unlikely name of Jane Doe, is living in Miami under an assumed name because she's on the run—from Africa, where, with her husband, she had been doing anthropological researh. Something happened over there that she could not have foreseen and did not bargain for. When Jane learns of the ritualistic murder of a pregnant woman in Miami's Overtown neighborhood, her heart skips a beat." Booklist

"Gruber keeps his far-flung locations, complicated characters and anthropological information perfectly balanced in this finely crafted, intelligent and original work." Publ Wkly

Gunesekera, Romesh

Heaven's edge. Grove Press 2002 234p $24

ISBN 0-8021-1735-X　　　　LC 2002-35335

"Set on an environmentally devastated tropical island . . . (this) novel follows a Londoner named Marc, who comes to the island to find his father but instead gets caught up in a passionate affair with an ecological activist." Publ Wkly

"Lurking within the story of Marc's exile is, of course, an allegory about the human condition. 'Heaven's Edge' is a somewhat self-conscious reworking of the Edenic myth, but what gives the novel its power is an awareness of the irredeemability of that condition." N Y Times Book Rev

Guterson, David

Our Lady of the Forest. Knopf 2003 323p $25.95

ISBN 0-375-41211-5　　　　LC 2002-43322

"When Ann Holmes starts having visions of the Virgin Mary, the bedraggled teen runaway becomes the last hope for the inhabitants of a dank, economically depressed logging town and the hordes of miracle-seekers who descend on it. In this panoramic, psychologically dense novel, she also becomes a symbol of the intimate intertwining of the sacred and the profane in American life." Publ Wkly

H

Haddon, Mark

The curious incident of the dog in the nighttime; a novel. Doubleday 2003 226p il $22.95

ISBN 0-385-50945-6　　　　LC 2002-31355

"The fifteen-year-old narrator of this ostensible murder mystery is even more emotionally remote than the typical crime-fiction shamus: he is autistic, prone to fall silent for weeks at a time and unable to imagine the interior lives of others. This might seem a serious handicap for a detective, but when Christopher stumbles on the dead body of his neighbor's poodle, impaled by a pitchfork, he decides to investigate. Christopher understands dogs, whose moods are as circumscribed as his own ('happy, sad, cross and concentrating'), but he's deaf to the nuances of people, and doesn't realize until too late that the clues point toward his own house and a more devastating mystery. This original and affecting novel is a triumph of empathy." New Yorker

Hadley, Tessa

Everything will be all right; a novel. Holt & Co. 2003 303p $23

ISBN 0-8050-7065-6　　　　LC 2003-49985

This novel "explores the many facets of womanhood as seen through the eyes of four generations of one English family. The narrataive centers on Joyce, whose father was killed at Dunkirk, a sensitive child who studies the females around her, gradually building an image of the woman she wishes to become. Through Joyce's adolescence, sexual awakening, motherhood, and middle age, Hadley paints a picture of unfulfilled high expectations." Booklist

Haigh, Jennifer

Mrs. Kimble. Morrow 2003 394p $24.95

ISBN 0-06-050939-2　　　　LC 2002-70304

The title "refers to three women, each of whom marries an opportunist named Ken Kimble. The first wife, Birdie, is Ken's student at a small Christian college. With her, he has two children. Then he seduces another student and deserts his family, leaving Birdie to bring up the children alone. The second Mrs. Kimble is a successful career woman, reassessing her priorities in the wake of her mastectomy. Ken capitalizes on Joan's neediness and sweeps her off her feet. He also ingratiates himself with her uncle, a real estate tycoon. When Joan and Uncle Floyd die, Ken inherits from both. The third Mrs. Kimble had been the first Mrs. Kimble's babysitter. . . . Original and compelling. Libr J

Hall, Brian, 1959-

I should be extremely happy in your company; a novel of Lewis and Clark. Viking 2003 419p $25.95

ISBN 0-670-03189-5　　　　LC 2002-66376

"Narrated in multiple distinct voices, this retelling of the story of Meriwether Lewis and William Clark's legendary expedition is less a historical blow-by-blow than an engaging character study of the two men. Hall focuses on a few significant episodes in the journey—such as the hunting accident that wounds Lewis and causes him to sink into his famous depression—as seen through the eyes of Lewis, Sacagawea, Clark and Toussaint Charbonneau, Sacagawea's French fur trader husband. The result is a memorable portrait of the expedition leaders." Publ Wkly

Hall, James W., 1947-

Off the chart; a novel. St. Martin's Minotaur 2003 337p $24.95

ISBN 0-312-27178-6   LC 2002-191965

"Thorn's long-ago fling with a beautiful woman named Anne Joy comes back to haunt him years later when Anne's brother, Vic Joy, a modern-day pirate along the Gulf Coast, decides he needs to add Thorn's five-acre property to his ill-gotten business and real estate empire." Publ Wkly

"Yes, we like to imagine ourselves wearing Thorn's deck shoes, in a full-frontal assault on all those who endanger our world, but Hall, unlike most thriller writers, portrays the collateral damage wreaked when rugged individualists go into overdrive. This remains one of the best series in the genre." Booklist

Hallgrímur Helgason, 1959-

101 Reykjavík; a novel; translated by Brian FitzGibbon. Scribner 2003 339p $23

ISBN 0-7432-2514-7   LC 2002-29434

"Hlynur Björn is, by his own admission, a 33-year-old mommy's boy. He lives at home, spends his days watching porn and surfing the Web, and his nights at Reykjavik's nightclubs drinking and taking Ecstasy. He assigns every woman he encounters a monetary value and refuses to commit to spending even a full night with his casual girlfriend, Hofy. When Hofy falls pregnant and his mother announces that her lesbian lover, Lolla, whom Hlynur slept with on New Year's Eve, is also pregnant, he must fight to protect his selfish and shallow way of life." Publ Wkly

"This novel uses caustic and irreverent humor to paint a vivid picture of Icelandic youth ideas and culture. . . . While the protagonist is confused, depressed, and futureless, the humor saves the book from being depressing." Libr J

Hambly, Barbara

Days of the dead. Bantam Bks. 2003 314p il maps $23.95

ISBN 0-553-10954-5   LC 2002-38571

"An extreme case of culture shock awaits Benjamin January. . .when he leaves cosmopolitan New Orleans, a city that loves life, for bellicose Mexico, a country that lives for its dead. Traveling with his bride, Rose, by overland coach in 1835, this Paris-trained surgeon (and former slave) encounters bloodthirsty bandits, fierce soldiers from Santa Anna's army, rebellious Yankees from uncivilized Texas and a hacienda teeming with feuding relatives on the country estate of the Spanish grandee Don Prospero's only son." N Y Times Book Rev

Hamill, Pete

Forever; a novel. Little, Brown 2002 613p $25.95

ISBN 0-316-34111-8   LC 2002-114241

"In 1740, an Irish Jew named Cormac O'Connor heads to New York in pursuit of the man who killed his father and gets tangled up in a rebellion against the English. Through a series of events involving an African slave with shamanistic powers, he is granted eternal life, provided that he never leaves Manhattan. There follows a tour of the city's history through Cormac's eyes: the political corruption and the poverty, but also the majestic growth of the metropolis through its culture, its buildings, and its people." New Yorker

Hansen, Brooks, 1965-

The monsters of St. Helena. Farrar, Straus & Giroux 2002 306p $24

ISBN 0-374-27019-8   LC 2002-23433

This novel speculates on Napoleon's "second exile on the remote Atlantic island of St. Helena, where he spent his remaining years dictating his memoirs. Because his island residence is incomplete, the emperor-turned-prisoner stays with the Balcombe family, whose 14-year-old daughter Betsy befriends him. . . . As a contrast, the island's haunted history is revealed through its slaves, who all know the story of St. Helena's first exile, fallen nobleman Fernando Lopez, and his connection to the island." Libr J

"Hansen's characters, St. Helena aside, are obstinately alive, with their own plots, hopes and limits, especially with their own faith. The book's risky shape comes to seem almost as disciplined as a history—a matter of respect for the records Hansen has so precisely imagined." N Y Times Book Rev

Hansen, Ron

Isn't it romantic?; an entertainment. HarperCollins Pubs. 2003 198p $17.95

ISBN 0-06-051766-2   LC 2002-69082

"Beautiful, self-possessed Parisian Natalie Clairvaux, a lover of all things American, decides to assuage her hurt feelings over her fiance's latest infidelity by taking a trip to the U.S. Appalled at Natalie's destination choice, the local travel agent grudgingly books her on a Greyhound See America tour. . . . When her fiance, Pierre, comes after her, they end up stranded by a flat tire in Seldom, Nebraska, and are lovingly embraced by the town's eccentric citizens." Booklist

"This is a preposterous plot, and at its best, 'Isnt It Romantic?' zips along like a Preston Sturges movie. Hansen slicks down his prose so the sentences are swift, and he punctuates them with a dry wit and some genuinely droll ripostes." N Y Times Book Rev

Hardie, Kerry

A winter marriage; a novel. Little, Brown 2003 394p $24.95

ISBN 0-316-07622-8   LC 2002-20781

"At a friend's wedding in England, widowed Hannie meets Ned Renvyle, a much older writer looking for a wife, and they agree to a pragmatic marriage—he gets a companion, she gets to share his money. Settling on Ned's farm in the Irish countryside, Hannie soon discovers that enduring the snooping of the snobbish community may be too high a price to pay for financial security, particularly when her disturbed teenage son, Joss, arrives." Publ Wkly

"This disquieting domestic drama effortlessly transforms itself into a taut psychological thriller featuring a harrowing back-story." Booklist

Harding, Paul

For works written by this author under other names see Doherty, P. C.

Harrar, George, 1949-

The spinning man. Putnam 2003 341p $24.95

ISBN 0-399-14983-X LC 2002-74532

This suspense novel "follows a philosophy professor under invesigation for the disappearance of a teenage cheerleader. Evan Birch gets pulled over by the police one evening on his way home from the supermarket with his 10-year-old twin sons. The police haul him in for interrogation, and he learns that a car much like his was spotted at the park where 16-year-old Joyce Bonner, a local high school student, was working the afternoon she disappeared. He's released after questioning, but damning circumstantial evidence continues to pile up." Publ Wkly

"A graceful and subtle writer, Harrar invites us to identify with the philosopher's struggles to maintain his mental equilibrium, even as the novel dangles the possibility that the mind might not always be in control of the body's behaviors." N Y Times Book Rev

Harris, Robert, 1957-

Pompeii. Random House 2003 278p $24.95

ISBN 0-679-42889-5 LC 2003-58446

A thriller about the "eruption of Mount Vesuvius in A. D. 79. It starts innocently enough; two days before the eruption, Marcus Attilius Primus, the engineer in charge of the massive Aqua Augusta Aqueduct, is summoned to the estate of Ampilatus. He is in the process of executing a slave for killing his fish. Attilius finds sulfur in the water and immediately realizes the problem is bigger than a few dead fish. With the approval of the famous admiral Pliny, Attilius sails to Pompeii and treks to the heart of the Aqua Augusta at the base of Mount Vesuvius. Attilius discovers the blockage that threatens to deprive a large chunk of the empire of water, but he is also troubled by the strange natural occurrences that may portend something far more serious than a blocked water supply." Booklist

"Lively writing, convincing but economical period details and plenty of intrigue keep the pace quick." Publ Wkly

Harrod-Eagles, Cynthia

Gone tomorrow; a Bill Slider mystery. Thomas Dunne Bks. 2002 362p $24.95

ISBN 0-312-30046-8 LC 2002-32475

"Dectective Inspector Slider investigates the murder of a fit, expensively dressed man whose body is left in a children's playground. He soon uncovers connections to drugs, scams, prostitution, and more." Libr J

Hart, Carolyn G.

Engaged to die; a death on demand mystery; [by] Carolyn Hart. Morrow 2003 311p $23.95

ISBN 0-06-000469-X LC 2002-70994

"Invited to a combined art opening and engagement party, mystery bookstore owner Annie Darling and her husband, Max, are present when the groom-to-be is found with his head bashed in. Circumstantial evidence points to one of Annie's young friends as the most promising suspect. After Max is deputized to help solve the case but Annie is not, Annie works on her own to exonerate her friend." Booklist

"The interplay between Annie and Max enhances the plot, where in lesser hands it would become the focus." Publ Wkly

Harvey, Jack See Rankin, Ian, 1960-

Haskell, John, 1958-

I am not Jackson Pollock. Farrar, Straus & Giroux 2003 180p $20

ISBN 0-374-17399-0 LC 2002-33889

Analyzed in Short story index

Contents: Dream of a clean slate; Elephant feelings; The judgment of Psycho; The faces of Joan of Arc; Capucine; Glenn Gould in six parts; Good world; Crimes at midnight; Narrow road

"Most of the nine stories are imaginative extrapolations of the lives of real people (or, in some cases, real animals), such as the eponymous painter and his wife, Lee Krasner; Psycho stars Janet Leigh and Anthony Perkins; Laika, the first dog in space; and Saartjie, the early 19th-century South African woman brought to London as the famous sideshow attraction the Hottentot Venus. . . . Haskell subtly explores questions of exploitation and agency through the eyes of his celebrity characters, winking all the while at his own attempts to get into their heads. His hypnotic writing creates its own genre, unsettling and quietly bizarre. Publ Wkly

Hassler, Jon

The Staggerford flood. Viking 2002 199p $24.95

ISBN 0-670-03125-9 LC 2001-56808

"A natural disaster threatens the unique rural charm of Hassler's Minnesota village in the latest installment in his ongoing series. . . . Agatha McGee is the 80-year-old sixth-grade teacher who is beginning to dread the onset of old age, so much so that a local radio personality suggests that she hold her own memorial party in advance to try to get a lift from the tribute. What invigorates Agatha instead is the threat of a flood, which distracts her from her preoccupation with local gossip and causes her to offer shelter to several troubled residents, including a combative mother and daughter as well as several friends and acquaintances." Publ Wkly

Hautman, Pete, 1952-

Doohickey; a novel. Simon & Schuster 2002 277p $24

ISBN 0-7432-0019-5 LC 2002-70671

"Nicholas Fashon and his pal Vince Love own a fashionable leather goods store in Tucson, Ariz. Nick's roguish granddad dies, leaving him a inheritance of useless inventions. Useless, that is, with one exception: a doohickey called the HandyMate, which performs numerous kitchen functions most efficiently. Yola Fuentes, a TV chef, is interested in the HandyMate and wants to use it on her TV show. Nick is grateful, especially since the building housing his store and the apartment upstairs containing all his worldly goods has just burned down." Publ Wkly

A "comic mystery that benefits greatly from deadpan humor; likable, eccentric characters; and a moral cleverly cloaked by the twisting plot." Booklist

Hay, Elizabeth

Garbo laughs. Counterpoint 2003 294p $25

ISBN 1-582-43291-0 LC 2003-11989

Hay, Elizabeth—*Continued*

A novel set in Ottawa. "Harriet, the Garbo-like star of the book, is a novelist who has developed the curious habit of writing but not mailing confiding letters to her hero, the then still-living film critic Pauline Kael, and discussing, at length, such burning cinematic questions as who is sexier, Cary Grant or Sean Connery, with her sweetly precocious and equality movie-mad son and daughter. As Harriet indulges her grand obsession with movies, she struggles with her less than passionate feelings for her real-life leading man and forges a warm but risky friendship with a new neighbor, the earthy Dinah." Booklist

"This rich, lovely novel makes us think about the ambivalences and contradictions of relationships and the patience of love." Quill & Quire

Haywood, Gar Anthony

Man eater; [by] Ray Shannon. Putnam 2003 280p $23.95

ISBN 0-399-14976-7   LC 2002-73965

"Production company executive Ronnie Deal has unwittingly bought herself a world of trouble. When she stops a thug from beating up a young woman, she has no idea that the man she attacks is Neon Polk, a hit man and psycho intimately familiar with all forms of violence. Now, Ronnie has added her name to Polk's unofficial hit list. Needing help, she turns to Ellis Langford, a recently released ex-con and aspiring screenwriter whose script happens to be in Ronnie's possession." Libr J

"Shannon adroitly threads plots and subplots together, occasionally smashing characters into one another with much brio and bloodshed." Publ Wkly

Hazzard, Shirley, 1931-

The great fire. Farrar, Straus & Giroux 2003 278p $24

ISBN 0-374-16644-7   LC 2003-49189

"The time is 1947-48, and the place is, primarily, East Asia. . . . Our hero, and indeed he fills the requirements to be called one, is Aldred Leith, who is English and part of the occupation forces in Japan; his particular military task is damage survey. He has an interesting past, including, most recently, a two-year walk across civil-war-torn China to write a book. In the present. . .he meets the teenage daughter and younger son of a local Australian commander. And, as Helen is growing headlong into womanhood, this novel of war's aftermath becomes a story of love—or more to the point, of the restoration of the capacity for love once global and personal trauma have been shed." Booklist

Heinrich, Will

The king's evil; a novel. Scribner 2003 195p $23

ISBN 0-7432-3504-5   LC 2003-42374

"Narrator Joseph Malderoyce knew passion only in his youth, when he vowed to be a painter, but that ambition was erased when an exhibition of Mondrians left him in hopeless awe. After working as a lawyer for many years, he resigns from his firm and moves to a remote rural village. . . . Joseph's quiet existence is abruptly altered when he discovers a strange teenager, Abel Rufous, asleep on his back porch. The boy has been beaten, and

Joseph invites him in, sympathetically offering him a room and assistance." Publ Wkly

"Offbeat but undeniably well written—there are intriguing digressions on such topics as Piet Mondrian and the history of tuberculosis—this first novel about facing the darker forces of one's personality has psychological, philosophical and even biblical overtones." Libr J

Helgason, Hallgrímur *See* Hallgrímur Helgason, 1959-

Heller, Zoe

What was she thinking?; notes on a scandal. Holt & Co. 2003 258p $23

ISBN 0-8050-7333-7   LC 2002-38809

"Barbara Covett, a sixtyish history teacher, is the kind of unmarried-woman-with-cat whose female friends sooner or later decide she is 'too intense.' Thus when a beautiful new pottery teacher, Sheba Hart. . .chooses Barbara as a confidante, she is deeply, even rather sinisterly, gratified. Sheba's secret is explosive: married with two kids, she is having an affair with a fifteen-year-old student. . . .Equally adroit at satire and at psychological suspense, Heller charts the course of a predatory friendship and demonstrates the lengths to which some people go for human company." New Yorker

Henry, Sue, 1940-

Death trap; an Alaska mystery. Morrow 2003 273p $23.95

ISBN 0-380-97883-0   LC 2002-33734

"Sidelined from sled-dog racing this season because of a knee injury, musher Jessie Arnold agrees to help out a friend by working the Iditarod booth at the Alaska State Fair. The fun of the fair ends abruptly for Jessie when a man is found dead in a pond on the grounds, and her beloved lead dog, Tank mysteriously disappears from the booth. . . . Interesting developments in Jessie's personal life will please fans of this long-running series." Booklist

Higgins, Jack, 1929-

Bad company. Putnam 2003 287p $25.95

ISBN 0-399-14970-8   LC 2003-41365

"As the war is drawing to a close in 1945, Hitler gives his diary to an aide for safekeeping. The diary contains an account of a meeting between representatives of Hitler and President Roosevelt at which they discussed ways to negotiate a peace treaty and then to attack Russia. The aide, Max von Berger, is now (in 2003) a billionaire industrialist and a silent partner with an international crime family. Seeking revenge for a killing, Berger vows to reveal the diary's secret that would destroy the current U.S. president. It's up to an American and a British agent to get the diary before it falls into the hands of the president's enemies." Booklist

Hillerman, Tony

The sinister pig. HarperCollins Pubs. 2003 228p $25.95

ISBN 0-06-019443-X   LC 2003-42316

Hillerman, Tony—*Continued*

"A barren desert landscape is quickly filled with Navajo tribal police, customs patrol officers, and the FBI when a dumped, unidentified body is discovered on the Navajo Reservation. The gathering of experts gives Hillerman the chance to bring back both Lieutenant Joe Leaphorn, whom he retired but can't bear to live without, and Officer Bernie Manuelito, now reassigned to the customs patrol and still ambivalent about her on-again, off-again romance with Sergeant Jim Chee." Booklist

"With his usual up-front approach to issues concerning Native Americans such as endlessly overlapping jurisdictions, Hillerman delivers a masterful tale that both entertains and educates." Publ Wkly

Hirshberg, Glen, 1966-

The Snowman's children. Carroll & Graf Pubs. 2002 324p $24

ISBN 0-7867-1082-9

"Troubled 29-year-old Mattie Rhodes returns to Detroit in search of hs childhood friend Theresa, a brilliant, strange, and mysterious girl who, even now, haunts him. For a few magical months in 1977, Mattie, Theresa, and their friend, Spencer, the lone black boy bused to their school as part of Detroits' desegregation mandate, form a special bond, united by their outsider status. At the same time, a serial killer called the Snowman has been preying on children, snatching them in broad daylight. . . . As Mattie and Spencer begin to sense that Theresa is in danger of slipping away from them and descending into mental illness, they concoct a desperate plan to save her and instead condemn their families to the nightmare of media publicity." Booklist

Hoffman, Alice

The probable future. Doubleday 2003 322p $24.95

ISBN 0-385-50760-7   LC 2003-40960

"In a New England family in which generations of women have magical powers, young Stella foresees a murder, a crime that her father is then accused of committing." SLJ

"Filled with vivid (if sometimes sketchy) characters and cinematic descriptions of New England landscapes, this book will be a hit wherever Hoffman is in demand." Libr J

Hoffman, Eva

The secret; a novel. PublicAffairs 2002 265p $25

ISBN 1-58648-150-9   LC 2002-73433

"The time is 2022, the place is Chicago, and Iris Surrey has an unusually close relationship with her chilly mother, Elizabeth. At 17, Iris is wearying of the odd stares she triggers in others, especially when her look-alike mother is with her. Iris wants to learn the identity of her father, which, alas, is not possible; the reader will figure out before Iris does that she is the product of genetic engineering. When Iris uncovers the truth, she goes on an emotional rampage, intent on tracking down any blood relatives in the hope that they will make her feel more authentic." Libr J

This work "is compelling throughout for Hoffman's prose, for her insights on identity, for her reflections on history." N Y Times Book Rev

Hoffman, William, 1925-

Wild thorn. HarperCollins Pubs. 2002 293p $24.95

ISBN 0-06-019798-6   LC 2001-58336

"Charley LeBlanc, the black sheep of a prominent family first introduced in Hoffman's Tidewater Blood, returns from Montana to his native Shawnee County in West Virginia for what he thinks will be a short visit. He is accompanied by his tough, sexy girlfriend, Blackie, whose hillbilly argot belies her extensive reading. When he calls on his old friend, the aging Aunt Jessie Arbuckle, he finds her isolated home crawling with police. She has been found dead under mysterious circumstances." Publ Wkly

"This entertaining murder mystery is replete with corrupt lawmen, betraying kin, dignified country folk, and the genteel residents of Wild Thorn manor. Further intrigue results over the true identity of two women: Esmerelda, who lives wild in the forest, and Jennie Bruce, the seductive mistress of Wild Thorn." Libr J

Holman, Sheri

The mammoth cheese; a novel. Atlantic Monthly Press 2003 442p $24

ISBN 0-87113-900-6   LC 2003-41796

This novel "begins with the media circus surrounding the birth of 11 infants to Manda Frank, a hapless young dog breeder living in the rural Virginia town of Three Chimneys. It's a situation ripe for satire or social commentary, but Holman isn't interested in anything so obvious. Her focus quickly widens to encompass a handful of Frank's neighbors and their ordinary, deeply eccentric lives." N Y Times Book Rev

Hospital, Janette Turner, 1942-

Due preparations for the plague. Norton 2003 401p $24.95

ISBN 0-393-05764-X   LC 2002-156598

"Lowell is a single father whose mother died when terrorists hijacked an Air France plane she was on in 1987. That event continues to haunt him and the other children of the victims, one of whom, Samantha, is convinced that the whole story of the hijacking has never been told and wants Lowell's help in unearthing it. When Lowell's father, a CIA agent, dies suspiciously and leaves his son incriminating evidence about the U.S.'role in Air France 64, Lowell reluctantly joins forces with Sam." Booklist

"Using the form of a politico-literary thriller, Janette Turner Hospital has attempted a meta-physical novel of evil. . . .'Due preparations for the Plague'—the title and the frequent quotes from Camus indicate the author's larger intentions—is a descent through Dantean circles of governmental conspiracy and betrayal." N Y Times Book Rev

Hosseini, Khaled

The kite runner. Riverhead Bks. 2003 324p $24.95

ISBN 1-57322-245-3   LC 2003-43106

"Amir, the son of a well-to-do Kabul merchant, is the first-person narrator, who marries, moves to California and becomes a successful novelist. But he remains haunted by a childhood incident in which he betrayed the trust of his best friend, a Hazara boy named Hassan, who re-

Hosseini, Khaled—*Continued*

ceives a brutal beating from some local bullies. After establishing himself in America, Amir learns that the Taliban have murdered Hassan and his wife, raising questions about the fate of his son, Sohrab. Spurred on by childhood guilt, Amir makes the difficult journey to Kabul, only to learn the boy has been enslaved by a former childhood bully who has become a prominent Taliban official." Publ Wkly

"Khaled Hosseini gives us a vivid and engaging story that reminds us how long his people have been struggling to triumph over the forces of violence." N Y Times Book Rev

Houellebecq, Michel

Platform; a novel; translated from the French by Frank Wynne. Knopf 2003 259p $25

ISBN 0-375-41462-2   LC 2002-40634

Original French edition, 2001

"Michel, a 40-year-old bachelor, is a civil servant working in the ministry of Culture. He falls for Valerie, a woman he first meets on a group tour vacation to Thailand. The point of his trip—which he pays for with money that he inherits when his father is murdered by the Muslim brother of his father's cleaning lady/lover—is to see if Thai prostitutes are as pretty, expert and reasonable as he imagines. . . . Valerie works for Aurore, a multinational hotel and resort chain. She and Michel persuade her boss, Jean-Yves Frochot, to invest in sex tourism resorts, but the plan goes terribly awry because of a terrorist attack by puritanical Islamic fanatics on a resort in Thailand." Publ Wkly

"Houellebecq can be a terrific writer, funny and prophetic, more feverishly alive to the world around him than are many authors more tasteful, less offensive, less willing to take risks." N Y Times Book Rev

House, Silas, 1971-

A parchment of leaves; a novel. Algonquin Bks. 2002 278p $23.95

ISBN 1-565-12367-0   LC 2002-66570

"In 1917 rural Kentucky, a young Cherokee woman named Vine, rumored to cast spells on unsuspecting men, falls in love with local Irishman Saul Sullivan, whom she eventually marries. . . (This novel) tells the story of Vine and Saul's tender relationship and the prejudice they face and eventually overcome." Libr J

"This is a moving love story set against a stunningly beautiful background, and House seems to capture it all—the deep emotion, the love of land, the customs of mountain people—in quietly eloquent prose." Booklist

House, Tom

The beginning of calamities; a novel. Bridge Works 2005 288p $24.95

ISBN 1-88259-369-3   LC 2002-152049

This novel is "set in the mid-1970s in a blue-collar Long Island town. Shy, awkward, 11-year-old Danny recreates the Passion of Christ as a school play to be performed for his fellow parochial school students during Holy Week. Impressed by his initiative, Danny's young teacher, Liz Kaigh, gets caught up in producing and directing the piece, whose troupe of players is eventually composed of the class misfits. The author effectively depicts Danny's constant personal angst and spiritual longings within the context of religious suffering but also manages to add a note of dark humor." Libr J

Huebner, Andrew

We Pierce; a novel. Simon & Schuster 2003 278p $24

ISBN 0-7432-1277-0   LC 2003-41618

This autobiographical novel "relates the story of two brothers: one whose sense of duty propels him into the Gulf War as a tank commander, the other whose equally strong sense of his duty to protest war leads him eventually to New York to ultimately fight a war of his own." Booklist

"The emotional impact builds even when the events being described are somewhat predictable, and the characters are richly individualized." Publ Wkly

Hulme, Juliet *See* Perry, Anne, 1938-

Hunt, Walter H.

The dark path. TOR Bks. 2003 413p $27.95

ISBN 0-7653-0606-9   LC 2002-38757

"A Tom Doherty Associates book"

Sequel to: The dark wing (2001)

"The war between the human and zor races has ended, and both have learned to coexist on the borders of the Solar Empire. When some Exploration Service vessels disappear, Ch'k'te, a young zor 'Sensitive,' senses a dark presence at the root of the trouble. Ordered to deal with the escalating series of events, Commodore Jacqueline Lapierre must draw upon her own skills, along with zor mysticism, to confront an enemy that threatens the existence of both races." Libr J

Hunter, Evan, 1926-

For works written by this author under other names see McBain, Ed, 1926-

Hustvedt, Siri

What I loved; a novel. Holt & Co. 2003 370p $25

ISBN 0-8050-7170-9   LC 2002-27358

The author "co-opts New York's competitive and faddish art world for its symbol-laden milieu. Leo Hertzberg, a thoughtful art historian, narrates a measured and mesmerizing tale of passion and tragedy that spans 20 years and involves his wife, Erica, a literary scholar, his close friendship with highly provocative painter Bill Wechsler; and his hidden infatuation with Bill's sexy muse and second wife, Violet, an expert in psychotic disorders associated with women's body images." Booklist

"The imprint of Henry James turns out to have reference not to the novel's prose style, which is cleanly colloquial, but to a tragic vision in which surface decorum hides subterranean upheaval. 'What I Loved' is a rare thing, a page turner written at full intellectual stretch, serious but witty, large-minded and morally engaged." N Y Times Book Rev

I

Iagnemma, Karl

On the nature of human romantic interaction. Dial Press (NY) 2003 212cmp il $22.95

ISBN 0-385-33593-8 LC 2003-40953

Analyzed in Short story index

Contents: On the nature of human romantic interaction; The phrenologist's dream; Zilkowski's theorem; The confessional approach; The Indian agent; Kingdom, order, species; The ore miner's wife; Children of hunger

"The meticulousness of science and mathematics is applied to the mysteries of love in Iagnemma's debut collection, which features eight complex, multilayered stories in which protagonists try to balance the demands of the heart against their need for rational, orderly thinking." Publ Wkly

Iles, Greg

The footprints of God. Scribner 2003 459p $25.95

ISBN 0-7432-3469-3 LC 2003-45733

As the novel opens Dr. David Tenant is "contemplating his life after friend and mentor Andrew Fielding is found dead in his lab. A stroke is the suspected cause, but David knows better because both men were part of an ultra-top-secret project known as Project Trinity, a quantum leap in the future of supercomputing and artificial intelligence. Both men had warned their managers about the experiment's dangers, and now David believes that he is next on the hit list." Libr J

"Readers interested in the exploration of religious themes without the usual New Age blather or window-dressed dogma will snap up this novel of cutting-edge science." Publ Wkly

Inman, Robert, 1943-

Captain Saturday; a novel. Little, Brown 2002 455p $24.95

ISBN 0-316-41502-2 LC 2001-23529

"Will Baggett has settled into a comfortable existence: he's a fixture of the Raleigh community as its most popular TV weatherman; his beatiful wife, Clarice, is a successful real estate broker; and his son, Palmer, is a medical student at UNC-Chapel Hill. Yet Will's seemingly perfect facade is destroyed when his news station is bought out and he is abruptly fired. This upset to his routine has a ripple effect; Clarice announces she wants a divorce, his relationship with Palmer is proven to be not as solid as he once believed, and Will finds himself accidentally embroiled in legal problems." Booklist

"Peopled with vivid, endearingly quixotic characters and filled with dead-on insights into a shallow New South that defines itself by club memberships and designer labels, this richly textured epic is paean to the vagaries of the human heart." Publ Wkly

Itani, Frances, 1942-

Deafening. Atlantic Monthly Press 2003 378p $24

ISBN 0-87113-902-2 LC 2003-45108

"Grania O'Neill has been deaf since an early childhod fever. . . . Leaving her intimate Canadian hometown for the Ontario School for the Deaf, she learns sign language and finds Jim, who expresses his love for her by describing beautiful sounds. Unfortunately for their marriage, Jim is off to the trenches of World War I, where the sounds (and sights) are horrifying indeed." Booklist

"This novel is not only a beautifully crafted love story but also an exploration of the possibilities of language and the eloquence of silence." Libr J

Iyer, Pico

Abandon; a romance. Knopf 2003 353p $24

ISBN 0-375-41505-X LC 2002-70059

"John Macmillan is a student at a Santa Barbara, Calif., university trying to finish his thesis on the lesser works of Sufi master Rumi. John begins searching the globe for a secret Islamic manuscript, reputedly smuggled out of Iran after the Shah's downfall, that may contain lost poems by Rumi. He travels through Syria, Iran, Spain and India; though the search is mostly fruitless, along the way he finds himself drawn into a romance with the flighty, fragile, slightly New Agey Camilla Jensen." Publ Wkly

"Iyer's writing is often poetic, and in presenting the Persian diaspora in Southern California, he has an intriguing way of peeling back familiar landscapes to reveal hidden sights." Booklist

J

Jaber, Diana Abu- *See* Abu-Jaber, Diana

Jaffe, Rona

The room-mating season. Dutton 2003 326p $24.95

ISBN 0-525-94713-2 LC 2002-73855

"The year is 1963, and college friends Leigh and Cady are determined to begin their adult lives amid the cosmopolitan social whirl of New York City. An ad for roommates brings two more young women into the circle: Vanessa, a sophisticated airline stewardess, and awkward, needy misfit Susan. . . . Jaffe traces the lives of her characters over the next four decdes with wit and poignancy." Booklist

Johnson, Adam

Parasites like us; a novel. Viking 2003 341p $24.95

ISBN 0-670-03240-9 LC 2002-41181

"Anthropology professor Hank Hannah studies the Clovis people, a prehistoric tribe of hunter-gatherers. His theory is that their hunting habits helped kill off 35 species of large mammals. The discovery of a Clovis arrowhead helps substantiate his claim, but disaster strikes when Hannah and two graduate students, publicity hound Brent Eggers and formidable Trudy Labelle, try to dig up the remains of a Clovis male. The police appear and Hannah is arrested for assaulting the officer who defiles the grave site. His stint at a luxury low-security prison, Club Fed, is interrupted by the outbreak of a deadly epidemic, transmitted from pigs to humans and triggered

Johnson, Adam—*Continued*

when Eggers and Labelle use the Clovis arrowhead to kill a pig." Publ Wkly

"Johnson relates all of this with great ingenuity and bravado—as well as a good deal of unfocused energy. . . . The most daring element in this heterogeneous mix, however, may well be the vein of earnest solemnity that Johnson adds to it. Unlike most satirists, he's not afraid to let the mask of irony fall occasionally." N Y Times Book Rev

Johnson, Diane, 1934-

L'affaire. Dutton 2003 340p $24.95

ISBN 0-525-94740-X   LC 2003-13725

"Amy Hawkins, a beautiful, naïve, suddenly very rich Califonian dot-com entrepreneur, comes to a posh ski resort in the French Alps as part of her plan for cultural self-improvement. When she generously pays for transporting the dying Adrian Venn, a publisher crushed in a landslide, back to his native England, her humanitarian gesture backfires with exquisite irony. Venn's two grown English children, his illegitimate French daughter, his new much younger American wife and their toddler son become embroiled in a classic scenario of quarreling heirs, each seething with expectations at the expense of the others." Publ Wkly

"Much of the wit comes from Johnson's shrewd view of her characters' cultural assumptions, which are both simplistic and devilishly on target." N Y Times Book Rev

Johnson, Stephanie, 1961-

The sailmaker's daughter. St. Martin's Press 2003 255p il map $23.95

ISBN 0-312-30693-8   LC 2003-40639

First published 1996 in the United Kingdom with title: The heart's wild surf

"The book follows 12-year-old Olive McNab during the month she is sent to her aunt and uncle's plantation while her mother is dying of influenza. Olive is haunted by ghosts of the family dead, appalled by her uncle's coarse brutality, fascinated by two free-spirited British lady travelers who are passing through, and, most of all, anguished by her mother's approaching death. In Johnson's poetic hands Olive and her eccentric family come to life." Libr J

Johnston, Wayne

The navigator of New York; a novel. Doubleday 2002 483p $27.95

ISBN 0-385-50767-4   LC 2002-71418

"Devlin Stead is the orphaned protagonist raised by his aunt and uncle in Newfoundland after his physician father dies in a polar expediation under the aegis of Robert Edwin Peary and Dr. Frederick Cook. The boy's sheltered existence is shattered when he receives a series of letters from Cook that reveal the explorer—who had committed an indiscretion with Devlin's mother—to be the boy's real father. Cook invites Devlin to New York, where he takes him under his wing and makes him an assistant." Publ Wkly

"Polar exploration—with its incredible hardships, its months of freezing isolation, darkness and despair—makes an irresistable metaphor for a lonely and uncertain childhood. The story itself is told through Devlin's deliberately understated narration and Cook's long expository letters and monologues, which can be tedious at times but which echo the straightforward humble-heroic tone of a Victorian explorer." N Y Times Book Rev

Jones, Edward P.

The known world. Amistad 2003 388p $24.95

ISBN 0-06-055754-0   LC 2003-40389

"Henry Townsend, born a slave, is purchased and freed by his father, yet he remains attached to his former owner, even taking lessons in slave owning when he eventually buys his own slaves. Townsend is part of a small enclave of free blacks who own slaves, thus offering another angle on the complexities of slavery and social relations in a Virginai town just before the Civil War." Booklist

"There are few certified villains in the novel, white or black, because slavery poisons moral judgements at the root. . . . The freshness of this story lies in its very incongruity and strangeness." N Y Times Book Rev

Jong, Erica

Sappho's leap; a novel. Norton 2003 316p $24.95

ISBN 0-393-05761-5   LC 2002-155113

A "interpretation of the life of the first known woman poet, Sappho, who lived on the island of Lesbos 2,600 years ago and wrote and performed poems of indelible candor and eroticism. Jong envisions Sappho as an ardent and adventurous soul who, while still in her teens, meet the love of her life (the rebel poet Alcaeus), reveals her poetic talents, and is forced into exile and marriage to a wealthy old drunk." Booklist

Jong's "effort to bring to life an ancient writer engrossed in politics, family and the creation of poety is a relief from the relentlessly everyday sincerity of much current 'women-oriented' writing." N Y Times Book Rev

Judd, Alan

Legacy. Knopf 2002 245p $24

ISBN 0-375-41484-3   LC 2002-16262

First published 2001 in the United Kingdom

This "spy thriller, set in the 1970s, begins when fledgling British agent Charles Thoroughgood receives an assignment: he is to persuade his former Oxford classmate, Viktor Koslov, now a liaison at the Soviet Embassy and apparently an undercover operative, to defect. But before he can do it, Koslov stuns him with the revelation that Thoroughgood's late father, an engineer who also had a military career, was working as a KGB agent." Publ Wkly

"Comparisons with John le Carre are inevitable, but Judd's style is more straightforward and his worldview far more benign. While fans of explosive action may find it slow going, this elegant and understated literary thriller is a worthy addition to the growing genre of historical espionage fiction." Libr J

K

Kafka, Franz, 1883-1924

Amerika; the man who disappeared; translated and with an introduction by Michael Hofmann. New Directions 2002 216p $23.95

ISBN 0-8118-1513-X

Original German edition, 1927; this translation first published 1996 in the United Kingdom

"Kafka left six completed chapters and a number of additional scenes, two of which appear in English for the first time in this new translation. . . . Anything by Kafka is worth reading again, especially in the hands of such a gifted translator as Hofmann." N Y Times Book Rev

Kalfus, Ken

The commissariat of enlightenment; a novel. Ecco Press 2003 295p $24.95

ISBN 0-06-050136-7   LC 2002-69308

"For Comrad Astapov of the Agitprop Section of the Commissariat of Enlightenment, the filmmaker protagonist of this début novel, 'life's struggle was not to control events, but the way in which they were remembered.' His story begins in 1910, at the press-besieged deathbed of Tolstoy, where his talent for manipulating film to satisfy events earns the notice of Stalin. Astapov's distortions are the perfect metaphor for Kalfus's own special effects: Stalin, of course, wasn't there when Tolstoy died. Preoccupied with truth, media, history, and politics, this novel shows its mechanisms proudly." New Yorker

Kaminsky, Stuart M.

Not quite kosher; an Abe Lieberman mystery. Forge 2002 254p $23.95

ISBN 0-312-87453-7

This installment "finds Lieberman trying to cope with a jewelry heist gone bad, a potential gang war, two corpses washed up from Lake Michigan and his grandson's bar mitzvah." N Y Times Book Rev

"Although Kaminsky can plot with the best of them, his characters are the real delights of the book." Publ Wkly

Keillor, Garrison

Love me. Viking 2003 272p $24.95

ISBN 0-670-03246-8   LC 2003-52540

This novel is "about fame, seduction and downfall as experienced by a Midwestern writer named Larry Wyler, whose common sense is hijacked by best-sellerdom. When his first novel, a prairie potboiler called 'Spacious Skies,' improbably takes off, so does Wyler. He abandons ho-hum St. Paul and his wife, Iris, for the diamond glitter of Manhattan, where he gets an apartment on Central Park, an office at The New Yorker and a killer case of creative constipation." N Y Times Book Rev

The author "blends humor and compassion with just a touch of cynicism, cooking up a funny, insightful, and touching story of ambition, sacrifice, and love." Booklist

Kellerman, Faye

Street dreams. Warner Bks. 2003 420p $25.95

ISBN 0-446-53131-6   LC 2003-45079

"Cindy, a rookie cop and Peter's 28-year-old daughter by his first marriage, takes center stage here. Both her rocky history with the department and with her dad come to the fore as she digs into the case of a developmentally disabled teenager who abandoned her baby, insists she was raped, and may have witnessed a murder. Following the strangely coincidental hit-and-run of another disabled teen from the same area, the case blossoms into a mystery that requires help from Peter." Booklist

Kempadoo, Oonya

Tide running. Farrar, Straus & Giroux 2003 215p $22

ISBN 0-374-27757-5   LC 2002-37914

This is the "story of a ménage à trois involving a beautiful Tobagan man and some recent arrivals—a wealthy mixed-race couple, recklessly 'flirting with newness' in a place that still bears the historical scars of the slave trade. With a finely tuned ear for the cadences of the Caribbean, Kempadoo, . . . examines the strange symbiosis between the newcomers, seduced by local color, and the impoverished islanders, hungry for consumer goods. As the trio's relationship presses to its disastrous conclusion, she succeeds in turning an unsettling tale into an exploration of the global politics of desire." New Yorker

Kemprecos, Paul

(jt. auth) Cussler, C. White death

Keneally, Thomas

Office of innocence. Doubleday 2003 319p $25

ISBN 0-385-50763-1   LC 2002-73653

A novel "about one young priest's crisis of faith in Sydney during World War II. Father Frank Darragh already feels conflicted about being out of the fighting when his regular duties as a soft-hearted confessor at St. Margaret's begin to put him in touch with war widows and American GIs. He is especially intrigued by Kate Heggarty, who seeks spiritual guidance when she's tempted to cheat on her P.O.W. husband. The monsignor objects to Father Frank's becoming so involved in her case, which explodes in the young priest's face when Kate turns up strangled." Libr J

Keneally moves his "protagonist, as confessor, from the banal to the transcendent: from insipid negotiations with schoolchildren to a primal reckoning in a war-ravaged landscape; from an innocence barely aware of its own spiritual vanity to a disillusioned acceptance of the ubiquity of sin and the stubborn mystery of fate." N Y Times Book Rev

Kerr, Katharine

Snare; a novel of the far future. TOR Bks. 2003 591p $27.95

ISBN 0-312-89045-1   LC 2002-40947

"A Tom Doherty Associates book"

"Three very different groups of human settlers go, not all willingly, to the planet Snare: a band of Islamic fundamentalists, a group of horse tribes and the pragmatic Cantons people. All descend on Snare's indigenous repitilian species the ChaMeech, and eight centuries of territorial and social turmoil follow." Publ Wkly

"Compelling male and female characters and a thoughtful premise make this epic adventure a strong addition to most sf collections." Libr J

Keyes, J. Gregory

The Briar king; [by] Greg Keyes. Del Rey Bks. 2003 552p $23.95

ISBN 0-345-44066-8   LC 2002-31166

The author "inaugurates the Kingdoms of Thorn and Bone quartet with this epic high fantasy. The inhabitants of this splendid and dauntingly complex parallel world, Everon, are mostly descended from folk magically transported from our world. This is not quite the land of Faerie although the Briar King resembles the old Celtic horned god Cernunnos, while Keyes brings his expertise as a fencing teacher to the swordplay, here called dessrata. The Empire of Crotheny faces war with its arch-rival, the Hanzish, and magical intrigues aimed at preventing the land from having a born queen (as opposed to a king's consort)." Publ Wkly

Kidd, Sue Monk

The secret life of bees. Viking 2002 301p $24.95

ISBN 0-670-89460-5   LC 2001-26310

This is the "tale of a 14-year-old white girl named Lily Owen who is raised by the elderly African American Rosaleen after the accidental death of Lily's mother. Following a racial brawl in 1960s Tiburon, S.C, Lily and Rosaleen find shelter in a distant town with three black bee-keeping sisters." Libr J

"Lily is a wonderfully petulant and self-absorbed adolescent, and Kidd deftly portrays her sense of injustice as it expands to accommodate broader social evils." N Y Times Book Rev

Kim, Suki, 1970-

The interpreter. Farrar, Straus & Giroux 2003 294p $24

ISBN 0-374-17713-9   LC 2002-72120

This novel introduces Korean American "Suzy Park, a 29-year-old interpreter whose work involves her in a bevy of agencies throughout the five boroughs, from the Immigration and Naturalization Service to the criminal courts. Park is blasé about her occupation until a routine translating job reveals that her greengrocer parents were not murdered by random violence, as the police had indicated, but instead had been shot by political enemies. These data provide fodder for Park, and the novel tracks her investigation into what really happened." Libr J

"This is an intriguing, tortured portrait of a second-generation Korean-American by a promising young writer." Publ Wkly

King, Laurie R.

Keeping watch. Bantam Bks. 2003 383p $23.95

ISBN 0-553-80191-0   LC 2002-34266

"At its simplest, this is the story of a man who helps rescue women and/or children from dangerously abusive men. King's lengthy, brilliantly executed backstory of Allen Carmichael's experiences in Vietnam, his disastrously unhappy return home and his eventual discovery of his 'calling' showcase some of her finest writing. Now in his early 50s, Allen is ready to retire from his dangerous vocation, to settle on his remote island and perhaps serve as a consultant to those who continue the struggle. But his last rescue, that of a 12-year-old boy trapped in a horrible situation, continues to haunt him." Publ Wkly

King, Roger, 1947-

A girl from Zanzibar. Books & Co./Helen Marx Bks. 2002 307p $14.95

ISBN 1-885586-60-4 (pa)   LC 2002-105487

A picaresque novel about a young East African woman's adventures and loves across a dozen years and three continents.

"Marcella is the author's mouthpiece, his stage manager, theorizing, summing up the action, signaling transitions, and at times these extra roles blur her outline. But the minor characters are just themselves, seen whole with tragic clarity." N Y Times Book Rev

King, Ross, 1962-

Domino. Walker & Co. 2002 435p $26

ISBN 0-8027-3378-6   LC 2002-29620

"When a talented young artist, Sir George Cautley, goes to London from Shropshire in 1780 to make something of himself, he meets a glamorous, mystifying woman named Lady Petronella Beauclair. As he paints her portrait, she tells him the labyrinthine story of an old man named Tristano, one of Europe's most renowned castrati from decades ago, who is a dormant social presence in London. As Cautley begins studies with Sir Endymion Starker, a famous artist he meets while gambling, he also makes the acquaintance of Starker's mistress, Eleanora, who has her own sad tale to tell." Publ Wkly

"Replete with mystery and suspense and immersed in vivid historical details, this work is also a sharp, philosophical musing on the disguises of the world and the search for the truth that lies beneath." Libr J

Knight, Michael, 1969-

Goodnight, nobody. Atlantic Monthly Press 2002 160p $23

ISBN 0-87113-867-0   LC 2002-27944

Analyzed in Short Story index

Contents: Birdland; Feeling lucky; Killing Stonewall Jackson; The end of everything; The mesmerist; Keeper of secrets, teller of lies; Mitchell's girls; Ellen's book; Blackout

"Stylistically, Knight slaloms through old-fashioned noir and snarky postmodernism, and from Barthelmean set pieces to a riff on Stonewall Jackson that evokes one of Barry Hannah's Civil War fever dreams." N Y Times Book Rev

Knode, Helen

The ticket out. Harcourt 2003 340p $24

ISBN 0-15-100184-7   LC 2002-7804

The morning after a party, film critic Ann Whitehead "discovers aspiring moviemaker Greta Stenholm in the bathtub, dead from knife wounds. Even though the knife used to kill Greta belongs to her, Ann's primary concern is using the story as her ticket out of the movie-reviewing business and into feature writing. Even as she patiently answers taciturn Detective Doug Lockwood's questions about the murder scene, she's busily hiding evidence. . . . . Her increasingly intimate relationship with the complicated Lockwood is the high point in this very entertaining novel." Booklist

Knox, Elizabeth, 1959-

Daylight. Ballantine Bks. 2003 356p map $23.95

ISBN 0-345-45795-1 LC 2003-544868

"Saint or vampire? The identity of the Blessed Martine Raimondi, a French nun murdered by the Nazis in 1944 for her part in the daring cave escape of rebel partisans, is only one question answered in this illuminating tour-de-force set in the south of France. . . . Brian 'Bad' Phelan, a New South Wales bomb tech and expert 'caver' on paid injury leave, helps retrieve Martine's blistered corpse outside a cave near the Italian border and discovers she bears a shocking resemblance to a woman he'd encountered years before in another flooded cave. He's further struck by Martine's resemblance to Eve Moskelute, the subject of a painting by Jean Ares, her Picasso-esque deceased husband. The author constructs an impressive mystery that dissects the meaning of miracles while putting a fresh spin on the vampire archetype." Publ Wkly

Koeppen, Wolfgang, 1906-

A sad affair; translated with an introduction by Michael Hofmann. Norton 2003 176p il $23.95

ISBN 0-393-05718-6 LC 2003-2212

Original German edition, 1934

This novel "follows the uncertain steps of young Friedrich, a university student who falls in love with an actress named Sibylle. Beautiful and unconventional in a Sally Bowles kind of way, Sybille has the usual ingénue's coterie of lovestruck suitors orbiting around her, and Friedrich is quickly drawn into what looks like a hopeless obsession. In this flowing translation by Michael Hofmann, Koeppen's narration is ellipitical and dreamlike." N Y Times Book Rev

Koontz, Dean R. (Dean Ray), 1945-

By the light of the moon; [by] Dean Koontz. Bantam Bks. 2002 431p $26.95

ISBN 0-553-80143-0 LC 2002-29902

The author "introduces readers to a twentysomething trio consisting of artist Dylan O'Conner, his autistic younger brother, Shep; and a stand-up comedienne named Jilly Jackson. One momentous evening, these threeunexpectedly find themselves coping with the bizarre effects of mysterious injections forced upon them by mad scientist Lincoln Proctor in an Arizona motel. With a generous helping of dark humor, Koontz quickly charges his characters with the task of harnessing their paranormal abilities as weapons against real-world violence and evil in a setting littered with present-day totems ranging from fast-food restaurants to sensation-mongering radio personalities." Libr J

The face; [by] Dean Koontz. Bantam Bks. 2003 608p $26.95

ISBN 0-553-80248-8 LC 2003-40354

"The eponymous Face is the world's biggest movie star; he doesn't appear in the novel, but his smart, geeky 10-year-old-son, Fric, takes center stage, as does Ethan Truman, cop-turned-security chief of the Face's elaborate estate and Fric's main human protector when one Corky Laputa, who's dedicated his life to anarchy, decides to sow further disorderby kidnapping this progeny of the world's idol. . . . Koontz's characters are memorable and his unique mix of suspense and humor absorbing." Publ Wkly

Krentz, Jayne Ann, 1948-

For works written by this author under other names see Quick, Amanda, 1948-

Kress, Nancy

Crossfire. TOR Bks. 2003 364p $245

ISBN 0-7653-0467-8 LC 2002-36671

"A Tom Doherty Associates book"

"Jake Holman, founder of the Mira Corporation, leads 6,000 private citizens in flight from a troubled Earth to the planet Greentrees, where the expedition gets caught in the crossfire between two alien races: the Furs, DNA-based humanoids who first settled the planet; and the Vines; sentient plants who arrived after the Furs, their deadly enemies of long standing. . . . Fans of serious SF will enjoy this tale of bravery, travel, adventure, and personal and social crisis." Publ Wkly

Krieg, Joyce

Murder off Mike. St. Martin's Minotaur 2003 290p $23.95

ISBN 0-312-31026-9 LC 2002-35389

Shauna J. Bogart "commands the afternoon news and talk block on Sacramento's only surviving independent radio station. In the midst of fielding calls and promos one afternoon, Bogart gets an especially . . . strange call in which the caller claims to have witnessed the murder of Dr. Hipster, the star rock dj at Shauna's station. Dr. Hipster doesn't arrive for his show and, hours later, is found dead, with a suicide note that blames Shauna Bogart." Booklist

"Politics, greed and murder combine with an intriguing behind-the-scenes look at contemporary talk radio in Krieg's superb debut." Publ Wkly

L

Lackey, Mercedes

Joust. DAW Bks. 2003 373p il $24.95

ISBN 0-7564-0122-4 LC 2003-544990

Vetch, an Altan serf, must learn the secret of the Tian jousters and their dragons in order to save his people

"This uplifting tale, which contains a valuable lesson or two on the virtues of hard work, is a must-read for dragon lovers in particular and for fantasy fans in general." Publ Wkly

Lahiri, Jhumpa

The namesake. Houghton Mifflin 2003 291p $24

ISBN 0-395-92721-8 LC 2003-41718

"A novel about assimilation and generational differences. Gogol is so named because his father believes that sitting up in a sleeping car reading Nikolai Gogol's 'The Overcoat' saved him when the train he was on derailed and most passengers perished. After his arranged marriage, the man and his wife leave India for America, where he eventually becomes a professor. They adopt American ways, yet all of their friends are Bengalis. But for young Gogol and his sister, Boston is home, and trips to Calcutta to visit relatives are voyages to a foreign land." SLJ

Lahiri, Jhumpa—*Continued*

"Its incorrigible mildness and its ungilded lilies aside, Lahiri's novel is unfailingly lovely in its treatment of Gogol's relationship with his father. This is the classic American parent-child bond." N Y Times Book Rev

Lambrecht, Patricia *See* Tracy, P. J.

Lambrecht, Traci *See* Tracy, P. J.

Landay, William, 1963-

Mission flats; [by] Bill Landay. Delacorte Press 2003 369p $23.95

ISBN 0-385-33614-4   LC 2002-34963

Maine police "Chief Truman, the narrator, stumbles upon the body of a Boston D.A. in a lakeside cabin. The Boston PD muscles him out of the case, but Truman, undeterred by the all-but-certain knowledge that the murder belongs to the controlling gang in the toughest Boston neighborhood, putzes around on his own. Truman is aided by a retired Boston cop who teaches him fascinating things about motives, blood-spatter patterns, and staged crime scenes." Booklist

Langton, Jane

The deserter; murder at Gettysburg. St. Martin's Minotaur 2003 322p il $23.95

ISBN 0-312-30186-3   LC 2002-191961

"Homer Kelly's wife, Mary, wants to clear the name of her Civil War ancestor, purported to have been a deserter. As the narrative alternates between past and present, the Kellys find evidence of false identity and murder." Libr J

"The suspense builds as the author adroitly shifts between past and present. Period photos, an 1860 playbill for the Hasty Pudding show, quotations from Walt Whitman and loads of Harvard lore add historical weight." Publ Wkly

Lansdale, Joe R., 1951-

A fine dark line. Mysterious Press 2003 307p $24.95

ISBN 0-89296-729-3   LC 2002-71387

A regional mystery "which harks back to 1958. Thirteen-year-old Stanley Mitchel, Jr., has enough on his hands just growing up in Dewmont, Tex., when he literally stumbles on a buried cache of love letters. Stanley pursues the identity of the two lovers with help from the projectionist at his family's drive-in, an aged black man who quotes Sherlock Holmes and doesn't mince words about the world's injustices. As the truth of a gruesome 20-year-old double murder comes to light in the sleepy town, so do the facts of life, death, men, women and race for young Stanley." Publ Wkly

"Stanley doesn't unravel everything, but race and power, and what people do to each other in the name of desire and religion, coalesce to a mighty climax." Booklist

Laskas, Gretchen Moran

The midwife's tale. Dial Press (NY) 2003 243p $23.95

ISBN 0-385-33551-2   LC 2002-41010

"Set in pre-World War I West Virginia, this novel flows along like the tributaries that feed the book's Appalachian foothills, as narrator Elizabeth Whitely traces the arc of four generations of midwives in her family, she being the last of the line. Poverty, lack of clean water, unemployment, an influenza epidemic, and severe weather also figure in this often melancholy tale. Laskas has injected many period details into her first book and a lot of verve into her characters to make them come alive." Libr J

Laskowski, Tim, 1957-

Every good boy does fine; a novel. Southern Methodist Univ. Press 2003 176p $23.95

ISBN 0-87074-477-1   LC 2003-40726

"Robert was a recent college graduate with a promising future as a pianist when he fell in a mountain-climbing accident. After weeks in a coma and years in a nursing home, he is placed in a rehabilitation program. At the novel's beginning, he is accepted into an accelerated program that might prepare him for relatively independent living—if he can adapt." Libr J

"Laskowski keeps the focus on Robert's daily struggles in the early going, but as the book progresses he begins to pose wrenching questions about the nature of illness and sanity. The book closes with an elegiac recovery fantasy that serves as a poignant reminder of the strength of the human spirit in the face of devastating disability." Publ Wkly

Lawton, John, 1949-

Old flames. Atlantic Monthly Press 2003 416p $24

ISBN 0-87113-864-6   LC 2002-28025

"April 1956, Nikita Krushchev is in London on a diplomatic errand. Chief Inspector Frederick Troy of Scotland Yard is assigned as a bodyguard to the Russsian leader. But he has a secret mission, too: Troy, fluent in Russian, is to spy on Khrushchev (who doesn't know the British cop speaks his language) by evesdropping on private conversations and reporting back to his superiors. It's a tough assignment, with a handful of tricky moral qualms, and it gets a heck of a lot tougher when a Royal Navy diver turns up dead." Booklist

"Lawton has created an effective genre-bending novel that is at once a cerebral thriller and an uproarious, deliciously English spoof." Publ Wkly

Le, Thi Diem Thuy, 1972-

The gangster we are all looking for. Knopf 2003 160p $18

ISBN 0-375-40018-4   LC 2002-33999

"The nameless first-person narrator is born in Vietnam, carried across the ocean by her father and 'washed to shore' in Linda Vista, a section of San Diego. Her 'Ba' finds work as a house painter, a welder and finally a gardener. It is two years before her mother joins them and her parents' tempestuous marriage moves to center stage, but the father is always a haunted, brooding presence in this drama of the narrator's coming-of-age." N Y Times Book Rev

"The story opens slowly but gathers strength, and though it remains somewhat muted, Le's lyrical writing and skill with the telling vigette will reward patient readers." Libr J

Le Guin, Ursula K., 1929-

Changing planes; illustrated by Eric Beddows. Harcourt 2003 246p il $22

ISBN 0-15-100971-6   LC 2002-14919

Analyzed in Short story index

Contents: Sita Dulip's method; Porridge on Islac; The silence of the Asonu; Feeling at home with the Hennebet; The ire of the Veksi; Seasons of the Ansarac; Social dreaming of the Frin; The royals of Hegn; Woeful tales from Mahigul; Great Joy; Wake Island; The Nna Mmoy language; The Building; The fliers of Gy; The Island of the Immortals; Confusions of Uñi

This is "philosophical fiction in the manner of Jonathan Swift and Jorge Luis Borges. . . . The narrator explains that a friend of hers, suffering from the 'tense misery, indigestion and boredom' of airport waiting rooms, discovered that with a slight twist of her mind she could transport herself to other 'planes' of existence. The 15 tales that follow are reports, ranging from the satirical to the gnomic, abut the strangely familiar societies one encounters during 'interplanary travel.'" N Y Times Book Rev

Lear, Peter *See* Lovesey, Peter

Lee, Mark, 1950-

The canal house. Algonquin Bks. 2003 353p $23.95

ISBN 1-56512-379-4   LC 2003-40401

This is the "story of the life and death of war correspondent Daniel McFarland, who after a brush with death in Uganda develops a new sense of mission and responsibility toward those whose wracked lives he is covering. He is drawn into an affair with Julia Cadel, an English doctor who idealistically ministers to the suffering in war zones, and the book's title refers to a brief idyll they share in London before setting out again on dangerous missions. Their new one is in East Timor." Publ Wkly

"Lee is a foreign correspondent who creates a powerful aura of realism that will forever alter your perception of the news." Booklist

Lefcourt, Peter

Eleven Karens; a novel. Simon & Schuster 2003 223p $24

ISBN 0-684-87034-7   LC 2002-21792

Lefcourt's "novel is essentially a series of short stories that reflect a statistical quirk—11 of his protagonist's loves have been named Karen. These femmes fatales range from the girlish—a kissing partner whom Lefcourt's hero pretends to marry in the fifth grade—to the matronly, as in the married fellow tourist who lures the narrator into an afternoon of stockings and heels in a Paris hotel." N Y Times Book Rev

"A blithe bacchanal, a lurid love song, one part travelogue, one part spoof, Lefcourt's narcissistic novel would work equally well on the big screen." Booklist

LeGuin, Ursula *See* Le Guin, Ursula K., 1929-

Lehane, Dennis

Shutter Island. Morrow 2003 325p $25.95

ISBN 0-688-16317-3   LC 2003-48744

"From the 1993 perspective of the prologue, Shutter Island is one of those unpopulated islands in Boston's outer harbor that always look so mysterious from a distance and so scruffy up close. But in 1954, when the United States marshall Teddy Daniels and his partner, Chuck Aule, alight on its rocky shores to hunt for an escaped murderess, this bleak spot is home to Ashecliffe Hospital, a maximum-security institution for the criminally insane. . . . The atmosphere is properly dark and moody, and so long as Teddy and Chuck stick to the manhunt and their investigation of Ashecliffe's creepy medical staff, they play their roles with muscle and grace." N Y Times Book Rev

Lelchuk, Alan

Ziff; a life? : a novel. Carroll & Graf Pubs. 2003 408p $25

ISBN 0-7867-1115-9   LC 2002-191184

"Dimming literary light Danny Levitan takes a last shot at glory by penning a biography of his onetime mentor and sometime friend, Arthur Ziff, a great American writer whom many Jews consider a traitor, and whose sex-charged novels have been overlooked by the Pulitzer and Nobel committees. What gives this story frisson is author Lelchuk's similar relationship with Philip Roth." Booklist

Leon, Donna

Uniform justice. Atlantic Monthly Press 2003 259p $24

ISBN 0-87113-903-0   LC 2003-44326

In this Guido Brunetti mystery "the Venetian police detective and family man is summoned to the exclusive San Martino Military Academy, where Cadet Ernesto Moro has been found dead, hanging in the lavatory." Publ Wkly

"As a thinking man, Brunetti reads Cicero for moral direction, looks to his wife for doses of cynical realism and humbly consults his secretary, the terrifyingly efficient Signorina Elettra, on practical matters. But it is as a man of sensibility that this endearing detective most engages us." N Y Times Book Rev

Leonard, Elmore, 1925-

When the women come out to dance, and other stories. Morrow 2003 228p $24.95

ISBN 0-06-008397-2   LC 2002-26426

Analyzed in Short story index

Contents: Sparks; Hanging out at the Buena Vista; Chickasaw Charlie Hoke; When the woman come out to dance; Fire in the hole; Karen makes out; Hurrah for Capt. Early; The Tonto woman; Tenkiller

"Reading the clipped, unfailingly accurate dialogue that comes out of the mouths of Leonard's characters can make you feel as if you're in the presence of a writer who is both ventriloquist and psychic. It's not just that Leonard captures the cadences and elisions of each character's speech, it's that he has an uncanny sense of knowing what each will say next." N Y Times Book Rev

Leroy, Margaret

Postcards from Berlin; a novel. Little, Brown 2003 391p $22.95

ISBN 0-316-73813-1   LC 2003-40069

Leroy, Margaret—*Continued*

"On the surface, Catriona (Cat) Lydgate enjoys a contented, middle-class life with a devoted husband, two lovely daughters, an elegant home, and a room to call her own: an attic where she dabbles at art. Things begin to unwind when Daisy, her younger daughter, comes down with the flu, which develops into a mysterious, malingering illness that causes her to stop eating and leaves her lethargic and achy. As specialist after specialist can find no physical explanation for the illness, they begin to suspect psychological causes." Libr J

"The resolution of Leroy's novel has a fairy-tale aspect, but fairy tales can nevertheless be very absorbing. Despite the occasional straining of her plot, Leroy succeeded in making me care about these characters; even at my most incredulous." N Y Times Book Rev

Lescroart, John T.

The first law; a novel; by John Lescroart. Dutton 2003 403p $25.95

ISBN 0-525-94705-1   LC 2002-37902

"The popular lawyer-cop team of Dismas 'Diz' Hardy (lawyer) and Abe Glitzky (cop) returns for another episode of legal maneuvering on the streets of San Francisco. The bullet wound sustained by Abe in Lescroart's last adventure. . . confines him to a desk job, so he's no help to Diz when he goes up against the Patrol Special, a private-enterprise neighborhood security system supervised by the SFPD. It seems that Diz's good friend, John Holliday, a bar owner in one of the patrolled areas, is fingered as a murder suspect; however, John contends the corrupt beat 'cops' framed him. . . . Lescroart's expert crafting turns this legal thriller into quite a wild ride." Booklist

Lethem, Jonathan

The fortress of solitude; a novel. Doubleday 2003 511p $26

ISBN 0-385-50069-6   LC 2003-43535

"Dylan Ebdus is a white kid on a black-and-brown street. As he strugles through public school in 1970s Brooklyn, he is 'yoked'—put in a headlock—and frisked for change on a daily basis. Testing into a good Manhattan school, he steps into a long-lasting role: vulnerable among street kids, he's street-smart compared to his new, privileged pals, and loathes himself as a poseur with both crowds. When he finds a ring that grants the power of flight, he's afraid to use it, but his black friend, Mingus, is not." Booklist

"The plot manages to encompass pop music from punk rock to rap, avant-garde art, graffiti, drug use, gentrification, the New York prison system—and to sing a vibrant, sometimes heartbreaking ballad of Brooklyn throughout. Lethem seems to have devoured the '70s, '80s, and '90s—inhaled them whole—and he reproduces them faithfully on the page, in prose as supple as silk and as bright, explosive and illuminating as fireworks." Publ Wkly

Lewis, Jim, 1963-

The king is dead. Knopf 2003 259p $24

ISBN 0-375-41417-7   LC 2002-43288

Walter Selbly "was born in 1925 and became a World War II hero, lawyer, and indispensable aide to the governor of Tennessee. His life seemed complete when he marrried beautiful Nicole Lattimore, whom he adored, and they had a son, Frank, and a daughter, Gail. Then, on a single day, Walter's professional and personal lives were destroyed, and his young children were left without parents. Thirty-five years later Frank Cartwright (with his adoptive parents' name), an attractive, womanizing actor whose career is languishing, is provoked by a film proposal from a fabled dowager to find his roots. . . . Even if the parts of this novel outshine the whole, Lewis' language often soars." Booklist

Lightman, Alan P., 1948-

Reunion; [by] Alan Lightman. Pantheon Bks. 2003 231p $23

ISBN 0-375-42167-X   LC 2002-34575

"Charles, a 'small-college professor' in his early 50's, more or less amicably settled into domestic banality in a leafy suburb, decides to attend his 30th college reunion. Once back at his unnamed alma mater. . .he is struck with eidetic force by recollections of his first passionate love affair, with an aspiring ballerina, Juliana. A narrative of this love affair and reflections upon it form the bulk of the novel." N Y Times Book Rev

"Lightman infuses even the simplest scenes with quiet menace as he explores the cataclysmic power of both erotic love and shocking betrayal." Booklist

Ligon, Samuel

Safe in heaven dead. HarperCollins Pubs. 2003 245p $23.95

ISBN 0-06-009910-0

"After stealing nearly half a million dollars of money skimmed by his bosses at the County Executive's office and deserting his wife, son and daughter, Elgin is mowed down by a bus 'while pursuing a woman he could not live without'—a woman who is a graduate student by day and and a high-priced call girl by night. How Elgin winds up in this predicament is the complex morality tale that Ligon tells in flashbacks that alternate between a third-person account shadowing Elgin's cross-country flight in search of salvaton and a first-person narration by Carla, the cynical young woman who has captured his heart." N Y Times Book Rev

Lindsey, David L.

The rules of silence; [by] David Lindsey. Warner Bks. 2003 405p $24.95

ISBN 0-446-53163-4   LC 2002-33059

"Multimillionaire Titus Cain is approached with a strange proposition: if he doesn't give a certain man $64 million, this same man will kill off some (or perhaps all) of Cain's friends and loved ones. The money has to be given to the extortionist in such a way that no one suspects anything is going on. . . and if Cain even tries to seek help, the killings will start instantly. . . . Lindsey's novels sometimes suffer from lethargy, as though he's just sort of wandering through his story, but this one moves swiftly to its rousing finale." Booklist

Lipman, Elinor

The pursuit of Alice Thrift; a novel. Random House 2003 269p $23.95

ISBN 0-679-46313-5   LC 2002-31864

Lipman, Elinor—*Continued*

"The eponymous Alice is a sleep-deprived surgical intern at a Boston hospital. A graduate of MIT and Harvard and a congenital workaholic, she's also devoid of social skills, a sense of humor or elementary tact. Though miserably unequipped with self-esteem, Alice is an intelligent, well-brought-up offspring of upper-middle-class parents. Why, then, does she fall prey to the romantic blandishments of Ray Russo, a vulgar loudmouth and con artist who—it turns out—lies every time he opens his mouth? That Lipman can make this story plausible, and tell it with humor, pschological insight and rising suspense, is a triumph." Publ Wkly

Lively, Penelope, 1933-

The photograph. Viking 2003 231p $24.95

ISBN 0-670-03205-0 LC 2002-32420

Widower "Glyn Peters, a famous British archeologist, discovers a compromising photograph of his wife, Katherine Targett, sealed in an envelope in a closet at home. Peters specializes in excavating the long defunct gardens, buried fields and covered-over roads of the British landscape. Reverting to professional habits, he treats Kath's infidelity as a sort of archeological dig. The photo depicts Kath and Nick Hammond, the husband of Kath's sister, Elaine, surreptitiously holding hands on some outing, with Elaine and Mary Parkard, Kath's best friend, in the background. Glyn decides to interview this cloud of witnesses, beginning with Elaine." Publ Wkly

"Lively's characters are shallow, their efforts at introspection often hilarious, but they are all obliged to confront their complicity in the premature death of a woman they each claim to have loved." N Y Times Book Rev

Llosa, Mario Vargas *See* Vargas Llosa, Mario, 1936-

Llywelyn, Morgan

1949; a novel of the Irish Free State. Forge 2003 414p $25.95

ISBN 0-312-86753-0 LC 2002-32525

"A Tom Doherty Associates Book"

Sequel to: 1921

"The story focuses on the indomitable Ursula Halloran. . .a young woman who first works for the Irish radio service and later the League of Nations. The unwed Ursula discovers how oppressive the new Catholic state can be when she becomes pregnant and must flee the country. Eventually, Ursula must choose between the two men in her life, one an Irish civil servant, the other an English pilot." Publ Wkly

"Llywelyn's great strength is her ability to communicate sweeping historical events through the eyes of both passive bystanders and active participants." Booklist

Loo, Tessa de

A bed in heaven; translated from the Dutch by Ina Rilke. Soho Press 2003 120p $21

ISBN 1-56947-316-1 LC 2002-30295

Original Dutch edition, 2000

"When the novel opens, narrator Kata Roszavolgyi, in her 40s, has just buried her father and is now 'lying in bed with his son.' Kata recalls growing up in Holland in the 1950s with a Dutch mother and Hungarian Jewish father, the latter a renowned composer. As a teenager she falls in love with another student named Stefan; as they grow closer, Kata learns that Stefan's mother, Ida Flinck, hid Kata's father from the Nazis during WWII. From there, the revelations pile up. . . . As the novel moves toward a climactic encounter between Kata's father and Stefan, de Loo explores the legacy of the war—loss, guilt, families set adrift—for the generation of Europeans born in its wake." Publ Wkly

Lovesey, Peter

The house sitter. Soho Press 2003 346p $25

ISBN 1-56947-326-9 LC 2002-42626

"Initially brought in as an auxilliary police consultant, Bath's Inspector Peter Diamond soon proves himself indispensable to a missing person case turned murder investigation. A woman from Bath discovered dead on a Sussex beach turns out to have been strangled—apparently right there in the midst of a crowd. The main witnesses, a family of three, seem to be hiding something. The victim was a psychological offender profiler, apparently working on the case of a serial murderer." Libr J

"The identity of the killer, when finally revealed, is genuinely startling, and not because of authorial obfuscation. The writing is as smooth as polished steel." Publ Wkly

Lowell, Elizabeth

Die in plain sight. Morrow 2003 385p $24.95

ISBN 0-06-050412-9 LC 2003-40606

"Art buyer and struggling southern California artist Lacey Quinn shows a few of her grandfather's paintings to renowned artist Susa Donovan, in the area for a charity event. The paintings are mostly landscapes, but also include a few samples from his dark later work, including detailed depictions of murder and death by fire and drowning. Believing that the landcapes are really the work of famous California plein air painter Lewis Marten, Susa asks Lacey to have them professionally appraised. Lacey resists Susa's pleas, fearing that her grandfather may have been guilty of forgery, but she discovers something far more complicated and horrifying. The murders her grandfather depicted actually took place." Publ Wkly

Ludington, Max

Tiger in a trance. Doubleday 2003 386p $24

ISBN 0-385-50704-6 LC 2002-35116

"Prep school dropout Jason Burke is the first-person narrator, dealing drugs, selling T-shirts and worshipping the guitar solos of Jerry Garcia on the group's 1985 tour. In a swirl of partying and sex, Jason pairs up first with Jane, the alluring girlfriend of a fellow dealer, then becomes more seriously involved with 17-year-old Melanie, a precocious, one-armed groupie. The novel turns darker when Jason learns that another brief rendezvous with a Dead fan has produced a child, and the darker still when he falls into the abyss of heroin addiction." Publ Wkly

This is a "road novel, and Jason is the latest incarnation of an American character passed down from Walt Whitman to Jack Kerouac: the soulful rebel with an enormous appetite for life." N Y Times Book Rev

Ludlum, Robert, 1927-2001

The Janson directive. St. Martin's Press 2002 547p $27.95

ISBN 0-312-25348-6 LC 2002-5136

Ludlum, Robert, 1927-2001—*Continued*

"The hero is Paul Janson, a private security consultant who retired a few years ago after a notorious career as the U.S. government's go-to guy for nasty jobs no one else was willing to take. Against his better judgment, Janson accepts an assignment to rescue Peter Novak, a Nobel Peace Prize-winning philanthropist and international troubleshooter held captive by Islamic extremists on an island in the Indian Ocean. . . . Extremely engaging and agonizingly suspenseful, Ludlum's plot bolts from scene to scene and locale to locale—Hungary, Amsterdam, London, New York City—never settling for one bombshell when it can drop four or five." Publ Wkly

M

MacDonald, Patricia J.

Not guilty; [by] Patricia MacDonald. Pocket Bks. 2002 357p $24.95

ISBN 0-7434-2355-0   LC 2001-59102

"Keely Bennet comes home from work one day to find her husband dead from a self-inflicted gunshot wound and her nine-year-old son cowering in the closet beside him. Several years later, her world is almost back on track; she has fallen in love, remarried, and given birth to a beautiful baby girl. But her son, Dylan, now 14, remains scarred by his dad's suicide and has grown sullen and resentful of his mom's new life. When violence strikes the family for a second time, all signs point to Dylan as the culprit." Booklist

Mackin, Edward, 1929-

For works written by this author under other names see McInerny, Ralph M., 1929-

Maillard, Keith, 1942-

The clarinet polka. Thomas Dunne Bks. 2003 406p $24.95

ISBN 0-312-30889-2   LC 2002-32511

"Jimmy Koprowski returns from his stint in the Air Force in 1969 consigned to his boyhood attic bedroom and a minimun-wage job at a TV repair shop. He drifts into an alcohol-fueled, sexually charged affair with a doctor's wife and engages in ongoing arguments about his 'life plan' with his hard-working dad. . . . Then his ethnmusicologist sister decides to start an all-girl polka band, and that's when he meets singer Janice Dluwiecki." Booklist

"Jimmy is a wry, down-to-earth, irresistable narrator, and Maillard draws all the characters in the working-class community with compassion and obvious affection. This moving, well-drawn story of sin and redemption in a fading industry town may remind readers of Richard Russo." Publ Wkly

Manicka, Rani

The rice mother. Viking 2003 432p $24.95

ISBN 0-670-03192-5   LC 2002-32421

"When 14-year-old Lakshmi marries a widower of 37, she believes that she is leaving her Sri Lankan village for a life of luxury in Malaysia. Instead, she endures hardship and poverty, giving birth to six children in the years before the Japanese invasion of World War II. In this gripping multigenerational saga, the tumultuous history of Malaysia becomes the backdrop for Lakshmi's indomitable spirit. The barbarity of the Japanese, postwar prosperity, the bursting of the Southeast Asian financial bubble, the vice trades of opium, gambling, and sex—all take their toll on Lakshmi's children and grandchildren." Libr J

Mankell, Henning, 1948-

Dogs of Riga; a Kurt Wallander mystery; translated by Laurie Thompson. Norton 2003 326p $24.95

ISBN 1-56584-787-2   LC 2002-30503

Original Swedish edition, 1992

"Set against the chaotic backdrop of eastern Europe after the fall of the Berlin Wall, Mankell's intense, accomplished mystery, the last in his Kurt Wallander series. . . explores one man's struggle to find truth and justice in a society increasingly bereft of either. Here the provincial Swedish detective takes on a probably fruitless task: investigating the murders of two unidentified men washed up on the Swedish coast in an inflatable dinghy." Publ Wkly

Firewall; translated by Ebba Segerberg. New Press (NY) 2002 405p $25.95

ISBN 1-56584-767-9   LC 2002-25543

Original Swedish editon, 1998

A mystery featuring Swedish police inspector Kurt Wallander. A "criminal mastermind is about to press the button and send the global financial network into free fall when his partner is murdered, giving Wallander a window of opportunity to scotch this mischief and let us use our A.T.M.'s again. Although things get pretty tense at the end in Ebba Segerberg's well-paced translation, this a thinking man's thriller bearing the messsage that no infernal machine is a match for a decent man with a sense of good and evil." N Y Times Book Rev

Mankind (Wrestler) *See* Foley, Mick, 1965-

Marías, Javier, 1951-

The man of feeling; translated from the Spanish by Margaret Jull Costa. New Directions 2003 182p $22.95

ISBN 0-8112-1531-8   LC 2002-153935

Original Spanish edition, 1986

"While in Madrid to perform the role of Cassio in Verdi's 'Otello,' a Spanish tenor meets a man whose job is to amuse the neglected wife of a powerful Brussels banker. The paid companion invites the singer on his outings with the woman, setting the stage for an affair. . . . (This). . . would seem to offer little more than banal melodrama. Everything depends, however, on how the plot unfolds. Marias avoids a straightforward delivery in favor of a digressive narrative that moves back and forth in time. . . . This suggestive indirection perfectly suits Marias's preoccupation: the erotic imagination." N Y Times Book Rev

Marlowe, Hugh, 1929- *See* Higgins, Jack, 1929-

Marsten, Richard, 1926-

For works written by this author under other names see McBain, Ed, 1926-

Marston, Edward

The vagabond clown. St. Martin's Minotaur 2003 292p $24.95

ISBN 0-312-30789-6   LC 2002-191950

"Lord Westfield's Men, the actors' troupe for which Bracewell works as stage manager, are forced to leave their theater after a violent act of sabotage trashes the place. Worse, someone has killed one of Westfield's friends during the melee. Bracewell struggles to save the troupe and its reputation. An outstanding historical." Libr J

Martin, Steve, 1945?-

The pleasure of my company; a novella. Hyperion 2003 163p $19.95

ISBN 0-7868-6921-6   LC 2003-49954

This work features "one of the odder yet more charming protagonists in recent fiction, Daniel Pecan Cambridge, a gentle soul suffering from a mild mix of autism and obsessive-compulsive disorder. Daniel, 33, lives in a rundown Santa Monica apartment, his life constricted by an armor of defensive habit. . . his dull days punctuated only by imagined romances and visits by his student social worker, lovely and kind Clarissa. Daniel's ways (a product of child abuse, Martin shows with subtlety) are challenged when Clarissa and her infant son, Teddy, move in to escape an abusive husband. . . . This novella is a delight, embodying a satisfying story arc, a jeweler's eye for detail, intelligent pacing and a clean, sturdy prose style." Publ Wkly

Martin, Valerie

Property. Talese 2003 196p $23.95

ISBN 0-385-50408-X   LC 2002-66846

This work "presents itself as a novel about the abuse of power within the loveless marriage between an antebellum plantation owner and his wife, their private suffering amplified by the social context of slavery. Bondage and its invitation to brutality are not unexplored terrain, but embedded within what might be mistaken as a morality play is a more subtle and compelling story—a contest of wills between two women, Manon Gaudet and Sarah, the slave she received from her aunt as a wedding gift." N Y Times Book Rev

Mawer, Simon, 1948-

The fall; a novel. Little, Brown 2002 370p $24.95

ISBN 0-316-09780-2   LC 2002-73193

"The book takes as its starting point the horrible accident of its title, with James Matthewson, a renowned but now middle-aged mountain climber, tumbling from the face of a Welsh cliff that he should not have been attempting by himself. He dies almost instantly, leaving behind a widow, an estranged best friend and a number of mysteries, among them why he would be climbing such a difficult route without ropes or a helmet. Could the veteran climber have been trying to commit suicide? It's a question for which the bulk of the novel is designed to provide an answer" N Y Times Book Rev

"Intricately weaving time and place, from the bombed-out ruins of World War II London to isolated Alpine mountain peaks, Mawer crafts a sinuously devastating tale of foridden love and faithless betrayal. A haunting and mesmerizing novel from an expert storyteller." Booklist

Mayer, Eric

(jt. auth) Reed, M. Four for a boy

Maynard, Joyce, 1953-

The usual rules. St. Martin's Press 2003 390p $24.95

ISBN 0-312-24261-1   LC 2002-36754

"Set both in Brooklyn and the small town of Davis, Calif., following the events of September 11, the book tells the coming-of-age story of a girl whose mother goes to work one morning and doesn't come back. Wendy, who must bear the burden of having the last conversation with her mother end in anger, must also help care for her four-year-old half-brother, Louie, while her stepfather, Josh, struggles to deal with his own grief. Attempting to escape her depressing surroundings and numb state of mind, Wendy leaves her family and best friend to live in California with her estranged father." Publ Wkly

Maynard's "gift for creating realistic and hearfelt domestic moments succeeds in convincing us that Wendy has found a reason to go on in the midst of her tremendous sorrow." N Y Times Book Rev

Mayor, Archer

The sniper's wife. Mysterious Press 2002 312p $23.95

ISBN 0-89296-767-6   LC 2002-67183

This mystery delves into the troubled past of "Detective Willy Kunkle, of Joe Gunther's Vermont Bureau of Investigation. When Kunkle learns that his ex-wife Mary overdosed on heroin in Manhattan, he hastens there to identify her body. Suspecting murder, he convinces Ward Ogfden, a high-ranking NYPD detective, to reopen the case. In tracing Mary's life in New York, Kunkle revisits his own Manhattan childhood, membership in the NYPD, the trauma of Vietnam and strained relations with his dysfunctional family. When he's arrested during a raid on an illegal club, Joe and detective Sammie Martens, Kunkle's lover, come to New York, and the two country cops prove they're as astute as their city counterparts." Publ Wkly

"Mayor writes a tough story for his tortured protagonist, and the unfamiliar setting brings out a new, edge-of-the-knife side of his incisive descriptive powers." N Y Times Book Rev

McBain, Ed, 1926-

Fat Ollie's book; a novel of the 87th Precinct. Simon & Schuster 2002 271p $25

ISBN 0-7432-0270-8   LC 2002-75830

This installment features "Det. Oliver Wendell Weeks of the 88th Precinct. Fat Ollie, of the gross appetite and the even grosser ignorance of political correctness. . . . Two major crimes occur at almost the same time: the shooting of Councilman (and possible mayoral candidate) Lester Henderson as he is getting ready for a rally and the theft of the just completed manuscript of Ollie's first novel, Report to the Commissioner. Ollie enlists Carella's help (Henderson lived in the 87th) and pursues both the murderer and the thief." Publ Wkly

"In McBain's howlingly funny sendup, the novel is pure drivel; but Ollie loved it, and darned if we don't like him for that." N Y Times Book Rev

McCaffrey, Anne

Acorna's rebels; [by] Anne McCaffrey and Elizabeth Ann Scarborough. Eos 2003 308p $24.95

ISBN 0-380-97899-7   LC 2002-73873

In this sixth title in the series "Acorna continues to hunt for her beloved life-mate, Aari. . . . She travels aboard the starship Condor to the planet Makahomia, which she finds in the grip of a plague killing the sacred temple cats. Acorna fights a desperate reaerguard action against the plague with her horn's healing power, but the mystery clearly lies deeper." Publ Wkly

McCann, Colum, 1965-

Dancer; a novel. Metropolitan Bks. 2003 336p $26

ISBN 0-8050-6792-2   LC 2002-71879

"A fictionalized account of the life of Rudolph Nureyev—the Cold War danseur noble lauded as the world's first 'pop star dancer'—as told by those who knew him. Among the narrators are the irrepressible Yulia, the daughter of Nureyev's first ballet teacher, Margot Fonteyn, Rudik's brilliant dance partner; Victor, a gay hustler from the Lower East Side with a penchant for blow; bath houses, and back talk; and others." Libr J

"It's hard to tell what a reader unfamiliar with the outlines of Nureyev's life might make of 'Dancer.' Much, deliberately, is left unsaid. Reduced to words, the dance evaporates—only passion and the personal can make it move again." N Y Times Book Rev

McCann, Maria, 1956-

As meat loves salt. Harcourt 2002 565p pa $15

ISBN 0-15-601226-X   LC 2002-68546

"A Harvest original"

"Set against the tumultuous backdrop of seventeenth-century England, McCann's debut novel. . . re-creates the religious and political tensions of a nation torn apart by civil war. An educated servant, Jacob Cullen, flees his loyalist household to avoid prosecution for the shocking murder of a young boy. Guilty of homicide, he compounds his sins by brutally raping his young bride. After joining Cromwell's New Model Army, he becomes obsessed with revolutionary Christopher Ferris' radical idea of establishing a commune. McCann doesn't flinch from the dark side of this erotic adventure." Booklist

McCullough, Colleen, 1937-

The October horse; a novel about Caesar and Cleopatra. Simon & Schuster 2002 792p $28

ISBN 0-684-85331-0   LC 2002-32753

This sixth and final volume in the Masters of Rome series "traces the last days of the Roman Republic, including the events leading up to the assassination of Julius Caesar and the aftermath of that famous murder. Here, that most renowned of Romans, at the height of his power, and Cleopatra, his illustrious mistress, are at center stage." Booklist

"Though some readers may find the sheer wealth of detail occasionally tedious, the book will find a niche among those who can appreciate the scholarship and research that contributed to recreating Caesar's remarkable career." Libr J

McDermid, Val

The distant echo. St. Martin's Minotaur 2003 404p $24.95

ISBN 0-312-30199-5   LC 2003-52902

"Winter of 1978, St Andrews University, Scotland. Four drunken young students on their way home from a party stumble upon local barmaid Rosie Duff, who has been raped, stabbed, and left to die. Unable to save her, the men become suspects in the case but are never formally charged. The stigma and shame of the experience follows these men into their adult lives. About 25 years later, two of the four men have been murdered. The remaining two, Alex Gilbery and the Rev. Tom Mackie must identify their friends' killer before they become the next victims of this revenge murder spree." Libr J

"Individually, the characters are sensitively drawn. Collectively, they present the inscrutable face of closed-off communities so terrified of change they would kill for peace." N Y Times Book Rev

McDermott, Alice

Child of my heart. Farrar, Straus & Giroux 2002 242p $23

ISBN 0-374-12123-0   LC 2002-69764

Fifteen-year-old "Theresa's Irish-American 'well-read but undereducated' parents have little money but plenty of foresight; when they see that their only daughter will be beautiful, they move to East Hampton, Long Island, summer playground of New York's richest, in the hopes that Theresa's beauty will eventually win her a wealthy husband." Publ Wkly

This is a "summer idyll in which a cat is hit by a car, a dog is shot, the heroine loses her virginity, and her fairy-like cousin succumbs to a fatal disease and want of parental love. All this loss—of innocence, of dearly loved creatures—and yet, there is not a word of sentimentality or taste of treacle. On the contrary, Child of My Heart is a golden and luminous memory retrieved by a narrator who has achieved a cool and slightly ironic distance from one of those summers in the late fifties or early sixties." Commonweal

McElroy, Joseph

Actress in the house; a novel. Overlook Press 2003 432p $26.95

ISBN 1-58567-350-1   LC 2002-34555

The plot of this novel turns "literally on the impact of a single glimpsed action—an actor slapping an actress with unfeigned force during a performance of a play—as it registers in the mind of Bill Daley, a man in the audience. The fact of the slap then gathers implication and mystery as Daley returns to the theater after hours and meets the actress, Becca; and finally spirals outward as the two get involved and begin, as any couple might, to ask questions and tell their stories." N Y Times Book Rev

"McElroy's prose, especially his dialogue, is enigmatic and layered with meaning, and the mood he creates is both subtly threatening and achingly wistful. Over a 40-year career, McElroy has been compared to William Gaddis, Don DeLillo, and Thomas Pynchon. This absorbing and unsettling novel, his first in 14 years, may finally bring him the wider recognition he deserves." Booklist

McGarrity, Mark, 1943-2002 *See* Gill, Bartholomew, 1943-2002

McGarrity, Michael

Everyone dies; a Kevin Kerney novel. Dutton 2003 273p $23.95

ISBN 0-525-94761-2   LC 2003-9208

In this installment "an unidentified psycho has his sights set on Kerney, his family, and his soon-to-be-born child. . . . McGarrity contrasts the painstaking investigatory work that leads to identifying a suspect with the personal crisis Kerney and his wife, Sara, face. Uncertain about how a child will affect their relationship, the couple must now contend with a much more immediate threat to their lives." Booklist

"Michael McGarrity is one of those low-key pros who keep the genre honest with realistic crime stories and plain-talking cops who know the procedures." N Y Times Book Rev

McGhee, Alison, 1960-

Was it beautiful?; a novel. Crown 2003 240p $23

ISBN 0-609-60978-5   LC 2002-10841

"William T. Jones, age 50, is barely going through the motions, trapped in the unspeakable hell unique to parents who outlive their children. After watching in helpless horror as a train kills his beloved only child, William J., he is fired from his job, and his wife, as ruined by suffocating sadness as her husband, moves in with her sister. Meanwhile, Sophie, William T.'s treasured daughter-in-law, seeks oblivion in the arms of a local carpenter. Nothing that William T. loved—not his land, not his friends, not the rhythms of nature's inevitable cycles—can break through the guilt that bleaches any shred of joy from his forever-altered heart." Libr J

McInerny, Ralph M., 1929-

Celt and pepper; [by] Ralph McInerny. St. Martin's Minotaur 2002 210p $22.95

ISBN 0-312-29117-5   LC 2002-69938

"After a young Notre Dame professor/Poet dies unexpectedly, Professor Roger Knight. . . suspects murder. His erudition, coupled with assistance from his brother Philip, a private investigator, ultimately leads to a killer. Solid plotting from a practiced hand." Libr J

Last things; a Father Dowling mystery; [by] Ralph McInerny. St. Martin's Minotaur 2003 307p $24.95

ISBN 0-312-30899-X   LC 2003-40641

"Father Dowling first becomes involved with the Bernardo family when Eleanor Wygant asks him to try to persuade her niece, Jessica Bernardo, to stop writing a novel based on the Bernardo family. Eleanor is afraid of the resultant scandal if her long-buried secret is revealed. . . . There is a murder for Father Dowling to solve, of course, but this time McInerny seems more interested in exploring the motivations and entwined family relationships of his characters. There's also plenty of the Catholic minutiae that Father Dowling fans enjoy." Booklist

McMurtry, Larry

By sorrow's river; a novel. Simon & Schuster 2003 347p (Berrybender narratives, Book 3) $26

ISBN 0-7432-3304-2   LC 2003-53892

"In this third volume of McMurtry's Berrybender Narratives, Lord Berrybender and his obnoxious, sniveling brood are, surprisingly, still alive on the dangerous Great Plains of Wyoming and Colorado. The wry story of mountainman adventure and European stupidity, set in the 1830s, is just as wacky and gruesome as its predecessors." Publ Wkly

The wandering hill; a novel. Simon & Schuster 2003 302p (Berrybender narratives, Book 2) $26

ISBN 0-7432-3303-4   LC 2002-30595

"In the second installment of 'The Berrybender Narratives,' a tetralogy that opened with Sin Killer, McMurtry continues the saga of the aristocratic Lord Berrybender and his entourage. Having abandoned the luxury steamer on which they traveled up the Missouri River because it was stuck in the ice, the party of 17 family members, servants, and numerous hangers-on waits out the winter at a trading post on the Yellowstone before moving on." Libr J

"The landscape is stunningly beautiful, but the beauty is often disrupted by spasmodic, gruesome violence. Nonetheless, this novel is an engrossing, exciting, and sometimes heart-rending saga of the American West that shows McMurtry at his best." Booklist

Meloy, Maile

Liars and saints; a novel. Scribner 2003 260p $24

ISBN 0-7432-4435-4   LC 2002-30852

"The Santerres, starting with lovely Yvette and uptight Teddy, a World War II marine, are hardly a typical Catholic family. When their eldest daughter gets pregnant in high school, Yvette concocts an elaborate ruse and convinces Teddy that the baby is theirs. Similar secret begettings, concealed identities, and hidden anguish occur in each subsequent generation as Yvette becomes increasingly religious and Teddy struggles to love his rule-breaking progeny." Booklist

"Meloy's unerring mastery of narrative is remarkable. The disciplined economy and resonant clarity of her prose allow her to present a complex story in swift, lean chapters. The alternating points of view of eight main characters shine with authenticity and illuminate the moral complexities felt by each generation." Publ Wkly

Melville, Jennie

See also Butler, Gwendoline

Mendelson, Cheryl

Morningside Heights; a novel. Random House 2003 326p $24.95

ISBN 0-375-50836-8   LC 2002-31760

The first title of a projected trilogy. The "intersecting lives of a group of Manhattanites living in the staid but rapidly changing Upper West Side neighborhood of Morningside Heights near Columbia University are the focus of this [novel]. . . . Opera singer Charles Braithwaite; his wife, Anne, a pianist; and their three (soon to be four) childen are the novel's ostensible protagonists. The books's real hero, however, is their beloved neighborhood, which they fear they will soon have to leave, unable to afford their cramped apartment." Publ Wkly

"With her motley cast, Mendelson paints an accurate, often comical portrait of the Upper West Side." N Y Times Book Rev

Mertz, Barbara, 1927-

For works written by this author under other names see Peters, Elizabeth, 1927-

Mewshaw, Michael, 1943-

Shelter from the storm; a novel. Putnam 2003 280p $23.95

ISBN 0-399-14988-0   LC 2002-74640

In this thriller "a feral child from the steppes of Central Asia becomes the bargaining chip in a hostage negotiation. Scarred hero Zack McClintock, a private-sector intelligence agent, travels to ex-Soviet territory in search of his kidnapped son-in-law and finds plenty of people with plenty to hide. . . .This is the sort of intelligent and morally ambitious thriller—like those of Craig Nova or Paul Watkins—that offers a welcome change from typical fare." Libr J

Meyer, Carolyn

Brown eyes blue; a novel. Bridge Works 2003 228p $23.95

ISBN 1-88259-368-5   LC 2002-12674

"Daughter Dorcas' return home is prompted by a call from a friend who tells her about the scandal caused by her mom's latest art exhibit. Instead of the pastoral Amish scenes for which she is know, Lavinia's latest show consists of brilliantly executed, graphic nudes. Dorcas, too, feels reckless and buys an old mansion to convert into an inn, and in the process remakes her own life. Then granddaughter Sasha shows up pregnant and with a lesbian partner." Booklist

"Little do these women guess how much they have in common—shared passions, losses and secrets that lead them to question the choices they have made in their lives. Meyer weaves the story of three generations of women who, with their distinctive voices, will endear themselves to readers." Publ Wkly

Michaels, Barbara, 1927-

For works written by this author under other names see Peters, Elizabeth, 1927-

Miller, Risa

Welcome to Heavenly Heights. St. Martin's Press 2003 230p $23.95

ISBN 0-312-30180-4   LC 2002-31876

This novel follows a group of American Jews who have settled in the West Bank. "Tova struggles with flashes of homesickness and worries about the changes this new life has wrought in her daughter. Nathan and Sandy argue over how to discipline their boisterous and impulsive son, Yossi. Mr. Stanetsky, a Holocaust survivor, carries a dog-eared photograph of his parents and sister with him as he collects rent from his tenants. In the backgrouond, the threat of violence and political upheaval are a constant rumble." Booklist

The author "has peered inside Tova's life to show us the search for joy that lies at the heart of her religious ritual and the beauty of people like her who devote themselves to that search. And then Miller has broken our hearts—with Tova's—byshowing us how horrible it is when the poetic liturgical metaphors of Judaism become the terrible realities of nationalism, when holiness tries to reconcile itself with the inevitable human corruption of statehood." N Y Times Book Rev

Millhauser, Steven

An adventure of Don Juan

In Millhauser, S. The king in the tree: three novellas p55-137

The king in the tree

In Millhauser, S. The king in the tree: three novellas p139-241

The king in the tree: three novellas. Knopf 2003 241p $23

ISBN 0-375-41540-8   LC 2002-72956

Analyzed in Short story index

"An excitable widow leads the reader on a tour of her house—apparently being offered for sale—in the harrowing 'Revenge'. . . . 'An adventure of Don Juan' finds the famous philanderer, bored with a lifetime of easy conquests, leaving the Continent for a change of scenery on his friend's English estate, where he will experience unrequited desire for the first time. Millhauser retells the tragedy of Tristan and Isolde in the title story. . . . Millhauser's precision, coupled with his brave imagination, makes these stories as smart and fresh as they are grim." Publ Wkly

Revenge

In Millhauser, S. The king in the tree: three novellas p1-53

Mitchard, Jacquelyn

Twelve times blessed. HarperCollins Pubs. 2003 532p $25.95

ISBN 0-06-621475-0   LC 2002-31781

"True Dickinson has everything: a loving 10-year-old son, Guy; a successsful business; and a cadre of friends who mostly fill the empty places in her life—until she falls for Hank Bannister, a restaurateur 10 years her junior." Booklist

"Mitchard infuses the courtship and domestic life with gentle humor." Publ Wkly

Mitchell, James C., 1942-

Lovers crossing. St. Martin's Minotaur 2003 294p $23.95

ISBN 0-312-31530-9   LC 2003-41350

"Roscoe Brinker, a Tuscon-based private detective and former INS agent, left the service after being shot in the line of duty by, he suspects, a fellow agent. A local business mogul, Mo Crain, hires him to look into the murder of Crain's wife, Sandra, who worked along the border as a nurse helping abandoned and battered children. Sandra seems to have had few enemies, but as Brinker's investigation proceeds, it seems that her death might be linked to a smuggling operation, and to Henry Sanchez, the corrupt INS agent that Brinker believes shot him." Publ Wkly

"The instantly likable Brinker is full of surprises, and the secondary characters who surround him also have great depth." Booklist

Modesitt, L. E., Jr.

Legacies. TOR Bks. 2002 558p $27.95

ISBN 0-7653-0561-5   LC 2003-268209

"A Tom Doherty Associates bk."

First title in the author's Corean chronicles. "As the son of a Nightsheep herder, Alucius learns the survival

Modesitt, L. E., Jr.—*Continued*

skills necessary to protect his valuable flock from the sand wolves and other strange predators, that dwell in the cold northern lands. He also realizes the more subtle ways of his talent, a magical ability common to those with herder blood. When the armies of Madrien invade his home, Alucius goes off to war, only to be captured and forcibly conscripted into the enemies' slave armies. Careful to hide his Talent, Alucius dreams of escape and revenge. . . Modesitt excels at portraying the everyday lives of people caught up in world-shaking events, thus making his characters both believable and sympathetic." Libr J

Moloney, Susie

The dwelling; a novel. Atria Bks. 2003 408p $25

ISBN 0-7434-5662-9   LC 2003-276274

In this tale of a haunted house, "Moloney attempts to depict 362 Belisle as a being with a mind of its own, beckoning realtor Glenn Darnley throughout the multiple showings of the house, and claiming or rejecting its inhabitants. The tenants seem quite ordinary until mysterious events begin to occur, each episode terminating at a horrifying moment before Moloney launches into the next inhabitant's story. Newly widowed Glenn's travails connect the sagas of her three buyers, as her thoughts of her dead husband fill the gaps between stories." Publ Wkly

The house "is a character in its own right, but Moloney . . . has thankfully peopled the narrative with other well-developed characters as well, ones with such recognizable strengths and weaknesses that the reader actually cares about their outcomes. The ending is horrible but poignant and exactly fitting." Libr J

Moon, Elizabeth

The speed of dark. Del Rey Bks. 2002 340p $23.95

ISBN 0-345-44755-7   LC 2002-20771

Set in the near future, this novel "depicts an autistic adult struggling with a momemtous decision. Lou Arrendal functions on a fairly high level: he has a job with a pharmaceutical company and leads a quiet, independent life. . . . When an experimental treatment offers Lou a chance to reverse his autism, he must choose between remaining himself or possibly becoming a different person." Libr J

"Moon is effective at putting the reader inside Lou's mind, and it is both fascinating and painful to see the behavior and qualities of so-called normals through his eyes." Booklist

Moorcock, Michael, 1939-

The skrayling tree; the albino in America. Warner Bks. 2003 330p $24.95

ISBN 0-446-53104-9   LC 2002-27247

"In the sequel to The Dreamthief's Daughter, Oona, protagonist of the earlier book, has married Ulric von Bek, last of his line of Grail Defenders. On vacation in Canada, Ulric is abducted, allegedly to fight a wind demon leading an army bent on destroying a golden city that possesses the Skrayling Tree, a key support of the Multiverse of Moorcock's Eternal Champion yarns.

Meanwhile, Oona is in a Native American universe, enlisted by the shaman White Crow to fight pygmies who threaten a golden city. In another universe, Oona's father, Elric, seeking those who forged his black sword, ends up in Vinland's City of Gold, asked to help pygmies there, whose gold has been stolen by an evil giant named . . . White Crow." Booklist

"The tale's power stems largely from the astounding lyricism of the author's prose, the only flaw being the sometimes stilted and overly expository dialogue about the nature of the Multiverse." Publ Wkly

Moore, Christopher, 1957-

Fluke, or, I know why the winged whale sings. Morrow 2003 321p $23.95

ISBN 0-380-97841-5   LC 2002-43231

Nate Quinn "studies whales, operating a small research unit in Lahaina in Maui along with Clay Demodocus, a famous undersea photographer, and two seasonal hires: Amy Earheart, supposedly a grad student from Woods Hole Institute, and Kona, a dreadlocked Hawaiian stoner. When Nate spots a humpback whale with 'Bite Me' tattooed on a tail fluke, mysterious disasters start to strike. Then Nate, out with Amy, is swallowed by the tattooed humpback . . . . The tattooed one is a living ship, a simulacrum of a humpback run by a crew of humans and 'whaley boys' human/whale cross breeds . . . [The] characters are perfectly calibrated, part credible human beings and part clever caricatures. This cetacean picaresque is no fluke—it is a sure winner." Publ Wkly

Morgan, Richard K.

Altered carbon. Del Rey Bks. 2003 375p pa $13.95

ISBN 0-345-45768-4   LC 2002-31165

First published 2002 in the United Kingdom

"In the 25th century, it's difficult to die a final death. Humans are issued a cortical stack, implanted into their bodies, into which consciousness is 'digitized' and from which—unless the stack is hopelessly damaged—their consciousness can be downloaded ('resleeved') with its memory intact, into a new body. While the Vatican is trying to make resleeving (at least of Catholics) illegal, centuries-old aristocrat Laurens Bancroft brings Takeshi Kovacs (an Envoy, a specially trained soldier used to being resleeved and trained to soak up clues from new environments) to Earth, where Kovacs is resleeved into a cop's body to investigate Bancroft's first mysterious, stack-damaging death." Publ Wkly

A "seamless marriage of hardcore cyberpunk and hardboiled detective tale." Times (London, England)

Moriarty, Laura

The center of everything. Hyperion 2003 291p $22.95

ISBN 1-401-30031-6   LC 2002-32898

This "is the story of Evenlyn Bucknow, who comes of age in a small Kansas town. Evelyn is 10 when the novel opens, an observer of the silent struggle between Tina, her wayward young mother, and Eileen, her quiet, religious grandmother. . . . Though Evelyn appears to be a mere observer of the tumultmous lives of her friends and family, it is she who will achieve her dreams with quiet determination. Evelyn is an intriguing, thoughtful narrator, and this novel is a truly exceptional coming-of-age story." Booklist

Morris, Scott, 1966-

Waiting for April; a novel; by Scott M. Morris. Algonquin Bks. 2003 340p $24.95

    ISBN 1-56512-370-0   LC 2002-38600

"Sanders Royce Collier arrives in the backwater Florida panhandle town of Citrus on Christmas Eve, 1965, to the accompaniment of portentous thunder and lighting . . . . [This novel] is narrated by Sander's teenage son, Roy, who pieces together the history of his father's fateful entanglement with Citrus's Lanier family." Publ Wkly

"Morris is an elegant, self-assured writer. His characters are authetic and overflowing with humanity. A genuinely evocative novel." Booklist

Morrison, Toni, 1931-

Nobel Prize in literature, 1993

Love. Knopf 2003 201p $23.95

    ISBN 0-375-40944-0   LC 2003-52737

"There were days, back in the 1940s and 1950s, when the Cosey Hotel and Resort was the place for blacks to vacation, dance, and dine. Bill Cosey, a charismatic figure greatly attractive to woman, ran the resort. But now Bill is dead, and the story is, as we see, not only a pean to past good times but also a portrait of Bill Cosey's power. . . . Now, in his absence, the women in his life jockey for their own power in the vacuum he left behind; their world now revolves around his will, scribbled many years ago on a dirty menu." Booklist

"Like all of Morrison's best fiction, this is a village novel. Race and racism, ancillary concerns in 'Love' for the most part, throw the small groups she writes about upon one another, steeping their passions. Even when the setting is contemporary, Morrison's books feel old fashioned, set in a world where the perpetual distraction of the media hasn't diluted people's fascination with their neighbors." N Y Times Book Rev

Mortimer, John Clifford, 1923-

Rumpole rests his case; [by] John Mortimer. Viking 2002 210p $24.95

    ISBN 0-670-03139-9   LC 2002-19046

Analyzed in Short Story index

Contents: Rumpole and the old familiar faces; Rumpole and the rememberance of things past; Rumpole and the asylum seekers; Rumpole and the Camberwell carrot; Rumpole and the actor Laddie; Rumpole and the teenage werewolf; Rumpole rests his case

"With Mortimer's greatly felicitous style and careful plotting, these stories are sheer, absolute reading pleasure." Booklist

Morton, Brian, 1955-

A window across the river. Harcourt 2003 289p $25

    ISBN 0-15-100757-8   LC 2003-5373

"Isaac and Nora—he's a photographer, she's a writer—were once a couple. After a five-year separation, a late-night telephone call draws them together, but their reunion . . . becomes increasingly problematic. Nora is ready to break up with her boyfriend, a professor who wants to become a 'public intellectual.' Isaac, who always believed that he and Nora were destined for one another, is frustrated by the world's indifference to his photography. What's more, he is about to become a char-

acter in one of Nora's unnervingly lifelike short stories. Morton is particularly skilled at describing the sharp rattle of artistic failure, and at bringing to life the streets and rooms of New York, where the fates of his lonely and desperate characters unfold." New Yorker

Moses, Kate

Wintering; a novel of Sylvia Plath. St. Martin's Press 2003 292p $23.95

    ISBN 0-312-28375-X   LC 2002-36753

"A fictionalization of the grueling months following the dissolution of Plath's marriage to Ted Hughes and leading up to her suicide at the age of 30 in 1963. 'Wintering' is beautiful and moving. The narrative voice is a distillation of Plath's diaries, letters and poems; with lyrical dexterity and great economy, Moses portrays a demanding, pitiless woman struggling against the stark fact of her husband's infidelity and her own inner demons." N Y Times Book Rev

Mosher, Howard Frank

The true account; concerning a Vermont gentleman's race to the Pacific against and exploration of the western American continent coincident to the expedition of Captains Meriwether Lewis and William Clark. Houghton Mifflin 2003 337p $24

    ISBN 0-618-19721-4   LC 2002-32804

"Private True Teague Kinneson, a Vermont school-teacher and inventor, writes to Jefferson to recommend himself for the expedition to the Pacific. When Jefferson announces that he's already appointed Captains Meriwether Lewis and William Clark, True, with his teenage nephew, Ticonderoga, in tow, heads West anyway, determined to reach the Pacific first. Ticonderoga narrates their adventures, describing with a straight face the schemes of his daffy uncle." Publ Wkly

"This picaresque tale provides a riotous fictional twist on a revered American legend, irresistibly insane, this novel celebrates the unique brand of homespun humor popularized in the tales of Mark Twain." Booklist

Mosley, Walter

Fear itself; a mystery. Little, Brown 2003 316p $24.95

    ISBN 0-316-59112-2   LC 2003-46092

"Set in 1955 Los Angeles, this . . . thriller finds Fearless and compatriot Paris Minton, the story's narrator, searching for a friend's missing husband. That seemingly simple task rapidly escalates into a case of multiple murders, blackmail, and a quest for a priceless heirloom that makes this Mosley's answer to the Maltese Falcon." Libr J

"It's a tossup which gives more pleasure in Mosley's vibrant views of neighborhood life, the high-stepping, free-talking who bob and weave their way through this convoluted plot, or the colorful local haunts like Henrietta's Gumbo House where they do their shuckin' and jivin'." N Y Times Book Rev

Six easy pieces. Atria Bks. 2003 278p $24

    ISBN 0-7434-4252-0

Analyzed in Short story index

Contents: Smoke; Crimson stain; Silver lining; Gator green; Gray-eyed death; Amber gate

"Mosley is as fine as ever, offering compelling com-

Mosley, Walter—*Continued*

mentary on black-white relations in 1964, writing in a style so simple that it deceives us into thinking wwriting great fiction is as easy as putting one foot in front of the other. It's not, but turning these pages is." Booklist

Mrazek, Robert J.

Unholy fire; a novel of the Civil War. Thomas Dunne Bks. 2003 299p $24.95

ISBN 0-312-30673-3   LC 2002-32512

"After being critically wounded in a Union battle fiasco, Lieutenant McKitredge is sent to a makeshift hospital on the outskirts of Washington, D. C. to die. Believing he has no chance of survival, well-meaning doctors continually dose him with laudanum. Defying the odds, kit survives, one of the many Civil War heroes to be rewarded with a serious opium addiction. Dispatched to the office of the provost marshal, he is assigned to investigate the cases of thieves, murderers, and deserters. Caught up in a murder case that seems to implicate General Joseph Hooker, he must unravel a perplexing mystery and foil a plot to assassinate the president." Booklist

"Mrazek's portrayal of Civil War battle is stark, graphic, bloody and exciting, and is only exceeded by his memorable description of Washington, D. C. as a Gomorrah on the Potomac." Publ Wkly

Muller, Marcia

Cyanide Wells. Mysterious Press 2003 292p map $24.95

ISBN 0-89296-781-1   LC 2002-45516

"Matt Lindstrom leaves the life he has rebuilt in British Columbia to search for his ex-wife, Gwen. After she vanished from their California home, innuendo that he had murdered her ruined him, forcing his relocation. He discovers that she's in a Soledad County town called Cyanide Wells, living with a lesbian lover and an adopted child. When he goes there—For revenge? for solace?—he discovers she has taken off again, this time with the child. He and Carly McGuire, publisher of the county newspaper and Gwen's partner, perform an uneasy dance as they try to bring her back." Booklist

Murakami, Haruki, 1949-

After the earthquake; stories; translated from the Japanese by Jay Rubin. Knopf 2002 181p $22

ISBN 0-375-41390-1   LC 2001-38829

Analyzed in Short story index

Original Japanese edition, 2000

Contents: UFO in Kushiro; Landscape with flatiron; All god's children can dance; Thailand; Super-frog saves Tokyo; Honey pie

"These six stories, all loosely connected to the disastrous 1995 earthquake in Kobe, are Murakami. . . at his best. The writer, who returned to live in Japan after the Kobe earthquake, measures his country's suffering and finds reassurance in the inevitability that love will surmount tragedy, mustering his casually elegant prose and keen sense of the absurd in the service of healing." Publ Wkly

Murphy, Garth

The Indian lover. Simon & Schuster 2002 439p $26

ISBN 0-7432-1943-0   LC 2002-29433

This novel "spans the years 1845 to 1851—the final days of California under the rule of Spain and Mexico—and follows the fortunes of a young Cupa Indian rancher and starry-eyed American pioneer." Publ Wkly

"Rich in characterization . . . this is an exhilarating adventure story that also imparts a full-bodied picture of a long-vanished way of life and a little-known historic conflict." Booklist

Murray, John, 1962-

A few short notes on tropical butterflies. HarperCollins Pubs. 2003 274p $24.95

ISBN 0-06-050928-7   LC 2002-68883

Analyzed in Short story index

Contents: The hill station; All the rivers in the world; A few short notes on tropical butterflies; White flour; Watson and the shark; The carpenter who looked like a boxer; Blue; Acts of wisdom, wisdom of man

"One has to admire Murray's range, his willingness to experiment. In some ways, he can be a very attractive writer—above all, in the understated modesty of his authorial presence." N Y Times Book Rev

Murray, Peter, 1952-

See also Hautman, Pete, 1952-

Myles, Symon, 1949-

For works written by this author under other names see Follett, Ken, 1949-

N

Nagata, Linda

Memory. TOR Bks. 2003 416p $26.95

ISBN 0-312-87721-8   LC 2002-43581

"A Tom Doherty Associates book."

"Jubilee and her brother Jolly grow up in the security of their mother's Temple, protected against the inexplicable phenomenon known as 'silver', which rises from the ground at night, obliterating anything that it touches. When the silver takes Jolly one night, Jubilee mourns her brother until the appearance of a mysterious man named Kaphiri arrives with the knowledge that Jolly might still be alive. Jubilee's voyage in search of her brother and of the hidden history of her civilization form a powerful coming-of-age story set against a world of high technology that seems magical in its manifestation." Libr J

Naslund, Sena Jeter

Four spirits; a novel. Morrow 2003 524p $26.95

ISBN 0-06-621238-3   LC 2003-51170

"During the civil rights conflict, Birmingham, Ala. was notorious for the ferocity of its racial bigotry: peaceful demonstrators attacked with fire hoses and dogs by police chief Bull Connor; the Klan-set explosion at a black church that killed four little girls. The four victims are only background figures in Naslund's . . . evocation of the city and the era, but they appear to several characters in the form of spirits who promise the reconciliation to come. The novel is constructed as a series of vignettes that follow a dozen or so characters whose lives finally intersect." Publ Wkly

Naslund, Sena Jeter—*Continued*

"Naslund has done something unusually fine—she's written a drifting collective portrait of a city in distress. The characters of 'Four Spirits' are deeply entwined, sometimes without knowing it." N Y Times Book Rev

Newman, Sandra, 1965-

The only good thing anyone has ever done. HarperCollins Pubs. 2003 389p $24.95

ISBN 0-06-051498-1   LC 2002-38737

"Chrysalis Moffat, a South American orphan, has grown into a psychologically unstable young woman living alone in the California mansion of her adopted parents, both dead. Her brother, Eddie, 'five foot seven inches of sheer depravity,' returns from a slacker trip around the world towing a fake Buddhist guru named Ralph, and together they open the Tibetan School of Miracles in the run-down mansion, selling enlightenment to spiritually destitute Californians. But this is just the first in a series of clever false fronts presented by this sprawling, globe-trotting novel, which hops from California to Colorado, Cairo to Kathmandu, exploring Chrysalis's and Eddie's messy lives and the source of their rampant dysfunctionality." Publ Wkly

Nichols, Leigh, 1945-

For works written by this author under other names see Koontz, Dean R. (Dean Ray), 1945-

Nunez, Elizabeth

Grace. Ballantine Bks. 2003 294p $23.95

ISBN 0-345-45533-9   LC 2002-26260

"Trinidad-born Justin Peters seemingly has it all: a beautiful, accomplished wife named Sally; a precocious four-year-old daughter; a fabulous brownstone in the hip Fort Greene section of Brooklyn; and a professorship at a public university. Everything is picture perfect until his mate blindsides him by confessing that she is unhappy and planning to move out, taking their child with her." Libr J

"This is a tender, graceful novel of personal amd material struggle that also explores the power of literature and poetry in everyday life." Booklist

O

Oates, Joyce Carol, 1938-

The tattooed girl; a novel. Ecco Press 2003 307p $25.95

ISBN 0-06-053106-1   LC 2002-192736

"When a reclusive, 38-year-old writer hires a near-illiterate young woman as an assistant at his suburban home in Carmel Heights, near Rochester, N. Y., he's unaware that a vehement anti-Semitism seethes beneath her tattoo-branded exterior. Renowned for The Shadows—his great early success, a novel based on his grandparents' experiences in Germany during the Holocaust—Joshua Seigl confuses his friends and sparks the anger of his hypomaniac sister, Jet, when despite their objections he refuses to fire the young woman." Publ Wkly

"Seigl's failure to cut it as a likable man is perhaps unintentional irony. His failure to understand his assis-

tant, on the other hand, is marvelously controlled satire. All the time he is patronizing her she is hating him, yet he just cannot see it. Oates's portrayal of the employer-employee relationship is wonderfully smart and subtle." N Y Times Book Rev

O'Connor, Joseph, 1963-

Star of the Sea. Harcourt 2003 386p $25

ISBN 0-15-100908-2   LC 2003-1984

"The Star of the Sea is a leaky old tub sailing from Ireland to New York in the terrible winter of 1847, carrying in its staterooms a reluctantly interwined collection of characters." N Y Times Book Rev

The author "brilliantly weaves together an intriguing plot, a cast of memorable characters, and some stunningly realistic dialog. Universal themes of love, loyalty, vengeance, and violence are explored in the context of a troubled class-ridden society convulsed by the catastropic potato blight." Libr J

Ōe, Kenzaburō

Nobel Prize in literature, 1994

Somersault; a novel; translated from the Japanese by Philip Gabriel. Grove Press 2003 570p $29.95

ISBN 0-8021-1738-4   LC 2002-29746

Original Japanese edition, 1999

This novel "takes place against the background of a religious cult's terrorist plan (even more drastic than Aum Shinrikyo's 1995 gas attack on the Tokyo subway), which is thwarted when the cult's leaders appear on television to renounce their creed—the 'smersault' of the title. Now, ten years later, the cult's charismatic guru is planning to reestablish his church. . . . Through the believers' motivations for joining the cult, Oe explores the struggle of contemporary Japanese to situate themselves between a traditional culture and the bullet-train pace of the boom years." New Yorker

O'Hagan, Andrew, 1968-

Personality. Harcourt 2003 311p $25

ISBN 0-15-101000-5   LC 2003-5369

"In a decayed resort town on the Isle of Bute in the nineteen-seventies, an Italo-Scottish family pins its hopes on the youngest member, Maria, who is working on her singing and her hair. At thirteen, she is wisked off to London, where she wins a talent contest on television. By sixteen, she is a famous pop singer. By twenty, she is anorexic and half-mad. (Soon she also has a homicidal admirer stalking her.) The analysis of her thoughts, a miasma of fear and narcissism, is the core of the novel. . . . At the same time, the book is so bustling and rich—we get every old lady and barfly on the island, with their letters, diaries, secrets—that the darkness seems lit from end to end." New Yorker

O'Nan, Stewart, 1961-

The night country; or, The darkness on the edge of town. Farrar, Straus & Giroux 2003 229p $23

ISBN 0-374-22215-0   LC 2002-44765

"The aftermath of a Halloween tragedy haunts a New England town on the one-year anniversary of a typical teen joyride that ended with a car wrapped around a tree. Toe, Marco, and Danielle were instantly killed. Kyle

O'Nan, Stewart, 1961-—*Continued*

lives on, sort of; a severe brain injury obliterates the rebel in him, the accident leaving him with the mind of a child. Tim, 'the lucky one' in the backseat, his arms around Danielle, survived but now has a death wish. Officer Brooks, the first on the scene, was terribly alterered by the event, and his life in shambles." Booklist

"O'Nan is wonderful at describing teenage ritual, the simultaneous desire for the comforting familiarity of friends and the lust for speed and novelty and excitement that will lift teenagers out of the confines of their suburban town, the routine of school, out of their own restless bodies." N Y Times Book Rev

O'Neal, Kathleen M.

See also Gear, Kathleen O'Neal

O'Neill, Anthony

The lamplighter; a novel. Scribner 2003 308p 308

ISBN 0-7432-4349-8   LC 2002-36453

"It is 1886. Although the new electric lamp has conquered Paris and London, it has yet to make its way to Edinburgh, whose medieval streets and modern boulevards are still illuminated at dusk by the 'leeries,' the traditional lamplighters. But someone—or something—is also coming out in the evenings, leaving a trail of horribly mutilated bodies: those of a professor, a lighthouse keeper, and a shady businessman. Assigned to the case is acting Chief Inspector Carus Groves." Libr J

O'Shaughnessy, Mary

For works written by this author in collaboration with Pamela O'Shaughnessy see O'Shaughnessy, Perri

O'Shaughnessy, Pamela

For works written by this author in collaboration with Mary O'Shaughnessy see O'Shaughnessy, Perri

O'Shaughnessy, Perri

Presumption of death. Delacorte Press 2003 390p $24.95

ISBN 0-385-33645-4   LC 2003-46199

"Nina Reilly, who is taking some time off after her clash with the California State Bar . . . visits old haunts in Carmel Valley with her longtime boyfriend, investigator Paul Von Wagoner, and her dog, Hitchcock. When Willis Whitefeather is accused of murder, it quickly becomes apparent that Nina will have more to contend with than the bothersome case of poison oak she has been nursing." Libr J

"Well-rounded and likable characters set against a richly described backdrop of some of the loveliest country in the world." Publ Wkly

Oster, Christian

My big apartment; translated and with an introduction by Jordan Stump. University of Neb. Press 2002 155p pa $20

ISBN 0-8032-3567-4; 0-8032-8612-0 (pa)

LC 2002-17977

Original French edition published, 1999

"In a nutshell, [this is] the story of a man who loses his keys and finds a life, sort of, maybe. That's all that really happens—well, that and a few laps in a pool and a driving lesson and an episiotomy. The specifics don't much matter anyway. This is simply the course the man, a Parisian called Gavarine, follows, and he has no more control over his fate than the leaf in the stream has over the eddy." N Y Times Book Rev

P

Packer, ZZ, 1973-

Drinking coffee elsewhere. Riverhead Bks. 2003 238p $24.95

ISBN 1-57322-234-8   LC 2002-73971

Analyzed in Short story index

Contents: Brownies; Every tongue shall confess; Our Lady of Peace; The ant of the self; Drinking coffee elsewhere; Speaking in tongues; Geese; Doris is coming

"The clear-voiced humanity of Packer's characters, mostly black teenage girls, resonates unforgettably through the eight stories of this accomplished debut collection. Several tales are set in black communities in the South and explore the identity crises of God-fearing, economically disenfranchised teens and young women." Publ Wkly

Page, Katherine Hall

The body in the lighthouse; a Faith Fairchild mystery. HarperCollins Pubs. 2003 327p $23.95

ISBN 0-380-97844-X   LC 2002-68859

"Intrepid part-time caterer/sleuth Faith Fairchild. . . vacations with her family on an island off the coast of Maine, but they don't get much relaxation. Ill feelings between year-round residents and summer visitors reach a crisis when a developer is found dead near the lighthouse. Faith investigates, with the usual spine-tingling results." Libr J

Palahniuk, Chuck

Diary; a novel. Doubleday 2003 260p $24.95

ISBN 0-385-50947-2   LC 2003-43900

This "is the story of a lonely artist named Misty Marie Wilmot and the spooky community of blue-blood islanders she's married into. . . . Her story takes the form of a diary written to her husband, Peter, who lies contorted and comatose in the hospital after a suicide attempt. On Waytansea Island, the Wilmot ancestral home, Misty struggles to take care of their daughter, Tabbi, and Peter's mother, Grace, while making ends meet as a maid at the island hotel." N Y Times Book Rev

"Catchy, jarring prose, cryptic pronouncements and baroque flights of imagination are instantly recognizable, and [the author's] sharp, bizarre meditations on the artistic process make this twisted tale one of his most memorable works to date." Publ Wkly

Paretsky, Sara

Blacklist; a V.I. Warshawski novel. Putnam 2003 415p $24.95

ISBN 0-399-15085-4   LC 2003-43157

Paretsky, Sara—_Continued_

"A dead reporter, a missing Egyptian boy wanted in connection with terrorist activities, and an elderly woman convinced that an intruder is in her family manse are all elements of Paretsky's . . . novel featuring Chicago private investigator V. I. Warshawski. As V. I. looks into these peoples' lives, she discovers connections among them. She uncovers a story of betrayal and secrets that spans several generations and involves Chicago's wealthiest families, the Red Scare, and the House Un-American Activities Committee hearings of the 1950s. As always, V. I.'s determined pursuit of the truth ensures at least a few heart-stopping moments." Libr J

Parker, Robert B., 1932-

Back story. Putnam 2003 291p $24.95

ISBN 0-399-14977-5   LC 2002-36901

"As the title implies, the story is full of references to the past, starting with an unsolved 1974 robbery in which a young California mother visiting her sister was shot dead when she went to cash some traveler's checks at the old Shawmut Bank in Boston. Spenser takes the case to give the victim's daughter peace of mind, only to discover that he has disturbed a cover-up involving the F.B.I., an organized crime figure and the remnants of a gang of counterculture revolutionaries." N Y Times Book Rev

"The repartee between Spenser and Hawk is fast and funny; the sentiment between Spenser and Susan and the musings about Spenser's code are only occasionally cloying; and there's a scattering of remarkable action scenes including a tense shootout in Harvard Stadium." Publ Wkly

Parker, T. Jefferson

Cold pursuit. Hyperion 2003 360p $23.95

ISBN 0-7868-6805-8   LC 2002-32940

"The murder of retired San Diego Port Commissioner and local politician Pete Braga falls in the lap of homicide detective Tom McMichael, whose family has a multigenerational feud going with the Bragas. Parker makes the most of a standard mystery device here—murder driven by a motive from the distant past—but the real joy of the novel is its remarkably evocative prose, which flows seamlessly from lyrical descriptions of rainy San Diego to crisp, no-nonsense dialogue." Booklist

Parkhurst, Carolyn, 1971-

The dogs of Babel. Little, Brown 2003 264p $21.95

ISBN 0-316-16868-8   LC 2002-43644

"When the book opens, Paul, a linguist who lives in suburban Virginia, has just learned that his wife, Lexy Ransome, has died in their backyard in a mysterious fall from an apple tree. Lorelei is the sole witness to this event, and Paul resolves to make her reveal what hapened. Never mind that she is a dog. He will each her to talk." N Y Times Book Rev

"As Paul slips into ever more desperate behavior, we hear an account of his and Lexy's courtship and marriage—the tender, tentative union of two damaged people. But then Paul contacts a man convicted of operating on dogs to install vocal chords, and what had been a poignant, affecting tale turns truly frightening . . . . Parkhurst delivers a remarkable debut in quiet, authoritative prose." Libr J

Parks, Suzan-Lori

Getting mother's body; a novel; [by] Suzanne Lori. Random House 2003 257p $23.95

ISBN 1-400-06022-2   LC 2002-31762

"Billy Beede is a girl with troubles. Unmarried, pregnant by a married man, and needing a lot of money fast, Billy decides to travel from Texas to Arizona to retrieve her dead mother's body, hoping to find a small fortune in jewels presumably buried in the grave." Libr J

"Set in the summer of 1963, and recounted in a slow, Southern drawl befitting the mood, the story unravels from a myriad of viewpoints, including the no-good custom coffin salesman who's fathered Billy's unborn baby, the one-legged neighbor in love with Billy, and her deceased mother's feisty lesbian lover." Publ Wkly

Patterson, Harry, 1929- _See_ Higgins, Jack, 1929-

Patterson, Henry, 1929- _See_ Higgins, Jack, 1929-

Patterson, James

Four blind mice; a novel. Little, Brown 2002 387p $27.95

ISBN 0-316-69300-6   LC 2002-67540

"Alex Cross is on the brink of retirement from the Washington Police Force when his best friend, John Sampson, comes to him with an urgent request. Sampson's friend, Sergeant Ellis Cooper, has just been convicted by a military court for the murders of three women. Cooper swears he's innocent, and Sampson believes him." Booklist

"The action leads, as is Patterson's custom, to a firecracker string of climaxes; the finale finds Cross handcuffed and stripped naked in deep woods, about to be killed. Throughout, Patterson expertly balances the conspiratorial action with intriguing developments in Cross's domestic life." Publ Wkly

The lake house; a novel. Little, Brown 2003 376p $26.95

ISBN 0-316-60328-7   LC 2002-36844

Sequel: When the wind blows (1998)

A thriller "about a group of children who have been genetically engineered to fly. . . . Beautiful Max and handsome Ozymandias lead the group of six children who are fighting to stay with Kit and Frannie, the couple that saved them from the School, where they were being held by the scientists who created them. The court returns the children to their biological parents, but only Max knows how much danger they're in. Max is privy to information about Resurrection, another project that is even more daring and groundbreaking than the one that created the children. . . . An unexpected and sweet romance between Max and Oz alleviates the nail-biting suspense somewhat, but as usual, Patterson gets his readers in his grip from page one and doesn't let go until the last page is turned." Booklist

Patterson, Richard North

Balance of power. Ballantine Bks. 2003 611p $27.95

ISBN 0-345-45017-5   LC 2003-51848

"Gun control and tort reform are the thorny issues tackled in this political drama, with Patterson hero Kerry Kilcannon ensconced in the White House and planning

Patterson, Richard North—*Continued*

his marriage to former television journalist Lara Costello." Publ Wkly

"This complex novel has a fascinating debate at its heart. To his credit, Patterson has done his research, and though it's clear which side he's on, he does a good job of presenting all the arguments." Booklist

Paul, Jim, 1950-

Elsewhere in the land of parrots. Harcourt 2003 405p $24

ISBN 0-15-100495-1   LC 2003-7918

When reclusive poet David Huntington "receives an exotic parrot from his father, his preferred life of airless solitude is turned upside down, and in frustration David soon tosses it out his apartment window. Little does he know that through that open window his carefully controlled and spiritless existence has begun its exit as well. David's guilty search for the bird serendipitously leads him into an adventure outside his quiet apartment and all the way to the swamplands of Ecuador, where a young researcher named Fern happens to be studying the same type of parrot in its native habitat." Libr J

"Paul's story successfully weds an odd theme —the ethology of parrots—to the perennial fascinations of human courtship behavior." Publ Wkly

Pawel, Rebecca, 1977-

Death of a nationalist. Soho Press 2003 262p $24

ISBN 1-56947-304-8   LC 2002-26921

"Madrid in 1939 is filled with bomb craters, desecrated churches and nearly abandoned streets, while black markets are just about the only markets with anything to sell. The hatreds and atrocities shared by the Nationalists (supported by the Communists) still simmer and erupt in sporadic violence. The Guardia Civil has the responsibility to maintain authority—and their enthusiasm and ruthlessnesss for enforcing order terrorizes the citizens. The intertwined fates of Sergeant Tejada Alonzo Leon of the Guardia Civil and that of Gonzalo Llorente, a wounded Republican in hiding are handled with unusual skill and subtlety." Publ Wkly

Pearl, Matthew

The Dante Club; a novel. Random House 2003 372p $24.95

ISBN 0-375-50529-6   LC 2002-17886

A literary thriller about a "serial murderer who draws gory inspiration from the torments of Dante's Inferno. . . . The author sets this novel in Boston in 1865, when Henry Wadsworth Longfellow, James Russell Lowell, and Oliver Wendell Holmes were translating Dante into English. As they work through the cantos, the Dante-inspired corpses arrive on cue, and the versifiers must turn detective." New Yorker

Pearson, Allison, 1960-

I don't know how she does it; the life of Kate Reddy, working mother. Knopf 2002 337p $25

ISBN 0-375-41405-3   LC 2002-66104

Kate "is the mother of a five-year-old girl and a year-old biy living in a trendy North London house with her lower-earning architect husband, and is a star at her work in an aggressive City of London brokerage firm. She is intoxicated by her jet-setting, high-profile job, but also is desperately aware of what it takes out of her life as a mother and wife." Publ Wkly

"What redeems I Don't Know how she do it, and makes it of more than passing interest, is Pearson's candor in presenting the very real tensions in Kates' life." Commentary

Pelecanos, George P.

Soul circus; a novel. Little, Brown 2003 341p $24.95

ISBN 0-316-60843-2   LC 2002-16207

"Strange and Quinn once again find themselves struggling to save even one not-yet-lost young soul from the ravages of drugs and violence, but this time their knightly pursuits are undermined by a growing sense of moral ambivalence." Booklist

"Pelecanos is fascinated with the way things work, and he takes apart the gun trade like an urban anthropologist, fitting the pieces into the drug business and the gang culture with an exactness that is breathtaking—and depressing. At the same time, he treats his criminals like human beings, talking their talk, driving their cars, listening to their music, getting into their world with something that can only be called sympathy." N Y Times Book Rev

Perdue, Lewis

Slatewiper. Forge 2003 367p $24.95

ISBN 0-7653-0111-3   LC 2002-45496

"A Tom Doherty Associates book"

"In Tokyo, a particularly violent and deadly plague has broken out. Inexplicably, it seems as if the virus only uses Koreans as its carrier. Enter Lara Blackwood, a genetic engineer recruited to fight this virus that somehow piggybacks itself on people with specific genetic characteristics. Ejected from her own company, Lara sees in this investigation her chance to get herself back in the research game, but she doesn't count on uncovering a genetic weapon of unimaginable power. . . . Perdue unflinchingly treads on Crichton's turf but emerges with a novel that feels fresh and original." Booklist

Perry, Anne, 1938-

No graves as yet; a novel of World War I. Ballantine Bks. 2003 642p $25.95

ISBN 0-345-45652-1   LC 2003-52233

'This is the debut novel in Perry's projected five-book series about a British family during World War I. The family in question includes brothers Matthew and Joseph Reavley and sisters Judith and Hannah, whose parents are killed in a car accident when the book opens. Reavley pere had been on his way to deliver a document that purports to be of national importance. Matthew, a trusted employee in the Intelligence Service, can't quite believe that the document could really threaten Britain's honor. Meanwhile, Joseph, an ordained minister and teacher of classical languages at Cambridge, struggles with the senseless murder of his brilliant protege." Libr J

"Perry's melancholy evocation of the 'eternal afternoon' that would soon turn to night all over England is lovely." N Y Times Book Rev

Seven dials. Ballantine Bks. 2003 345p $25.95

ISBN 0-345-44007-2   LC 2002-35605

Perry, Anne, 1938-—*Continued*

"When the Egyptian mistress of a senior cabinet minister is discovered in her garden in the middle of the night, using a wheelbarrow to dispose of the body of a junior diplomat, the apparent crime of passion turns into an international incident. Thomas Pitt. . . chafes at the order from Special Branch to extricate the government official, Saville Ryerson, from the affair; but he sees the gravity of the political situation. . . . Although the focus of the plot tends to drift, the visual panorama is voluptuous to behold." N Y Times Book Rev

Perry, Thomas

Dead aim; a novel. Random House 2002 366p $24.95

ISBN 1-400-06003-6   LC 2002-68100

"For someone who made millions in real estate and retired when he was 38, Robert Mallon lacks the wit and imagination to figure out how to enjoy his good fortune. Some nascent feelings are awakened in his anesthetized soul when he accepts a sexual favor from Catherine Broward, a young woman he pulls out of the ocean in front of his Santa Barbara beach house when she tries to drown herself. After Catherine turns around and kills herself anyway, the newly energized hero plays detective to determine the circumstances of her life and death." N Y Times Book Rev

Peters, Elizabeth, 1927-

Children of the storm. Morrow 2003 400p $25.95

ISBN 0-06-621476-9   LC 2002-41083

This installment, set in 1919, finds Amelia Peabody "back in Egypt, reunited with her extended brood of family and friends (a helpful preface sorts them all out) and anticipating an enriching season at the archaeological dig being excavated by her husband. In some respects, the story follows the formula of the 14 earlier books in this spirited series—precious tomb artifacts go missing and the logical suspect turns up dead, necessitating adventures filled with romance and fraught with peril." N Y Times Book Rev

Piazza, Tom, 1955-

My cold war; a novel. ReganBooks 2003 245p $24.95

ISBN 0-06-053340-4   LC 2003-46649

College professsor John Delano's "field is history and his specialty the Cold War period, but he is disdained by his fellow academics for his less-than-scholarly approach. His estrangement from his childhood and family is so complete that he doesn't use his birth name and hasn't spoken to his younger brother Chris in eight years. When Delano fails to progress on his latest book, a popular history of the images of the Cold War, he undertakes a journey to reconnect with Chris and the childhood he left behind." Libr J

"The trip is good for Delano, and it's good for this novel. 'My Cold War' works better when it's not in academic satire mode; there's a painful, penetrating authenticity in Delano's memories of growing up in a Long Island suburb during the cold war and in his portraits of his relationships with his volatile, loner father and emotionally fragile brother." N Y Times Book Rev

Pottinger, Stanley, 1940-

The last Nazi. St. Martin's Press 2003 324p $24.95

ISBN 0-312-27676-1   LC 2003-53852

"Melissa Gale, a lawyer and agent with an investigative unit of the FBI, is on the trail of the mysterious Adalwolf, a former assistant to Joseph Mengele, who aided in experiments on concentration camp prisoners. For Melissa it's not just a job, it's a personal mission because her grandmother died in a concentration camp. When she and her partner botch the swat team operation, their careers are put in jeopardy, and the elusive Nazi is emboldened to continue with his plot to develop a killer virus." Booklist

"Be prepared to feel horror for a villain who is not only the last Nazi but also one of the most terrifying." Libr J

Powell, Sophie, 1980-

The Mushroom Man. Putnam 2003 196p $23.95

ISBN 0-399-14963-5   LC 2002-21355

At the heart of this novel is a "child's invented fairy tale, set in a Welsh forest, about an amiable hermit who fashions umbrellas from wild mushrooms to protect the local fairy population from the rain. . . . Eleven-year-old Amy—a triplet who lives on a farm in the Welsh countryside with her identical sisters; her older brother, Joseph; and her widowed mother, Beth—is the creator of the tale. One night she tells it to her 6-year-old cousin, Lily, who's so enchanted that she sets out to find the mushroom man and goes missing in the process, thus setting the novel's plot in motion. . . . The Welsh countryside has never seemed so alluring, or the existence of simple magic, despite the nasty disappointments of adult life, so probable." N Y Times Book Rev

Powers, Richard, 1957-

The time of our singing. Farrar, Straus & Giroux 2002 631p $28

ISBN 0-374-27782-6   LC 2002-22397

"The book follows the mixed-race Strom family through much of the 20th century, from 1939—when German-Jewish physicist David Strom meets Delia Daley, a black, classically trained singer from Philadelphia—through the 1990s." Publ Wkly

"Powers's blending of unlikely tones in order to probe the problems of a society that continues to insist, all grays to the contrary, on seeing everything in terms of black and white is, more often than not, a fascinating, stimulating and moving artistic imagining of a harmony that continues to elude us in life." N Y Times Book Rev

Poyer, David

A country of our own; a novel of the Civil War at sea. Simon & Schuster 2003 429p $24

ISBN 0-684-87134-3   LC 2003-45435

Second volume in the author's Civil War at Sea trilogy

"Lt. Ker Claiborne has reluctantly relinquished his commission in the U.S. Navy and joined the Confederacy. He's an anomaly—a Virginian who opposes slavery. The plot follows Claiborne throughout the South and then across the Atlantic as captain of a highly successful and feared rebel commerce raider. There are enough spies, plots, battles, storms, and shipwrecks to satisfy any reader." Libr J

Pratchett, Terry

Monstrous regiment; a novel of Discworld. HarperCollins Pubs. 2003 353p $24.95

ISBN 0-06-001315-X   LC 2003-50800

"Polly Perks, an exuberantly determined Borogravian barmaid, decides to disguise herself as a man to infiltrate the Tenth Foot Light Infantry (aka the Ins-and-Outs) and find her missing soldier brother, Paul." Publ Wkly

"Pratchett revels in pricking pomp and assurance, but it isn't going too far to say that of late his real subject, like Wilfred Owen's, is the pit of war. Pratchett's approach may be less lyrical, but he can move from farce to sadness in seconds." N Y Times Book Rev

Night watch. HarperCollins Pubs. 2002 338p $24.95

ISBN 0-06-001311-7   LC 2002-68684

"Sam Vimes is living the good life. He's a duke, his lady wife is about to give birth to their first child, and he is no longer just a shoddy watch commander. Even so, he can't stop thinking about the good old days. He finds himself missing going on patrol, reading the streets, being part of the Watch rather than a nobleman who has to see the big picture. Suddenly, caught by a surge of occult energy, Vimes is back in the good old days. Somehow, they are less good than he remembered. And then he discovers he is responsible for the future: if he doesn't make history turn out the way he remembers it, he may never get home again." Booklist

Preston, Douglas

Still life with crows; [by] Douglas Preston and Lincoln Child. Warner Bks. 2003 435p $24.95

ISBN 0-446-53142-1   LC 2002-192401

FBI Agent Pendergast arrives "in tiny Medicine Creek, KS, just in time to investigate a series of gruesome murders. Life in rural Medicine Creek usually revolves around the local turkey-processing plant and growing corn, but all hell breaks loose when a female corpse is found in a clearing in a cornfield, surrounded by a ring of dead crows impaled on arrows." Libr J

Price, Richard, 1949-

Samaritan. Knopf 2003 377p $25

ISBN 0-375-41115-1

"Ray Mitchell, an Emmy-nominated TV writer who returned to teach pro bono at his old high school amid the projects of Dempsy, New Jersey, has had his head bashed in. Nerese Ammons, a cop 10 weeks from retirement, takes the case personally because of a good turn Ray did her when they were children. But Ray, deteriorating in the hospital, doesn't want to tell her who attacked him." Booklist

"'Samaritan' is two books. One belongs to Ray, the other to Nerese, a division emphasized by the use of cuts and jumps. Chapters recounting Ray's return to Dempsy are interspersed with scenes fo Nerese's investigation of the whos and whys of this return. The structure, though obtrusive, does its job, bringing stereoscopic depth to the events." N Y Times Book Rev

Pronzini, Bill

Spook; a nameless detective novel. Carroll & Graf Pubs. 2003 233p $25

ISBN 0-7867-1086-1

"The case seems simple enough. Spook, a homeless street person, becomes a fixture at a local business; its employees provide assistance as needed for the obviously mentally disturbed individual. He is murdered in an especially heinous assault. His unofficial 'family' wants San Francisco private investigator 'Nameless' to learn his real identity. Nameless hands the case over to his newly hired field operative, Jake Runyon, a former Seattle cop. . . . A fascinating entry in a series that continues to redefine noir fiction even as it honors its roots." Booklist

Proulx, Annie

That old ace in the hole; a novel. Scribner 2002 361p $26

ISBN 0-684-81307-6   LC 2002-30462

This novel's "hero, Bob Dollar, a decent sort who was abandoned at 8, is sent by his company to Woolybucket, Tex., to scout locations for factory hog farms, but is soon smitten with the high, flat country, the locals and their tales of stubborn ranchers, plagues of locusts and family farms undone by corporate greed." N Y Times Book Rev

Pye, Michael, 1946-

The pieces from Berlin. Knopf 2002 335p $24

ISBN 0-375-41436-3   LC 2002-20524

This novel "examines the shady life of fictional Lucia Muller-Ross, who spirited vanloads of valuable antiques entrusted to her by their Jewish owners out of Berlin and into Switzerland at the end of WWII. Sixty years later, Lucia is the elderly, proud and respected owner of an antiques shop in Zurich, when Sarah Freeman, a Holocaust survivor, spies in the store's window a table she once owned. Sarah's anguished need for emotional restitution sparks a tragic upheaval in Lucia's family." Publ Wkly

"Pye writes well, and this is a mature novel. It must also be said that it is not an easy novel, in its themes or its structure. A lot of assembling and clue-tracking is required to make sense of the narrative. It's a page-turner, but often one is turning the pages backward to find some lost, or tenuous, connection. Yet this hard work seems appropriate, even necessary." N Y Times Book Rev

Q

Quick, Amanda, 1948-

Late for the wedding. Bantam Bks. 2003 322p $24.95

ISBN 0-553-80271-2   LC 2002-34254

"The killer, an insider with easy access to the opulent homes of Regency England's elite, has left his calling card, a memento-mori ringMa jeweled, coffin-topped band with a white skull inside. He's clever, but not nearly clever enough to fool the fearless team of Lavinia Lake and Tobias March." Booklist

"As this engaging effort demonstrates, Quick has the Regency-murder mystery mix down to a fine science." Publ Wkly

Quill, Monica, 1929-

For works written by this author under other names see McInerny, Ralph M., 1929-

R

Raban, Jonathan

Waxwings; a novel. Pantheon Bks. 2003 281p $24

ISBN 0-375-41008-2   LC 2003-42997

"Tom Janeway is a professor of writing, a novelist and a public radio commentator; his wife, Beth, works for GetaShack.Com, a startup providing virtual neighborhood tours for prospective house buyers. They have a four-year-old son named Finn, and they appear content. Behind the happy facade, though, Beth has grown deeply unhappy with her self-absorbed husband. . . . Unfolding in counterpoint to Raban's chronicle of the rather civilized collapse of their marriage is the story of a shady Chinese immigrant called Chick; he survives a horrific journey to America and becomes an off-the-books contractor who bullies Tom into employing him to renovate their gloomy old house after Beth moves out." Publ Wkly

This novel "succeeds as a sharply observed satire of the Internet boom and as a bittersweet meditation the American dream." Libr J

Rae, Hugh C., 1935-

See also Stirling, Jessica

Raleigh, Michael

The Blue Moon Circus; a novel. Sourcebooks 2002 342p $22

ISBN 1-4022-0015-3   LC 2002-153628

"Although he is a circus man through and through, Lewis Tully has not been in the business since he was wiped out by a flood in 1919. When a poker game generates a fair amount of cash, he decides to give it one more go. From across the country, he summons veteran performers to create a small but special circus with unique acts. . . . Perhaps his most difficult task, though, is to take care of a nine-year-old orphan put in his care. Lewis then sets off to thrill the inhabitants of small western towns, many of whom have never seen a circus. This is a heartwarming, often humorous story filled with interesting circus lore." Booklist

Rampling, Anne *See* Rice, Anne, 1941-

Rankin, Ian, 1960-

Resurrection men; an Inspector Rebus novel. Little, Brown 2003 436p $23.95

ISBN 0-316-76684-4   LC 2002-16271

"It's the perfect cover. Edinburgh Detective Inspector John Rebus, the maverick's maverick, guilty of throwing a coffee cup at his superior officer, is sent to a remedial 'career counseling' course on being a better team player. But the fix is in; Rebus' real assignment is to investigate four Glasgow renegade coppers also forced to take the course." Booklist

"We are well and truly in Rankin country—a shady world where good and evil are relative terms and truth is an arbitrary concept." N Y Times Book Rev

Read, Piers Paul, 1941-

Alice in exile. St. Martin's Press 2002 344p $24.95

ISBN 0-312-30398-X

"As striking in her beauty as she is shocking in her behavior, Alice Fry has an uninhibited sexuality that makes her attractive to two very different men. Pregnant with fiance Edward Cobb's child, Alice is abandoned by him when her father becomes embroiled in a sexual scandal that threatens Cobb's political ambition. With no one to turn to and nowhere to go, Alice is rescued by Baron von Rettenberg, a womanizing Russian nobleman who hires her as his children's governess. . . . To read Read is to be caught up in an epic wonder of passion, scandal, adn international intrigue." Booklist

Reed, Mary

Four for a boy; [by] Mary Reed & Eric Mayer. Poisoned Pen Press 2003 328p il map $24.95

ISBN 1-59058-031-1   LC 2002-105066

A mystery set in sixth-century Constantinople. "The future emperor Justinian asks a young slave named John the Eunuch to investigate the murder of philanthropist Hypatius, struck down while examining the controversial Christ statue he and three others have given to the city's Great Church. . . . Written with humor and pathos, this superior historical is sure to please existing fans and send new ones in search of the rest of the series." Publ Wkly

Reichs, Kathleen J.

Bare bones; [by] Kathy Reichs. Scribner 2003 306p $23.95

ISBN 0-7432-3346-8   LC 2003-40725

"Tempe, a forensic anthropologist, is back home in Charlotte, N.C., anticipating a nice, long vacation from the county medical examiner's office, when a series of unnatural disasters drags her back to the lab. . . . Whether she's examining the pulverized remains of the victims of a suspicious plane crash or reassembling the bones of an illegally slaughtered bear, Tempe is a pro's pro at her job, but also a compassionate woman who isn't afraid to show her outrage at the cruelty done to man and beast for the sake of a dirty dollar." N Y Times Book Rev

Resnick, Mike, 1942-

The return of Santiago. TOR Bks. 2003 464p $25.95

ISBN 0-7653-0224-1   LC 2002-75660

Sequel to: Santiago (1986)

"A century after the alleged demise of the legendary Santiago, the greatest outlaw of the Inner Frontier, a petty thief named Danny Briggs stumbles upon a lost collection of poems by Black Orpheus, the interstellar bard whose verses immortalized Santiago. Inspired by his discovery, Briggs—now renamed Dante—sets off across the galaxy in search of someone to re-create the legend of Santiago and start a rebellion against the enemies of freedom." Libr J

"An eminently satisfying space western, with just the right mixture of fast-drawing gunmen and talented women to keep the action going." Booklist

Rice, Anne, 1941-

Blackwood Farm. Knopf 2002 527p $26.95

ISBN 0-375-41199-2   LC 2003-272519

Rice, Anne, 1941---*Continued*

In this ninth volume in the author's vampire chronicles "fledgling vampire Quinn Blackwood makes a desperate appeal to the older, stronger Lestat to save his loved ones from Goblin, a doppelganger out to destroy them. Since Quinn entered the dark world of the undead, the once caring and protective Goblin has amassed tremendous strength and a ruthlessness that cannot be controlled. Lestat is intrigued but refuses to make a decision until Quinn tells his life story. Slowly, the dark, Gothic settings and eccentric characters that make Rice's fiction so fascinating emerge." Libr J

Blood canticle. Knopf 2003 305p $25.95

ISBN 0-375-41200-X   LC 2002-192475

This tenth volume of the Vampire chronicles takes up where "Blackwood Farm ended, the now-doppelganger-free Quinn Blackwood and Lestat save Quinn's true love, the witch Mona Mayfair, from certain death by making her an immortal. In his effort to attain sainthood, Lestat must deal with a lot of metaphysical angst. The opulent Blackwood estate and its spooky swamps, as well as New Orleans and a Caribbean isle, provide the settings for many elegant costume changes as the exquisite vampiric triumvirate gleefully suck several deserving victims dry and lay waste to dozens of a drug lord's minions." Publ Wkly

Rice, Luanne

The secret hour. Bantam Bks. 2003 335p $22.95

ISBN 0-553-80224-0   LC 2002-27985

"Marine biologist Kate Harris travels from Washington, D.C., to Connecticut on a mision of love. She is searching for her missing sister, Willa, who disappeared six months earlier, and whom Kate believes might be a victim of a serial killer whose lawyer is John O'Rourke. . . . As John helps her, pursuing answers to questions that put them both at grave risk, their lives become deeply entwined. Rice's lyrical style reveals the mind of a serial killer and humanizes the dilemma of justice by the book versus justice for victims." Booklist

Richards, David Adams, 1950-

The bay of love and sorrows; a novel. Arcade Pub. 2003 307p $24.95

ISBN 1-55970-650-3   LC 2002-38348

"In the early Seventies, Michael Skid, the privileged son of a judge, returns to his hometown on the Oyster River in rural New Brunswick from his postgraduate wanders through India. He takes up with a dangerous crowd, including Everette Hutch, an ex-convict who makes a practice of surreptitiously taping his friends in order to blackmail them later, and his coterie of drug-using associates." Libr J

"Michael is as naive as the other downtrodden individuals Everette has chosen as pawns to carry out his darkly laid plans, and the tragic events that ensue will forever be ingrained in the minds of the townpeople residing in The Bay of Love and Sorrows. Richards' story falls into place with the ease of a domino rally, providing all of the elements for a riveting story." Booklist

Richler, Nancy, 1957-

Your mouth is lovely; a novel. Ecco Press 2002 357p $25.95

ISBN 0-06-009677-2   LC 2002-23521

This "novel summons up the lost world of the Russian shtetls around the Pripet marshes in Ukraine, and shows how those communities were first changed and then annihilated by the events that led, ultimately, to the Russian Revolution. At the center of Richler's tale is Miriam Lev, whose mother drowned herself when she was a day old, and who at age six is taken in hand by her father's new wife, Tsila, a harsh, beautiful seamstress who teaches Miriam the alphabet and dreams of another life. After an ill-starred and and painful series of events, Miriam ends up, at nineteen, in Siberia, having shot an officer of the Tsar at point-blank range. Miriam's hegira is told here as a letter to her own daughter, whom she hasn't seen since she gave birth to her, in prison. Richler's work recalls the stories of Isaac Babel, in which the knowable is charged with mystery." New Yorker

Ridley, John, 1965-

Those who walk in darkness. Warner Bks. 2003 310p $24.95

ISBN 0-446-53093-X   LC 2002-193352

This "novel questions the nature of heroism in a near future where cops battle mutated 'metanormals' with telepathy, pyrokinetics, and other superpowers. Officer Soledad O'Roark is a successful 'freak' killer, unquestioning in her belief that they are dangerous and need to be desroyed." Libr J

"For all the bleakness . . . Ridley makes it hard not to pull for Soledad. Readers will find themselves torn between sympathy, empathy, pity and disgust, often on the same page." Publ Wkly

Rikki *See* Ducornet, Rikki

Rinehart, Steven

Built in a day; a novel. Doubleday 2003 241p $23.95

ISBN 0-385-49855-1   LC 2003-41968

"Andrew, the antihero of this blackly humorous novel, is still in college in his 30s, has a job as a youth counselor that involves nothing more than hanging out with teens all day and is skilled at manipulating women. When his new wife dies, leaving him in charge of her teenaged sons and 16-year-old foster daughter, he finally has adult responsibility thrust upon him. He responds to his new role by taking his sexually precocious female charge to bed and making starry-eyed plans to marry her while also thinking about seducing her social worker." Publ Wkly

"The charm of the protagonist, clearly, is not the primary appeal of this novel. The charms of Rinehart's writing, however, more than countervail; though stripped-down and deadpan, his sentences pack a lot of raw, juicy comic power." N Y Times Book Rev

Riordan, Rick

Cold Springs. Bantam Bks. 2003 340p $23.95

ISBN 0-553-80236-4   LC 2003-40365

"Cold Springs is an east Texas wilderness boarding school for troubled teens. Haunted by his own unresolved guilt over his daughter's death from a heroin overdose nine years earlier, ex-teacher Chadwick now makes his living escorting children into this boot camp for losers, giving them a second chance whether they

Riordan, Rick—*Continued*

want it or not. When an ex-lover asks him to locate her self-destructive 15-year-old daughter and take her to Cold Springs, Chadwick finds himself involved in a case of blackmail, murder, and financial skullduggery." Libr J

Riordan's "voice is fresh yet sure, with insights so trenchant they nearly provoke tears. And Riordan's characters, even the minor ones, are achingly believable." Booklist

Robb, Candace M.

The cross-legged knight; an Owen Archer mystery; [by] Candace Robb. Mysterious Press 2003 321p $23.95

ISBN 0-89296-772-2   LC 2002-27248

"When William of Wykeman, bishop of Winchester, fears reprisal after being blamed for the death of a local knight by his irate family, Owen Archer. . . must protect him. In the meantime, Owen copes with wife Lucie's overwhelming sorrow upon losing the child she was carrying." Libr J

"Once again, Robb provides the reader with an evocative and suspenseful whodunit thoroughly bolstered by a wealth of authentic historical detail." Booklist

Robbins, David L., 1954-

The last citadel; a novel of the Battle of Kursk. Bantam Bks. 2003 421p $24.95

ISBN 0-553-80177-5   LC 2003-44304

"The battle for the Soviet city of Kursk in July 1943 during World War II involved two million soldiers. Code-named Citadel, it was Hitler's frenzied—and final—attempt to defeat Russia on the eastern front and was the largest buildup of German armed power of the war. Robbins re-creates the battle in this rousing novel: its characters being Hitler; his generals and advisers; Russian, German, and Spanish foot soldiers and tank drivers; fighter pilots (both men and women); partisans; and even elderly men and women digging trenches." Booklist

Robbins, Tom

Villa incognito. Bantam Bks. 2003 241p $27.50

ISBN 0-553-80332-8   LC 2003-40353

"The novel begins with the story of Tanuki, a badgerlike Asian creature with a reputation as a changeling and trickster and a fondness for sake. Also part of the cast is a beautiful young woman who may or may not have Tanuki's blood in her veins. . . and three American MIAs who have chosen to remain in Laos long after the Vietnam War. Events are set in motion when one of the MIAs, dressed as a priest, is arrested with a cache of heroin taped to his body. In vintage Robbins style, the plot whirls every which way, as the author, writing with unrestrained glee, takes potshots at societal pillars: the military, big business and religions of all ilks. The language is eccentric, electrifying and true to the mark." Publ Wkly

Roberts, Gillian

Claire and present danger. Ballantine Bks. 2003 244p $23.95

ISBN 0-345-45490-1   LC 2002-43654

"Because of disturbing anonymous letters, a rich old lady hires Philadelphia schoolteacher Amanda Pepper. . .to investigate the 'credentials' of her son's evasive fiancee. What Amanda finds may be murder, both past and present." Libr J

Robinson, Peter, 1950-

Close to home; a novel of suspense. Morrow 2003 389p $24.95

ISBN 0-06-019878-8   LC 2002-71901

"A moody chap on the sunniest of days, Peter Robinson's Yorkshire copper, Inspector Alan Banks, slips into a melancholy funk. . . when he returns to his boyhood home—indeed, to his own narrow bed in his old room in his parents' house—to help with an investigation into the death of a former schoolmate. Graham Marshall was 14 when he disappeared in 1965, and the belated discovery of his skeletal remains brings a rush of painful memories to the middle-aged detective who had been his best friend and the keeper of their secrets." N Y Times Book Rev

Robinson, Roxana

Sweetwater; a novel. Random House 2003 319p $24.95

ISBN 0-375-50916-X   LC 2002-31830

"A widow for two years, 47-year-old Isabel Green marries her ardent suitor, Paul Simmons, hoping that her affection for him will turn into love. During a visit to Sweetwater Lodge, the Simmons family's lakeside compound in the Adirondacks, she meets Paul's cold disapproving parents, Douglas and Charlotte. . . and his bachelor brother, Whit, with whom Paul maintains a vicious sibling rivalry. Fundamental issues soon convince Isabel that her marriage is a dreadful mistake." Publ Wkly

"Robinson writes big solid scenes bubbling with tension, that hold the reader's interest. She has always shown her characters' flaws, and the dark emotions stirred up by divorce and parenthood; here she has reached farther to relate her characteristic predicaments to the larger world outside." N Y Times Book Rev

Robinson, Spider

Callahan's con. TOR Bks. 2003 286p $23.95

ISBN 0-7653-0270-5   LC 2003-40285

"A Tom Doherty Associates book"

"When Jake Stonebender and his wife, Zoey, move to Florida and open up the Place, the latest incarnation of the unusual bar once known as Callahan's Place, he acquires a collection of strange friends, including a talking German shepherd, a merman, and a foul-mouthed parrot. An encounter with the Florida bureaucracy over the homeschooling of his hyperintelligent daughter, Erin, and the intrusion of the local Mafia result in a grand scheme to outwit both intrusions and rescue Jake's missing wife in the process. Robinson's latest entry in his Callahan series features more zaniness, good humor, and bad jokes." Libr J

Roquelaure, A. N. *See* Rice, Anne, 1941-

Roza, Luiz Alfredo García- *See* García-Roza, Luiz Alfredo, 1936-

Rozan, S. J.

Winter and night. St. Martin's Minotaur 2002 338p $24.95

ISBN 0-312-24555-6 LC 2001-48659

In this mystery featuring New York PIs Lydia Chin and Bill Smith it is "Smith's turn to tell the story, which here concerns his teenage nephew, Gary Russell, the athlete son of his estranged sister Helen. When Gary is arrested for pickpocketing in Manhattan, the boy asks for his uncle's help. Gary denies running away from his Warrenstown, N. J. home; he was doing something important. Then the boy vanishes, drawing Smith and Chin into a nightmarish case in which a small town's obsession with its high school football team overwhelms standards of justice and morality." Publ Wkly

Ruiz, Luis Manuel, 1973-

Only one thing missing; translated from the Spanish by Alfred Mac Adam. Grove Press 2003 308p $24

ISBN 0-8021-1730-9 LC 2002-29723

Original Spanish edition, 2000

"A distraught young woman living in Seville, Spain, Alicia has just lost her husband and only child in a horrible accident. She suffers from terrifying nightmares of wandering through a nameless city whose monuments and inhabitants begin appearing to her during waking moments. Carmen Barroso, the most sought-after psychotherapist in Seville. . . treats her with hynosis and medication but is strangely dismissive of her harrowing dreams. . . . Aided by her brother-in-law, Esteban, who loves her deeply, Alicia comes to realize that she is the victim of a sinister conspiracy with roots in devil worship." Libr J

"As translated by Adam, Ruiz's prose is ornate and word-drunk. Ruiz sometimes falls in love with the sound of his narrator's voice, but it is easy to forgive him." Booklist

Rush, Norman

Mortals; a novel. Knopf 2003 715p $26.95

ISBN 0-679-40622-0 LC 2002-43289

This "novel is about middle-class Americans in Botswana, Africa. . . . The protagonist is a minor secret CIA agent in the early 1990s with the region in turmoil as Mandela struggles to come to power across the border. Ray's not quite sure how he landed in his spy job, but he quite likes it. He's sure he's never been involved with anything really bad. What matters to him is his beautiful wife, Iris. After 17 years, he's still totally obsessed with every part of her body, every glance, every funny word. But is she having an affair with Morel, the black American doctor who believes the way to fix broken Africa is to get rid of Christianity? When Ray is sent on a bungled mission and lands up with the brutal apartheid paramilitary, Morel comes to the rescue, and the two bond in a prison cell." Booklist

"The richness of Rush's vision, and its stringent moral clarity, sweep the reader into his brilliantly observed world." Publ Wkly

S

Saberhagen, Fred, 1930-

Berserker's star. TOR Bks. 2003 368p $24.95

ISBN 0-7653-0423-6 LC 2003-41016

"A Tom Doherty Associates book"

A title in the author's far-future saga of interstellar warfare

"Wanted in parts of the galaxy for his theft of a powerful space cannon, pilot Harry Silver accepts a business proposition from a mysterious woman who claims she wants to rescue her husband from cultists on Maracanda, a pseudo-planet wedged between a black hole and a neutron star. En route, Silver discovers that his passenger's agenda is not quite what it seems and, after making planefall, he finds that Maracanda holds secrets and terrors beyond his worst fears. . . . Witty dialog, clever plot twists, and a likeably roguish protagonist make this a good selection for most sf collections." Libr J

Sagan, Nick, 1970-

Idlewild. Putnam 2003 275p $23.95

ISBN 0-399-15097-8 LC 2003-43152

"A young man wakes up in what appears to be a pumpkin patch; while he cannot remember his own name, he has the feeling that he has just survived an attempt on his life. He soon discovers that his nom de game is Halloween, that he is one of 10 students in some kind of exclusive school, and that someone is indeed trying to kill him." N Y Times Book Rev

Sallis, James, 1944-

Cypress Grove. Walker & Co. 2003 255p $24

ISBN 0-8027-3380-8 LC 2002-41480

"Turner ('just Turner'), a former Memphis cop who went to prison for something he'd like to forget, has dropped out of human circulation and buried himself in a cabin in the deep woods. Because Turner's communication skills are rusty, Sallis gives him a constrained narrative voice, the guarded speech of a man so wary of emotion that the very act of speaking seems to leave his throat raw. When the sheriff of this rural backwater asks for his help with a murdered drifter who was found with a wooden stake in his chest, Turner crawls out of hibernation." N Y Times Book Rev

Salvatore, R. A.

Immortalis. Ballantine Bks. 2003 487p il map $26.95

ISBN 0-345-44122-2 LC 2002-33046

"Jilseponie Wyndon is no longer Queen of Ursal. Her newly rediscovered, totally unscrupulous son, Aydrian, has usurped the throne. In alliance with the unscrupulous, perhaps even demon-possessed weretiger and Abellican priest Marcallo De'Unnero, Aydrian sets out to conquer the world, initially without any scruples as to who gets killed in the process. But the alliance begins to fray as De'Unnero realizes that his protégé is more magically potent and ruthless than he is." Booklist

"A satisfying tale of personal responsibility, forgiveness, and redemption, this conclusion to the second 'DemonWars' trilogy features strong, memorable characters and superb plotting and storytelling." Libr J

Sanchez, Thomas, 1944-

King Bongo; a novel of Havana. Knopf 2003 309p $25

ISBN 0-679-40696-4   LC 2002-40770

"The title character of Sanchez's latest novel is a Cuban American living in Havana in 1957, just before Castro's revolution. Ethnically and socially, Bongo is a man of two worlds, by day a mild-mannered insurance salesman, by night an acclaimed bongo drum virtuoso. Bongo's sister, a stunning exotic dancer known as the Panther, has not been seen since the night the Tropicana was bombed by terrorists. Bongo's desperate search for her takes him to every corner of the decadent city." Libr J

"The byzantine plot is neatly constructed and thoroughly involving but never an end in itself. Sanchez shows us a city and a people on the eve of revolution but filters it all through the emotions of a conflicted hero, sympathetic to the cause but loyal only to himself and those he loves. Havana is both setting and soul in this pulsing bolero of a novel." Booklist

Sandford, John, 1944-

Naked prey. Putnam 2003 359p $26.95

ISBN 0-399-15043-9   LC 2003-41364

Lucas Davenport "is now Director of Regional Studies in the Minnesota Bureau of Criminal Apprehension, which is a fancy name for the job of investigating difficult crimes as quickly as possible and answering to the governor of the state. Known for his ability to solve the unsolvable, he goes to a remote area of the state to discover why a black man and a white woman were hanged in a groove of trees. . . . Fast paced and full of surprises, this may be Sandford's best novel yet." Libr J

Sandlin, Tim

Honey don't. Putnam 2003 342p $24.95

ISBN 0-399-14998-8   LC 2002-031712

"Honey, a savvy Texas girl with a weakness for older guys, offers sexual consolation to a raunchy President on the prowl. Her Mafia-connected boyfriend interrupts the scene, and the POTUS croaks. What to do? Naturally, Honey and Jimmy try to get away with it, recruiting and otherwise comporting with a persistent reporter, Secret Service agents, a Redskins third-stringer, and other essential characters who populate Sandlin's wacky Washington." Libr J

Saramago, José

Nobel Prize in literature, 1998

The cave; translated from the Portuguese by Margaret Jull Costa. Harcourt 2002 307p $25

ISBN 0-15-100414-5   LC 2002-2355

Original Portuguese edition, 2000

"Widowed Cipriano Algor is a 64-year-old Portuguese potter who finds his business collapsing when the demand dries up for his elegant, handcrafted wares. His potential fate seems worse than poverty—to move with his daughter, Marta, and his son-in-law, Marcal Gacho, into a huge, arid complex known as 'The Center,' where Gacho works as a security guard. But Algor gets an order from the Center for hundreds of small ceramic figurines, a task that has Marta and Algor hustling to meet the delivery date." Publ Wkly

"As a further warning against the urge to seek safety on common ground—moving to the center, as it were—the writer highlights the menaces of cliche by parodying the worldly-wise narrative interventions of an earlier era. . . . Such deft manipulations in Saramago's style are brilliantly rendered in Margaret Jull Costa's agile English version of his Portuguese." N Y Times Book Rev

Saulnier, Beth

Ecstasy. Mysterious Press 2003 342p $23.95

ISBN 0-89296-750-1   LC 2002-26519

In this mystery featuring reporter Alex Bernier "Alex gets saddled with covering the Melting Rock Music Festival, a four-day annual event held in nearby Jaspersburg. . . . The story really begins, however, when one of the kids, and then another, dies of a drug overdose. Alex enlists the aid of her policeman boyfriend to determine if the overdose were truly accidental." Publ Wkly

Saylor, Steven, 1956-

Have you seen Dawn? Simon & Schuster 2003 342p $24

ISBN 0-7432-1366-1   LC 2002-70619

Rue Dunwitty "leaves her analyst job for a dot-com survivor in San Francisco to go on her annual visit to tiny Amethyst, Texas, where her beloved wheel-chair-bound grandmother awaits. After she arrives, Rue learns a local 17-year-old girl is missing and is shaken by the incursion of contemporary crime into the safe little backwater." Booklist

Scarborough, Elizabeth Ann

(jt. auth) McCaffrey, A. Acorna's rebels

Scholz, Carter

The amount to carry; stories. Picador 2003 208p $23

ISBN 0-312-26901-3   LC 2002-192667

Analyzed in Short story index

Contents: The eve of the last Apollo; A catastrophe machine; Blumfeld, an elderly bachelor; The menagerie of Babel; A draft of Canto CI; Altamira; Travels; At the shore; The nine billion names of God; Invisible ink; Mengele's Jew; The amount to carry

"In each keenly meta-physical fable Scholz, a connoisseur of the imagination, parses the language of science, literature, art, and music as he ponders the quintessentially human habit of telling stories, a valiant attempt to render sense out of the delirium of existence." Booklist

Schupack, Deborah

The boy on the bus; a novel. Free Press 2003 215p $23

ISBN 0-7432-4220-3   LC 2002-32179

"One afternoon, Vermont housewife Meg discovers that the boy on the school bus outside her door is almost, but not quite, her eight-year-old son, Charlie. . . . Meg's panic recalls her aloof, restless husband from his job in Canada and her bratty, rebellious teenage daughter from boarding school, but neither they nor the local sheriff nor the family doctor can verify Charlie's authenticity." Publ Wkly

"Motherhood with all its contradictions has rarely been shown so nakedly. Schupack gives us Meg's view and everyone else's in overlapping layers. . . . From beginning to end in this novel, nothing is ordinary, while at the smae time everything is." N Y Times Book Rev

Schwartz, Gil

See also Bing, Stanley

Schwarz, Christina

All is vanity; a novel. Doubleday 2002 368p
$24.95

ISBN 0-385-49972-8   LC 2002-67583

"This novel concerns a Manhattan schoolteacher named
Margaret who quits and tries her hand at writing about
something . . . far afield: the ennui of a Vietnam vet.
. . . [Later] Margaret ditches Vietnam, and secretly
bases her novel on her friend Letty's life. Letty's husband has a falshy new job at a museum in California,
and the couple's been spending crazy money trying to
seem less nouveau and more riche. Margaret encourages
Letty to spend without end." Newsweek

"Schwarz's portrait of the talentless, self-absorbed
Margaret is surgically accurate. . . . Anyone who has
ever tried to write and been blocked will howl with recognition at the indignities that befall the novelist. . . .
The novel is both a page turner and a cautionary tale of
consumerism run amok." N Y Times Book Rev

Scott, Anne

Calpurnia. Knopf 2003 293p $24

ISBN 0-375-41380-4   LC 2002-30096

"Elizabeth Oliver is overseeing the sale of an estate
called Calpurnia, a large Philadelphia mansion once
owned by Maribel Archibald Davies, painter and self-
appointed bohemian. As Elizabeth gathers, organizes, and
catalogs the items of the estate, she finds herself drawn
into the family's intimate relationships as well as the
mysterious circumstances surrounding Maribel's death."
Booklist

"Scott sets the book in the 1980's, before online antique auctions and the advent of dot-com billionaires who
might have competed fiercely to buy a flashy old pile
like Calpurnia. Her central theme, however, the impulse
to make and live with art, is timeless." N Y Times Book
Rev

Scottoline, Lisa

Dead ringer. HarperCollins Pubs. 2003 339p
$25.95

ISBN 0-06-051493-0   LC 2002-191931

A "legal caper featuring the lady lawyers of series heroine Bennie Rosato's Philadelphia law firm Rosato and
Associates. This time out it's Bennie playing the lead
role, as she fights to save her financially sinking firm;
mother her lovable partners, Mary DiNunzio and Judy
Carrier; solve the murder of a valuable client; and battle
her evil twin, Alice. . . . Bennie grows on you, and soon
enough you're rooting for the home team and laughing
at her corny jokes." Publ Wkly

See, Lisa

Dragon bones; a novel. Random House 2003
348p $24.95

ISBN 0-679-46320-8   LC 2002-24871

"The controversial construction of a massive dam on
the Yangzi River is the backdrop for the latest adventures of Liu Hulan, inspector in the Ministry of Public
Security in Beijing, and her husband, American lawyer
David Stark." Publ Wkly

"Hulan and David must overcome their estrangement
and work together to solve the crimes. In a land where
bribery and corruption are the norm, there are many suspects. The novel flows beautifully, engaging readers in
the mystery while gently introducing them to China's
rich cultural history." Libr J

Self, Will

Dorian; an imitation. Grove Press 2002 277p
$23

ISBN 0-8021-1729-5   LC 2002-29962

"In this retelling of Oscar Wilde's The Picture of Dorian Gray, most of the original's characters are cleverly
transmuted into their late-20th-century counterparts: dis-
solute Henry Wotton, now openly homosexual with a
nasty heroin habit; his protege, eager young video artist
'Baz' Hallward; and the title character, the quintessential
amoral narcissist. . . . Self uses Wilde's plot to examine
post-Stonewall gay life, from its drug-fueled hedonistic
excesses to the reckoning of the AIDs epidemic. The
novel skewers every layer of British society—street hus-
tlers, members of Parliament and the idle rich." Publ
Wkly

Shade, Eric, 1970-

Eyesores; stories. University of Ga. Press 2003
205p $24.95

ISBN 0-8203-2432-9   LC 2002-7151

Analyzed in Short story index

Contents: Eyesores; Blood; The heart hankers;
Superfly; A rage forever; Stability; Kaahumanu; A final
reunion; Hoops and wires and plugs; The last night of
the couonty fair; Souvenirs

A collection of stories set in a small Pennsylvania
town. "Windfall, recently bypassed by a freeway, is losing its blue-collar jobs and shuddering toward new life
as a destination for golfers. Residents are torn between
the desire for and the fear of change. . . . Shade captures perfectly the way in which it's hard to leave your
mistakes behind when you're surrounded by people who
remember when you made them." Booklist

Shaley, Tseruyah

Husband and wife; [by] Zeruya Shalev; translated from the Hebrew by Dalya Bilu. Grove Press
2002 311p $24

ISBN 0-8021-1718-X   LC 2001-58479

"Na'ama is a social worker who heals ailing young
mothers and their children, though she is unable to turn
an observant eye on the lives of her own husband and
child, or herself. When her husband, Udi, a healthy hik-
ing guide who periodically leaves the family for long,
solitary jaunts into nature, wakes up one morning unable
to move his legs, Na'ama begins an inner monologue,
wrestling over whether to take him to a hospital. . . or
whether to keep him at home, where she and their nine-
year-old daughter Noga can finally have a constant relationship with him." Publ Wkly

Shalev, Zeruya *See* Shaley, Tseruyah

Shamsie, Kamila, 1973-

Kartography. Harcourt 2002 305p $24

ISBN 0-15-101010-2   LC 2003-4989

Shamsie, Kamila, 1973——_Continued_

"Karachi, Pakistan's largest city, is a place under constant siege: ethnic, factional, sectarian and simply random acts of violence are the order of the day. This violence—and the lingering legacy of the civil war of 1971—is the backdrop for the story of Raheen and Karim, a girl and boy raised together in the 1970s and '80s, whose lives are shattered when a family secret is revealed. . . . This is a complex novel, deftly executed and rich in emotional coloratura and wordplay." Publ Wkly

Shannon, Ray _See_ Haywood, Gar Anthony

Shapiro, Dani

Family history. Knopf 2003 269p il $23
ISBN 0-375-41547-5   LC 2002-30183

"Disaster slams into the charmed lives of an arty couple in small-town Massachusetts when, after the birth of their second child, their teen-age daughter—a beautiful, athletic, straight-A student—suddenly becomes a foul-mouthed, self-mutilating terror. She injures her baby brother and makes a terrible accusation about her father that threatens to destroy the family entirely. The fierce emotional pitch would seem melodramatic were it not for Shapiro's understanding of the mother's anxious, guilt-ridden world." New Yorker

Shattuck, Jessica

The hazards of good breeding. Norton 2003 288p $23.95
ISBN 0-393-05132-3   LC 2002-14203

"Social comedy, with flashes of darker import, about an upper-crust Boston suburban family forced to come to terms with the pressures of contemporary life and the ways in which they succeed, or more frequently fail. . . . Shattuck is an observant and graceful writer, and contrives some elegant and touching scenes." Publ Wkly

Sher, Ira

Gentlemen of space. Free Press 2003 291p $23
ISBN 0-7432-4218-1   LC 2002-192807

This "novel is told from the perspective of Georgie Finch, whose father, Jerry—a high schol science teacher—wins a trip to the moon. Jerry's rise to celebrity status as an astronaut brings a crowd of media and the curious, who suddenly disrupt the lives of Georgie and his mother, Barbara, in the small community of Magnolia Court, Fl. While Jerry is on the moon, Barbara learns that he had an affair with Georgie's babysitter, who is now pregnant." Libr J

"Sher's affection for his characters is clear, and they shine with softly absurd humor. . .and a DeLillo-like nostalgia for Americana and belief. This is beautiful, eloquent first novel." Booklist

Sherrill, Martha

My last movie star; a novel of Hollywood. Random House 2003 349p $23.95
ISBN 0-375-50769-8   LC 2002-69707

"Fed up with her manipulataive editor, entertainment journalist Clementine James is packing up to move to her boyfriend's Virginia farm when Flame magazine asks her to write an in-depth profile of captivating actress Allegra Coleman. When their interview ends in a car crash, Clementine awakes to find herself a celebrity. Allegra has vanished, and Clementine was the last person to see her. Alegra's disappearance catapults her into instant superstardom." Booklist

"The novel is as much a celebration of screen legends (buffs will be drawn to Sherrill's filmography) as it is a cautionary tale." N Y Times Book Rev

Shigekuni, Julie

Invisible gardens. Thomas Dunne Bks. 2003 240p $23.95
ISBN 0-312-31183-4   LC 2003-41354

"Bittersweet story of a year in the life of Lily Soto, a Japanese American academic and mother of two young children who is married to a pathologist. The family lives in New Mexico, where Lily teaches at a college and her husband works at the morgue. Lily alternates between dutifully fulfilling her obligations as historian, wife, and mother and suffering a midlife crisis, which causes her to wonder about such basic issues as who she is and where she's headed." Libr J

"This is mostly a taut, well-modulated tale. Readers may be a bit baffled by the resolution, but Shigekuni beautifully describes Lily's subtle sense of isolation in her marriage." Publ Wkly

Shirley, John, 1953-

Demons. Ballantine Pub. Group 2002 372p $25
ISBN 0-345-44647-X   LC 2001-43478

"A Del Rey book"

This "apocalyptic tale, redolent with the terror of inexplicable carnage, is two novels in one: a first-person account of an initial advent of demons in everyday reality, followed by the story of their later return. Ira, narrator of the first, plays a significant role in the second, and Shirley links the two episodes nearly seamlessly. Ira reports a world gone mad with demonic possession, its people clinging to normality for dear life." Booklist

Shreve, Anita

All he ever wanted. Little, Brown 2003 310p $25.95
ISBN 0-316-78226-2   LC 2002-36847

"Escaping from a New Hampshire hotel fire at the turn of the 20th century, Prof. Nicholas Van Tassel catches sight of Etna Bliss and is instantly smitten. She does not reciprocate his feeling, for she has her own unrequited lust, for freedom and independence. That they marry guarantees tragedy. Nicholas tells the story in retrospect, writing feverishly on a train trip in 1933 to his sister's funeral in Florida." Publ Wkly

"Aside from an exchange of letters between his wife and his rival, everything is seen from the point of view of Nicholas, who grows increasingly jealous and pathetic, his motives couched in formal, self-justifying language that almost always sounds like a form of evasion. In the end, he admits, he's telling 'the story of a faintly ridiculous man,' but luckily it's a tale that also flirts with full-scale tragedy as well as the darkest kind of comedy." N Y Times Book Rev

Shriver, Lionel

We need to talk about Kevin. Counterpoint 2003 400p $25
ISBN 1-58243-267-8   LC 2002-152753

Shriver, Lionel—*Continued*

"This is the story, narrated in the form of letters to her estranged husband, of Eva Katchadourian, whose son has committed the most talked-about crime of the decade—a school shooting reminiscent of Columbine." Libr J

"It's a harrowing, psychologically astute, sometimes even darkly humorous novel, with a clear-eyed, hard-won ending and a tough-minded sense of the difficult, often painful human enterprise." Publ Wkly

Siegel, James, 1954-

Derailed. Warner Bks. 2003 339p $23.95

ISBN 0-446-53158-8   LC 2002-73572

Charles Schine "writes advertising copy and worries a lot about his stressed-out wife and diabetic daughter. Charles makes his fatal mistake one morning on the 9:05 commuter train from Babylon to Penn Station, when he looks up from his newspaper. . . and makes eye contact with a beautiful stockbroker named Lucinda. One thing leads to another, but their hotel tryst is interrupted by an armed intruder who rapes Lucinda, pistol-whips Charles and proceeds to blackmail them. Desperate, Charles resorts to criminal measures to stop this sadistic torment." N Y Times Book Rev

"With its clean prose, high-velocity plotting and just the right amount of emotional shading darkening its sharply drawn characters, this novel is the bomb." Publ Wkly

Siegel, Lee

Love and other games of chance; a novelty. Viking 2003 418p $27.95

ISBN 0-670-89461-3   LC 2002-29635

This novel is "organized as a game of Snakes and Ladders, with each chapter representing a square on the game board; the reader can choose between a traditional reading, from start to finish, and a playful one, letting the roll of the dice decide. The story follows Isaac Schlossberg, a swindler, circus performer and entertainer. As Schlossberg travels around the world (and across the board), his stunts—from childhood appearances in sideshow acts with his Jewish immigrant parents at the turn of the century to his attempts to beat Sir Edmund Hillary to the top of Mount Everest—are woven together into one exceptionally tall tale." Publ Wkly

Siegel, Sheldon

Final verdict. Putnam 2003 391p $25.95

ISBN 0-399-15042-0   LC 2002-37189

This legal procedural features "law partners Mike Daley and ex-wife Rosie Fernandez working together in their San Francisco firm, Fernandez, Daley and O'Malley. . . . Skid row resident Leon Walker, successfully represented by Michael and Rosie in a murder case 10 years earlier, reappears and seeks legal help once again. Leon is charged with the murder of Tower Grayson, a Silicon Valley venture capitalist found stabbed to death in a Dumpster behind a liquor store. Publ Wkly

"An ending that's full of surprises—both professional and personal—provides the perfect finale to a supremely entertaining legal thriller." Booklist

Silverberg, Robert

Roma eterna. Eos 2003 396p $25.95

ISBN 0-380-97859-8   LC 2002-35416

This is "a what-if history of the world, starting from the premise that the Roman Empire never fell. Spaning 1,500 years, the narrataive unfolds in a world without Christianity. It seems that the failure of the ancient Hebrews to escape Pharaonic oppression prevented the rise of mystical religious cults in the province of Syria Palaestina, thereby guaranteeing the survival of Roman hegemony down to the beginning of space travel. Silverberg, who has written numerous popular works of history and archaeology, brings his alternate Rome to life by blending invention with a dazzling array of details borrowed from the annals of the real Rome." N Y Times Book Rev

Simmons, Dan

Ilium. Eos 2003 576p $25.95

ISBN 0-380-97893-8   LC 2002-44791

"Restored to life by the 'gods,' a race of beings who dwell on the heights of Olympos, 20th-century scholar Thomas Hockenberry travels back in time to observe the events of the Trojan War, as chronicled in Homer's epic poem. There, one of the gods recruits him in a secret war against her brother and sister deities. Set in a far future in which the population of true humans is kept strictly regulated by extraplanetary forces and machine intelligences study Proust and Shakespeare as they perform their duties throughout the universe." Libr J

"For answers to the mysteries laid out in 'Ilium'— from the true identity of the Olympian gods to the fate of robots and humans and of the 'little green men' on Mars for whom communication means death—you will have to wait for the promised sequel. For now, matching wits with Simmons and his lively creations should be reward enough." N Y Times Book Rev

Simon, Roger Lichtenberg, 1943-

Director's cut; a Moses Wine novel. Atria Bks. 2003 241p $23

ISBN 0-7434-5802-8

"For some reason, agents interrogate Hollywood private investigator Moses Wine. . .about his possible links to terrorists. Shortly thereafter, Moses signs on (undercover) with a movie crew filming in Prague to investigate the distrubing appearance of symbolic plastic snakes on set and elsewhere. Lo and behold, terrorists kidnap him and the film's lead actress. The incident ends badly for the terrorists but results in Moses directing the film, supposedly about overcoming sins of the Holocaust. A particularly relevant plot, then, filled with action and suspense and set against arresting Czech backdrop." Libr J

Smiley, Jane, 1949-

Good faith. Knopf 2003 417p $26

ISBN 0-375-41217-4   LC 2002-73096

"Everyone trusts Joe Stratford, the affable Pennsylvania real-estate agent who narrates Smiley's ninth novel— his clients, his bankers, his boss, his boss's sexy married daughter, and even the irascible contractor who builds the most beautiful houses in the country. But when Marcus Burns, a charismatic I.R.S. agent turned developer, comes to town, Joe feels that no one else understands his potential the way Marcus does. With Joe as his partner, Marcus soon seduces half the county into investing in a development venture that he says will make everyone rich. It is hard to imagine a novelist better suited to taking on the S.& L. scandals of the nineteen-eighties than Smiley." New Yorker

Smith, April, 1949-

Good morning, killer. Knopf 2003 356p $24
ISBN 0-375-41240-9   LC 2002-35917

"This kidapping thriller starts off like most kidnapping thrillers, with the abduction of a pampered teenager, 15-year-old Juliana Meyer-Murphy, that has the local cops running around in circles. But we know we're in uncharted territory here when Juliana returns home, raped, battered and deeply traumatized, and Ana Grey, the F.B.I. agent assigned to the case, is so distressed by the girl's condition that she ignores procedures and starts acting on impulse. . . . A risk taker herself, Smith writes in the forceful style of a true literary maverick, someone who has earned the right to break a few rules." N Y Times Book Rev

Smith, B. J., 1957- *See* Smith, Brad, 1957-

Smith, Brad, 1957-

All hat; a novel. Holt & Co. 2003 308p $24
ISBN 0-8050-7217-9   LC 2002-27307

"His attempt to live 'a half-ass normal life' doomed out of the starting gate, ex-con Ray Dokes hatches a plot to swap racehorses before a race. Set in rural Onario and featuring an ensemble cast of delightfully eccentric, even downright loopy, characters, this big-hearted caper novel mixes laugh-out-loud-comedy with streaks of country noir that call to mind Daniel Woodrell." Booklist

Smith, Julie, 1944-

Mean woman blues. Forge 2003 304p $24.95
ISBN 0-7653-0552-6   LC 2003-40018

"A Tom Doherty Associates book"

"The Formosan termites that infest new Orleans every May haunt police detective Skip Langdon's dreams, an apt image for the gnawing fear that her happiness will collapse. That happiness is based on the fact that her long distance lover, a documentary filmmaker, has moved to New Orleans. Her fear is that her enemy, an evangelical fanatic who aspires to the mind control of Jim Jones, is coming back to kill her, after a disappearance of two years." Booklist

Smith, Mary-Ann Tirone, 1944-

She's not there; a Poppy Rice novel. Holt & Co. 2003 317p map $25
ISBN 0-8050-7223-3   LC 2002-68592

"FBI agent Poppy Rice is taking some time off with boyfriend Joe at his vacation home on Block Island. . . . Her enforced relaxation falls by the wayside after only a few days when she stumbles across the body of a teenage girl from the island's summer weight-loss camp." Booklist

"The ease with which Poppy gets technical support from Washington and manpower from the Rhode Island mainland is some stretch, but that doesn't take away from her shrewd analysis of the isolationist island mentality or her understanding of teenage behavior." N Y Times Book Rev

Smith, Rosamond, 1938-

See also Oates, Joyce Carol, 1938-

Solomon, Nina

Single wife; a novel. Algonquin Bks. 2003 307p $23.95
ISBN 1-56512-382-4   LC 2003-40406

"Most men who leave their wives have the courtesy to (at least) leave a note, but not journalist Laz Brookman. At the start of this. . . novel, he casually leaves his New York apartment one morning and never returns. . . . Anxious to save face and preserve the precarious normality of her life, and certain that he will soon return—mysterious several-day-long disappearing acts not being uncommon with her husband—Grace Brookman secretly begins living two lives, Laz's and her own." Publ Wkly

"Solomon tells a funny and bizarre story that is both hard to believe and hard to put down, with characters who are real, almost tangible. She captures the essence of the struggle for self." Libr J

Sparks, Nicholas

The guardian. Warner Bks. 2003 384p $24.95
ISBN 0-446-52779-3   LC 2002-192411

"On Christmas Eve, Julie Barenson, 25 years old and newly widowed, finds an unexpected present—a Great Dane pup that her late husband, Jim, had arranged for her to receive after her died from a brain tumor. . . . Julie's new dog, Singer, turns out to be a better judge of character than she, which is unfortunate because the dog nearly gives away the book's ending when he growls warily at Richard Franklin, the new man in Julie's life." Publ Wkly

Spencer, James, 1924-

The pilots. Putnam 2003 268p $23.95
ISBN 0-399-14973-2   LC 2002-73449

"There is a touch of Tales of the South Pacific to the adventures of Steve Larkin, a fighter pilot and the author's stand-in, who bails out of his plummeting aircraft and lands on a grimly hazardous jungle island inhabited by head-hunting, spear-toting savages. They capture and inmprison Steve in a fetid hut, and the situation seems bleak, but after some days of testing his intentions, two nubile young women make it clear he is welcome. . . . Scenes in Australia, where the pilots go for rest, are vivid and poignantly capture the pain of the women there who have lost their men. This is not self-conscious writing, but it successfully balances the beauty of flying with the terrors of life-and-death combat, and is a worthy addition to the literature of WWII." Publ Wkly

Spencer, Scott

A ship made of paper; a novel. HarperCollins Pubs. 2003 351p $24.95
ISBN 0-06-018534-1   LC 2002-68922

"Daniel Emerson is a New York City lawyer who has returned to his hometown of Leyden, N.Y., a picturesque Hudson Valley village, with his girlfriend Kate, a novelist, and her daughter, Ruby. Kate drinks and obsesses about the O.J. Simpson trial instead of writing fiction. Daniel finds himself falling in love with Iris Davenport, an African-American grad student at the local university. Iris is married to Hampton Welles, an investment adviser. The book records Iris and Daniel's affair from both perspectives and poses the question, is their fleeting happiness really worth so much ruin." Publ Wkly

Spencer, Scott—*Continued*

"The interracial aspect allows Spencer. . .to explore both subtle and overt forms of racism among liberals and conservatives and the heavy burden of living with a consciousness of race and the responsibility of setting an unimpeachable example." Libr J

Spiegelman, Ian, 1974-

Everyone's burning; a novel. Villard Bks. 2003 164p $18.95

ISBN 1-400-06056-7   LC 2002-33191

"A nightmarish tour of the drug-fueled subculture of Queens. Leon Koch, a recent high-school graduate, leads a streamlined existence: his goals are to avoid getting killed by any of the neighborhood psychopaths who might have any grievance (real or imagined) against him and to make sure he has enough cocaine and alcohol to cushion his bleak existence. He bounces from one dead-end job to another and seeks out sadomasochistic relationships with the equally damaged women who make up his world." Booklist

"Spiegelman's characters talk to one another like David Mamet's: in staccato bursts, with verve and irony." N Y Times Book Rev

Spiegelman, Peter

Black maps. Knopf 2003 285p $22.95

ISBN 1-4000-4075-2   LC 2003-273218

This mystery introduces John March, " a Manhattan P.I. who walks the mean streets of Beaver and Broad. As the rebel son in four generations of merchant bankers, who turned his back on the family business to become a cop . . . he's quick enough to grasp the byzantine forensic accounting procedures that fire up this technically accomplished financial mystery." N Y Times Book Rev

Standiford, Les

Havana run. Putnam 2003 304p $24.95

ISBN 0-399-15059-5   LC 2002-37021

John Deal "is rebuilding the failed Miami construction firm he inherited from his father, dead by suicide. Soon after moving to Key West to oversee a major construction contract, Deal is approached by Antonio Fuentes, a mysterious businessman, who attempts to hire him to oversee a huge rebuilding project in Havana, slated to begin once Castro has departed the scene. Deal has his suspicions, especially after Fuetes offers a check for a million dollars as a retainer." Publ Wkly

"Standiford does a superb job of setting up his complex plot, using the color-drenched, ever-threatening Havana landscape both to ratchet up the tension and to emphasize the otherworldly nature of this latest and most baffling call from the grave." Booklist

Stark, Richard

For works written by this author under other names see Westlake, Donald E.

Breakout. Mysterious Press 2002 299p $23.95

ISBN 0-89296-779-X   LC 2002-23492

This is an "entry in the Parker series. After a pharmaceutical heist goes south, Stark's strong, silent antihero faces a dose of hard time. While awaiting arraignment in an overcrowded detention center, Parker formulates an escape with the help of two fellow prisoners, a crooked defense attorney, and sometime-partner-in-crime Ed Mackey. A series of breakouts follow, as Parker and company hit pothole after pothole on their crooked road to freedom." Booklist

"Richard Stark (the name that Donald E. Westlake uses when he lets Parker off the leash) writes with ruthless efficiency. His bad guys are polished pros who think hard, move fast and turn on a dime in moments of crisis. And because talk doesn't come cheap, every bit of dialogue counts." N Y Times Book Rev

Steel, Danielle

Johnny Angel. Delacorte Press 2002 181p $19.95

ISBN 0-385-33549-0   LC 2001-37188

"Killed in a car crash after his senior prom, 17-year-old Johnny Peterson is sent back to earth as an angel. His mission: to fix certain troubles left unresolved at the time of his death involving his girlfriend, Becky, her impoverished mother and his dysfunctional family. . . . Steele's heartfelt depiction of the central relationship between Johnny and his mother is touching, and few readers will get through the revelation of Johnny's final gift with dry eyes." Publ Wkly

Steele, Allen M.

Coyote; a novel of interstellar exploration. Ace Bks. 2002 390p $23.95

ISBN 0-441-00974-3   LC 2002-74517

"At first, this novel. . . looks like a fairly conventional tale of high-tech intrigue—in this case, rebels against a right-wing American dictatorship plot to steal the prototype interstellar spaceship built to immortalize the government's ideology by planting a colony of fanatics on another star's planet. However, once the freedom seekers arrive on the new world, Coyote, things get a lot more interesting. Coyote, is habitable but alien, full of flora and fauna that upset the colonists' easy preconceptions." Publ Wkly

"A much-foreshadowed 'surprise' ending is by far the least of the surprises in Steele's bag of tricks. But each page of this novel bears evidence of fresh thought about the opportunities inherent in science fiction to take the familiar and make it new." N Y Times Book Rev

Steinhauer, Olen

The Bridge of Sighs. St. Martin's Minotaur 2003 278p $23.95

ISBN 0-312-30245-2   LC 2002-68127

"Set in 1948 in a small, unnamed Eastern European country devastated by WWII and still occupied by Russian troops, [this novel]. . . introduces 22-year-old homicide inspector Emil Brod of the People's Militia. Brod's police academy training has prepared him for neither the rude reception he receives from his homicide comrades nor the difficult and risky asignment handed him as his initiation." Publ Wkly

"This is an intelligent, finely polished debut, loaded with atmospheric detail that effortlessly re-creates the rubble-strewn streets of the postwar period in an Eastern state 'liberated' from German occupation by the Russians." Libr J

Stirling, Jessica

The piper's tune. St. Martin's Press 2002 486p $26.95

ISBN 0-312-28870-0   LC 2001-57854

"Eighteen-year-old Lindsay Franklin gets an unexpected jolt when her shipbuilding magnate grandfather gives her a share of the family business. At the same time, her all-too-charming Irish cousin, the womanizing Forbes McCulloch, comes to Glasgow to learn the family business from the bottom up and sets his sights on marrying Lindsay. The style and design of the cover give the impression that this is a historical romance, but the tale is much more than a formulaic love story. Stirling does a bang-up job of illustrating how character shapes a person's life." Publ Wkly

Stone, Robert, 1937-

Bay of souls. Houghton Mifflin 2003 249p $25

ISBN 0-395-96349-4   LC 2002-192171

"Michael Ahearn is a respected professor of literature at a small college in the upper Midwest, with a lovely wife and 12-yer-old son, but a vague dissatisfaction gnaws at him, exacerbated by a frightening incident while deer hunting and the near-death of his son from exposure. When Michael meets a new professor, the beautiful and electrifying Lara Purcell, he falls under her spell and launches an affair, endangering his marriage and his relationship with his son. At Lara's prompting, Michael travels with her to her Caribbean island home of St. Trinity, a nation rife with political violence, where Lara hopes to repossess the soul she believes has been captured by a voodoo goddess." Publ Wkly

"Unusual (for Stone) in is brevity, this is a highly concentrated work, probably the least violent yet most unnerving of his novels. And the philosophical conflict dramatized in it ends surprisingly, in a way that provokes new questions about what Stone is up to in his writing." N Y Times Book Rev

Stone, Zachary, 1949-

For works written by this author under other names see Follett, Ken, 1949-

Stroby, Wallace

The barbed-wire kiss. St. Martin's Minotaur 2003 340p $24.95

ISBN 0-312-30034-4   LC 2002-35879

"Ex-cop Harry Rane, recovering from the death of his wife and forced into semi-retirement by a bullet wound, comes to the rescue of his longtime friend Bobby. Bobby has made a big mistake: he has invested money with a partner for a 'one-time' drug buy. The partner has disappeared with the cash, but the supplier, a suspicious character under scrutiny by New Jersey cops, still wants his money." Libr J

"Although the story advances predictably. . . Stroby does wonders with his blue-collar characters, the hardworking fishermen and mechanics and bar waitresses who put their hand to petty crime the way they play the lottery—to try their luck and get a thrill, the way they did when the seashore was a kinder place to live." N Y Times Book Rev

Stubbs, Harry Clement *See* Clement, Hal, 1922-2003

T

Taibo, Paco Ignacio, 1949-

Returning as shadows; [by] Paco Ignacio Taibo II; translated from the Spanish by Ezra E. Fitz. St. Martin's Press 2003 455p $24.95

ISBN 0-312-30156-1   LC 2002-35388

"As this sequel to The Shadow of a Shadow (1991) begins, it is 1941, and Mexico, a neutral country, is buzzing with crypto-Nazi espionage. The Germans have three aims: to secure coffee beans for a caffeine-addicted Adolf Hitler, to establish a covert submarine base in the Gulf of Mexico and to complete some occult process involving Hitler's former adviser and guru, Eric Jan Hanussen. Hanussen, who has broken with the Nazis, is disguised as an inmate in a Mexico city nuthouse. His roommate, ex-lawyer Alberto Verdugo, rules as a sort of narrating magus over the story." Publ Wkly

"Unlike some other writers who use the thriller genre, [the author] has a novelists's sensibility, the education of a truly literary man and the notebook of a journalist—which means that in his books the world in all its oddity is always bigger, much bigger, than just the plot." N Y Times Book Rev

Tawada, Yoko, 1960-

Where Europe begins; translated from the German by Susan Bernofsky; from the Japanese by Yumi Selden; with a preface by Wim Wenders. New Directions 2002 208p $23.95

ISBN 0-8112-1515-6   LC 2002-5196

Analyzed in Short story index

Contents: The bath; The reflection; Spores; Canned foreign; The talisman; Raisin eyes; Storytellers without soul; Tongue dance; Where Europe begins; A guest

"Tawada's stories shift between the transparent and the opaque, even on the same page; they agitate the mind like songs half remembered or treasure boxes whose keys are locked within." N Y Times Book Rev

Taylor, Sarah Stewart

O' artful death. St. Martin's Minotaur 2003 277p $23.95

ISBN 0-312-30764-0   LC 2002-191963

"Art historian Sweeney St. George's interest in an unusual late-Victorian gravestone sculpture takes her to a former art colony in Vermont. Her arrival coincides with the suspicious death of an old local lady who believed that the young woman in the grave Sweeney is seeking was murdered. Sweeney investigates, attempting to find out who carved the beautiful monument and what really happened to the young woman. Her search into local family backgrounds inevitably turns up clues to the old lady's murder as well." Libr J

Sweeney is a "vivid and attractive sleuth, and the iconography of graves and death, hidden meanings in diaries and inscriptions, and some complicated personal relationships sweep one past an overstuffed plot and a slightly wobbly denouement. Rich and rewarding reading." Booklist

Templeton, Edith, 1916-

Gordon. Pantheon Bks. 2001 226p $22

ISBN 0-375-42194-7   LC 2002-70427

Templeton, Edith, 1916--—*Continued*

First published 1966 in the United Kingdom under the pseudonym Louise Walbrook

"This eerie tale of sexual obsession is narrated by a young woman adrift in London just after the Second World War. She meets a 'frightening, sinister, implacable' psychiatrist who, over all protest, invades her, body and mind, arousing previously unsuspected tastes for submission and humiliation. One part 'Story of O' to two parts Muriel Spark, the book beautifully evokes the tightened belts and loose morals of postwar London." New Yorker

Teran, Boston

The prince of deadly weapons. St. Martin's Minotaur 2002 371p $24.95

ISBN 0-312-27118-2   LC 2002-69839

The serpentine plot "has Rudd—supposedly blinded early on in a subway attack, but even this is left in doubt at the end—investigating the death of the man whose corneas he inherited by infiltrating a gang of smugglers and killers whose nastiness is exceeded only by their ineptitude." Publ Wkly

"This thriller combines a feverish New Journalism writing style with the kind of philosophical ruminations popular in freshman dorms after all the pot has been smoked. . . . For every over-amped paragraph . . . Teran uncorks a passage of startling power and beauty. With a bit more restraint, he might have delivered one of the year's most powerful noir novels." Booklist

Thomas, Chantal, 1945-

Farewell, my queen; a novel; translated by Moishe Black. Braziller 2003 239p $22.50

ISBN 0-8076-1514-5   LC 2003-45192

Original French edition, 2002

"For 11 years, in her post as deputy reader to Marie Antoinette, [Agathe-Sidonie] Laborde's devotion to the vain and moody queen never wavered. Then, as the storming of the Bastille rocked the Bourbon dynasty, Laborde's own life began to unravel. . . . In Moishe Black's excellent translation . . . Versailles is transformed from the seat of power into the last retreat of a disintegrating monarchy. In language both vivid and elegant, the novel also captures the mood of panic that soon had servants and soldiers fleeing their posts, and nobles, clergy and hangers-on looking to save their skins." N Y Times Book Rev

Thomas, Scarlett

Dead clever; a novel. National Bk. Network 2003 285p $24.95

ISBN 1-932112-01-4   LC 2002-40564

"Having dumped her boyfriend, job, and London flat to return home to Devon, Lily Pascale takes on part-time work at the local university, filling in for an instructor who quit. On her first day, a student is brutally raped and murdered. Lily begins sleuthing when another student, who tried to tell her that he witnessed the girl's murder, dies of a purported drug overdose." Libr J

"When [Lily] discovers an insidious drug cult on campus with a sinister leader, what was hitherto a tale of amateur detection becomes a Sax Rohner-type thriller." Publ Wkly

Timm, Uwe, 1940-

Morenga; translated from the German by Breon Mitchell. New Directions 2003 340p $25.95

ISBN 0-8112-1514-8   LC 2002-15248

Original German edition, 1978

This novel is "an oddly fragmented montage that offers a . . . view of the title figure, a charismatic black South-West African who led the Hottentot and Herero uprising against the Germans after the Boer War. The initial protagonist is a fictional German military veterinarian . . . . The early chapters concern the mysterious fate of a colleague who disappears from [the veterinarian's] unit. From there, Timm turns to the uprising itself, his depiction of Morenga's role broken up by snapshots of secondary characters." Publ Wkly

The "fragmentary approach has great cumulative moral power, making us consider all sides of the story without forgetting that there were victims who deserve some remembrance." N Y Times Book Rev

Tolkien, Simon, 1959-

Final witness; a novel. Random House 2003 283p $24.95

ISBN 0-375-50882-1   LC 2002-21316

Published in the United Kingdom with title: The stepmother

"The book pits 16-year-old Thomas Robinson against the beautiful, social-climbing Greta Grahame, who married Thomas's father, Sir Peter Robinson, a prominent politician, soon—very soon—after Lady Anne Robinson was killed. Thomas, who witnesed his mother's murder by two armed robbers, alleges that Greta was behind the killing. His courtroom testimony alternates with Greta's, and with a third-person narrative that at times contradicts both of the witnesses and keeps the reader in suspense. . . . The book is fast paced and crisply plotted." Publ Wkly

Tolstaîâ, Tat´iana, 1951-

The slynx; [by] Tatyana Tolstaya; translated by Jamey Gambrell. Houghton Mifflin 2003 278p $24

ISBN 0-618-12497-7   LC 2002-27627

Original Russian edition, 2000

In a postapocalyptic Russia, "in a society turned primitive by nuclear holocaust, people hunt mice and tremble at the mention of a mysterious forest creature called the slynx; of course, they are utterly ignorant, as books are banned. . . . Benedikt, scribe to the tyrant who rules this sorry land . . . has yet to read a book, but in the course of the novel he discovers the libraries owned by the Oldeners, those who recall the world before the fateful blast. Not surprisingly, he finds that literature is both liberating and dangerous." Libr J

"It takes some time for a plot to develop, but Tolstaya sketches a vivid picture of life in this permanent winter. . . . In this extended fable, she captures the Russian yearning for culture, even in desperate circumstances. Gambrell ably translates the mix of neologisms and plain speech with which Tolstaya describes this devastated world." Publ Wkly

Tolstaya, Tatyana *See* Tolstaîâ, Tat´iana, 1951-

Tracy, P. J.

Monkeewrench. Putnam 2003 373p $23.95

ISBN 0-399-14978-3   LC 2002-68139

Tracy, P. J.—*Continued*

"When people start dying in strange ways in Minneapolis, everyone wonders what the murderer will do next—everyone except the employees of Monkeewrench Software, who are all too aware that their new serial-killer computer game is the model for the crimes. They go to the police with the what, where, and when of the next murders and quickly become suspects themselves." Booklist

"Unlike the conventionally dimwitted cops and hick sheriff's deputies, Grace and her four geek partners in the software company . . . add real flavor to the proceedings with their colorful jargon and quirky personas. These techno-nerds may be freaks—and one of them may even be a killer—but they have style." N Y Times Book Rev

Tremain, Rose

The color. Farrar, Straus & Giroux 2003 382p $25

ISBN 0-374-12605-4   LC 2002-192528

This novel, set in the mid-19th century, centers on Joseph and Harriet Blackstone, who have married and emigrated to New Zealand in search of a better life. "Together with Joseph's mother, they attempt to build a farm on the flats outside of Christchurch, but when Joseph finds gold in the creek, he becomes obsessed by 'the color', as the fabulous metal is known. Abandoning both women, he travels by ship to the west coast, where he encounters hundreds of other desperate men and the clamorous, filthy, dehumanizing conditions in which they live. . . . By the time [Harriet] does join him, each of them despises the other, yet the discovery of gold binds them in a new way." Publ Wkly

"As the story gathers momentum, it widens . . . . Tremain's excursions into the minds of her Maori and Chinese characters are written with a blend of sympathy and irony that sabotages our expectations of things exotic and inscrutable." N Y Times Book Rev

Tremaine, Jennie *See* Chesney, Marion

Trigiani, Adriana

Lucia, Lucia; a novel. Random House 2003 263p $24.95

ISBN 1-400-06005-2   LC 2003-46612

"Kit, an aspiring playwright, agrees to afternoon tea with 'Aunt' Lu, an old, but still elegant, fellow tenant. Kit's casual question about Lue's frequently worn mink coat is rewarded by the story of two pivotal years in Lucia Sartori's life. For the bulk of the novel, we are swept back to Greenwich Village in the early 1950s, where we meet Lucia's family. Beautiful and talented Lucia, who works in the custom dress shop at B. Altman's, wants to retain her maiden name after marriage, continue in a nonfamily business, and delay having children, all taboo for an Italian Catholic. Then she meets the irresistible John Talbot, and Lucia's happy life seems destined to unravel." Libr J

"This old-fashioned drama wears its heart on its sleeve—subtlety is not its strong suit—but readers will laugh with and weep for Lucia and her lost dreams." Publ Wkly

Truman, Margaret, 1924-

Murder at Ford's Theatre. Ballantine Bks. 2002 326p $24.95

ISBN 0-345-44489-2   LC 2002-74748

"When the body of congressional intern Nadia Zarinski turns up outside the stage door of Ford's Theatre, D.C. police detectives Mo Johnson and Rick Klayman, who happens to be a Lincoln buff, are assigned the case. Nadia worked in the office of Senator Bruce Lerner, ex-husband of Clarise Emerson, head of Ford's Theatre and nominee for chair of the National Endowment for the Arts. Once Clarise determines with Klayman's help that her son, Jeremiah, was the last to see Nadia alive, she appeals to former attorney Mackensie 'Mac' Smith to represent him." Publ Wkly

Truong, Monique T. D.

The book of salt; [by] Monique Truong. Houghton Mifflin 2003 261p $24

ISBN 0-618-30400-2   LC 2002-192152

"From a few lines in The Alice B. Toklas Cook Book, Truong reimagines the Vietnamese cook who was hired by the famous residents at 27 Rue de Fleurus. Binh, as he calls himself, is an exile from his homeland, where he was denounced because of a homosexual relationship and banished by his brutal father. After three years at sea, Binh ends up in Paris, where he answers Toklas's ad. . . and enters the household of Gertrude Stein." Publ Wkly

"Truong is tapping some trendy territory here: the postcolonial perspective; the book derived from a minor character in another well-known book. . .; the gay novel; the novel of exile. And Truong's central character, the gay Asian houseboy, is something of a stereotype in itself. But nothing in this distinctive novel feels secondhand." N Y Times Book Rev

Turner, Frederick W., 1937-

1929; [by] Frederick Turner. Counterpoint Bks. 2003 390p $25

ISBN 1-58243-265-1   LC 2002-154007

"A brilliant cornet player with an amazing ear, [Bix Beiderbecke] drank himself to death at the age of 28 with illegal Prohibition liquor. . . . Turner offers a fictional take on Beiderbecke's life, giving readers a . . . picture of what life was like for jazz musicians in the years leading up to the Great Depression." Publ Wkly

"Written in a period-appropriate overheated, romantic prose, and incorporating memorable appearances by Capone, Bing Crosby, Maurice Ravel, Paul Whiteman, and Clara Bow, the book is by turns corny, intoxicating, and ineffably sad, like the 'hot' music it is designed to evoke." New Yorker

Turow, Scott

Reversible errors. Farrar, Straus & Giroux 2002 433p il $28

ISBN 0-374-28160-2   LC 2002-70891

"In 1991, three people were brutally murdered in a Kindle County diner. Prosecutor Muriel Wynn and detective Larry Starczek ferreted out Rommy Gandolf, who soon confessed to the crime. Ten years later, Rommy is on death row, just weeks away from his execution. Arthur Raven has been appointed as his lawyer, but he can't imagine that anything new will turn up despite

Turow, Scott—*Continued*

Rommy's claims of innocence. Then Erno Erdai steps forward." Booklist

"What Turow has done, in book after book, is to give us page turners that are also pleasing literary artifacts, mysteries that are also investigations into coomplex human emotions." N Y Times Book Rev

U

Ullman, Ellen

The bug; a novel. Talese 2003 355p $23.95

ISBN 0-385-50860-3   LC 2002-73289

A "novel about the fate of a programmer, Ethan Levin, who wrestles with an ineradicable bug in the heroic era of computing. It is 1984, and Telligentsia is an information technology startup engaged in creating a database and an interface to access it. . . .The story is narrated by Roberta Walton from the perspective of 2000, remembering her first IT job as a quality-checker for Telligentsia, which she takes after a failed bid for an academic job in linguistics." Publ Wkly

"With her thrilling and intellectually fearless first novel, 'The Bug'—which might have been subtitled 'The Postmodern Prometheus,' after Mary Shelley—Ullman reinvents the story of Frankenstein and his sentient beast as an allegory for the birth of the computer." N Y Times Book Rev

Unsworth, Barry, 1930-

The songs of the kings; a novel. Doubleday 2003 338p $26

ISBN 0-385-50114-5   LC 2002-66845

"A stubborn wind from the northeast ushers in rough times for the House of Atreus, and the Greek ships, en route to Troy, remain trapped in the straits at Aulis. Unsworths' retelling of the story, familiar from Euripides, of the sacrifice of Iphigeneia to appease the gods so that the boats can sail is a bold, modern tale with cynical riffs on the themes of duty and power, truth and fiction. His Greek warriors are schemers and media-savvy self-promoters who are desperate to look good in the sung reports that are their equivalent of the news media—songs that are, we realize, the seeds of the Homeric tradition." New Yorker

Upadhyay, Samrat

The guru of love. Houghton Mifflin 2003 290p $23

ISBN 0-618-24727-0   LC 2002-32234

Ramchandra, a math teacher in 1990s Kathmandu, Nepal, has "become infatuated with one of his tutees, 15-year-old single mother Malati. Unable to endure his obsession, his wife, Goma, has fled to her parents' home with pubescent Sanu and her younger brother, Rakesh. But nothing—neither infidelity nor her rich parents' scorn for a son-in-law who can barely afford a dilapidated apartment with outdoor plumbing—diminishes Goma's love for Ramchandra." Publ Wkly

The author "excels at depicting the thousand small cuts that afflict a middle-class married man having an affair. . . . The writing is emotionally restrained and doesn't call attention to itself. There are no lyrical bursts of exuberance over the country's beauty or the torments of love. At points the novel is excessively terse; when three words would have sufficed, Upadhyay uses two. In spite of that it is gripping, because you like the characters so much, and wish them well." N Y Times Book Rev

Updike, John

Seek my face. Knopf 2002 276p $23

ISBN 0-375-41490-8   LC 2002-18442

"The action of the novel, such as it is, takes place over a single early-April day at the house in the Vermont countryside of the septuagenarian Hope Chafetz, an artist in her own right and, more famously, widow of the action painter Zack McCoy and ex-wife of the Pop artist Guy Holloway. Kathryn, an ambitious young journalist, has come up from New York to interview this living repository of the history of postwar American art. Through the course of the long day the two women talk, attended by a tape recorder, that ubiquitous tool of contemporary journalism." N Y Times Book Rev

"Despite its uncomplicated premise, the novel achieves a remarkable depth of characterization and a glowing beauty in its articulation of the artistic sensibility." Booklist

V

Vanderbes, Jennifer

Easter Island; a novel. Dial Press (NY) 2003 304p $24.95

ISBN 0-385-33673-X   LC 2002-31588

This novel "parallels two stories: that of Elsa Pendleton, who travels to Easter Island in 1913 with her much older husband and her mentally impaired sister to study the toppled moai statues, and of Dr. Greer Farraday, who in the 1970s escapes grief after the death of her famed scientist husband, accused of fraud, by studying ancient pollen on the island. Both women have been suppressed by circumstance—Elsa, always her sister's caretaker, has made a bid for security by marrying a colleague of her father after his death, and Greer battles prejudice against women scientists." Libr J

"Vanderbes knows how to craft suspense, and the narratives—while packed with vivid historical and scientific detail—move forward on the strength of her fully realized characters." Publ Wkly

Vargas Llosa, Mario, 1936-

The way to paradise; translated by Natasha Wimmer. Farrar, Straus & Giroux 2003 373p $25

ISBN 0-374-22803-5   LC 2003-56379

This is a dual fictional biography of "early-nineteenth-century French-Peruvian workers' rights activist Flora Tristan and her grandson, famous painter Pual Gauguin. In alternating chapters, the author. . . fashions portraits of these two vibrant individuals as he follows Flora in touring France to carry out her campaign to promote labor organization and equality in marriage, and Paul in awakening to his innate sexuality, to say nothing of tapping into his formidable artistic talent, by abandoning France for the South Pacific." Booklist

"A whiff of the lecture hall is detectable all through

Vargas Llosa, Mario, 1936——*Continued*

this book. (Some passages have more dates than an almanac.) But the juxtaposition of Tristan's and Gauguin's stories is fascinating all the same. In their different ways, both were moralists and proselytizers." N Y Times Book Rev

Varley, John, 1947-

Red thunder. Ace Bks. 2003 411p $23.95

ISBN 0-441-01015-6   LC 2002-38231

"When a Chinese spacecraft, Heavenly Harmony, threatens to land on Mars a few days before the U.S. shuttle vehicle Ares Seven, washed-up ex-astronaut Travis Broussard, his brilliant but uncoventional cousin, Jubal, and four kids from Florida decide to build their own private spaceship, Red Thunder, and get there first in this riveting SF thriller. . . . With hilarious, well-drawn charracters, extraordinary situations presented plausibly, plus exciting action and adventure, this book should do thunderously well." Publ Wkly

Vasilikos, Vasiles *See* Vassilikos, Vassilis, 1934-

Vassilikos, Vassilis, 1934-

The few things I know about Glafkos Thrassakis; translated from the Greek by Karen Emmerich. Seven Stories Press 2002 356p $24.95

ISBN 1-58322-527-7   LC 2002-13866

Original Greek edition, 1978

The author "takes as his territory the lawless borderlands between literature and life. Narrated by an unamed biographer (who keeps reminding the reader how much he looks like his subject), the novel purports to tell the life story of the Greek writer Glafkos Thrassakis, which is in turn the pen name of Lazarus Lazaridis, who bears more than a passing resemblance to Vassilis Vassilikos himself. Biographer and subject, subject and author, fiction and fact: masks and doubles proliferate. The result is a deft and witty reflection on writing as well as a moving portrait of the artist as political exile." N Y Times Book Rev

Vera, Yvonne, 1964-

The stone virgins. Farrar, Straus & Giroux 2003 184p $20

ISBN 0-374-27008-2   LC 2002-25004

"As white rule in Rhodesia ends and the nation of Zimbabwe is born, sisters Thenjiwe and Nonceba can finally look forward to full lives, Thenjiwe finding love in their rural village and Nonceba discovering knowledge in boarding school. But when the new president sends forces to the province of Matabeleland to rid the country of his rivals, the sisters and their village are once again terrorized." Libr J

"Vera's impressionistic writing can make it difficult to grasp the political context and chronology of the war, but it perfectly captures the terrifying chaos of the fighting, as well as the rhythms of provincial African life." Publ Wkly

Vernon, Olympia

Eden. Grove Press 2003 272p $23

ISBN 0-8021-1728-7   LC 2002-33863

"Fourteen-year-old Maddy Dangerfield is called upon to help her cancer-afflicted aunt Pip live out her last days. Maddy's mother, Faye, can't forgive her sister's betrayal of her with her own husband. Maddy is caught in the vortex of unresolved conflicts among the adults: a stoic, overworked mother who can't make peace with a dying sister; an alcoholic husband addicted to gambling; and a fiery aunt who has lived her life on her own terms. The small black community of Pyke County, Mississippi, is also saturated with unresolved conflicts, seething resentments, and violence. . . .Vernon's writing is lyrical and emotionally powerful." Booklist

Vida, Vendela

And now you can go; a novel. Knopf 2003 189p $19.95

ISBN 1-400-04027-2   LC 2002-35688

"An armed man waylays a twenty-one-year-old woman, Ellis, in Riverside Park, seeking a partner in suicide, but she survives. . . . Ellis alternately fends off and submits to the consolations of various men; thinks about the child an infertile couple conceived with her eggs; broods over her father's four-year disapearance and unexplained return; jets off to the Philippines on a volunteer mission; then, back in Manhattan, cuts her hair into a mullet. There's plenty of mordant humor along the way." New Yorker

W

Walbrook, Louise *See* Templeton, Edith, 1916-

Walker, Dale L.

(ed) Westward. See Westward

Wallace, Daniel, 1959-

The Watermelon King. Houghton Mifflin 2003 226p $23

ISBN 0-618-22138-7   LC 2002-75941

"Lucy Rider drives into Ashland, AL, on a hot day in 1982 and unintentionally changes the nature of the quiet little town forever . . . . Known as the Watermelon Capital of the World, Ashland celebrates each watermelon crop with a festival, crowning a watermelon king and orchestrating his performance in a fertility rite for the following year's crop. The fertility ritual leads to Lucy's death and to the gradual decline of the town. Eighteen years later, Thomas Rider drives into Ashland, seeking information about his mother and his own roots, and Ashland again takes a Rider to its collective hearts, again leading to tragedy and loss." Libr J

"This is a unique and spellbinding novel, an unforgettable southern tall tale with extraordinary characters." Booklist

Wallach, Janet, 1942-

Seraglio. Talese 2003 316p $24.95

ISBN 0-385-49046-1   LC 2002-28698

Based on fact, "this book traces the life of Aimée du Buc de Rivery . . . who was kidnapped at age 13 en route to her home in Martinique. Her pirate captors take her to the Turkish sultan, who enslaves her in the sera-

Wallach, Janet, 1942-—*Continued*

glio . . . . There, Aimée befriends Tulip, the black eunuch responsible for her welfare. Tulip recounts Aimée's reluctant initiation into the harem as Nakshidil, her dramatic development from slave girl to woman of pleasure, and her incredible transformation into the valide sultan (mother of the sultan) . . . assisting him in his controversial attempt to westernize 19th-century Turkey." Libr J

"It is to Wallach's credit that at no point does her story seem preposterous. The intrigue and drama of the palace are balanced by capable, authoritative prose and admirable restraint, resulting in a novel at once serious and enchanting." Publ Wkly

Walsh, Michael

And all the saints. Warner Bks. 2003 383p il $24.95

ISBN 0-446-51815-8   LC 2002-31123

This novel is the fictional autobiography of Owen ("Owney") Madden, "raised in New York's infamous Hell's Kitchen (though born of Irish parents in England). Early on, Madden set his mind on becoming the first among the gangsters and, thus, to have the city at his feet. . . . [During Prohibition, he] carved out a turf that included ownership of the famed Cotton Club. A major influence with Tammany Hall and even Hollywood (he was one of Mae West's lovers and was responsible for George Raft's success), Madden later devoted his 'talents' to making Hot Springs, Arkansas, a major center of gangsterism." Booklist

"Walsh spices up the novel with cameo appearances by George Raft, Jack Johnson, Duke Ellington and Lena Horne . . . . The subplot about Madden's attempts to keep his louche buddies away from his sister, May, is lifeless, but the novel is saved by a crisp, compelling finale. In all, a lively slice of gangster life." Publ Wkly

Wangerin, Walter

Saint Julian; a novel; [by] Walter Wangerin, Jr. HarperSanFrancisco 2003 xxiii, 210p $19.95

ISBN 0-06-052252-6   LC 2002-32842

This story, supposedly narrated by an old priest, is based on the medieval legend of St. Julian the Hospitaller, a gifted but violent young man with a dark devotion to the hunt. A dying stag told Julian that he would one day kill his own parents, and although Julian fled from home, years later he unknowingly carried out the prophecy. Then, horrified by what he had done, he sought to atone by building shelters for the poor and sick and by carrying people across a swift river. In succouring a ghastly leper, he encountered Christ himself and won forgiveness.

"Full of mystical and spiritual undertones, this dark novel of depravity and deliverance casts a spell heightened by the author's ability to immerse himself—as the narrator—in the culture, the language, and the moral fabric of another time and another place." Booklist

Waters, Mary Yukari

The laws of evening; stories. Scribner 2003 177p $23

ISBN 0-7432-4332-3   LC 2002-29429

Analyzed in Short story index

Contents: Seed; Since my house burned down; Shibusa; Aftermath; Kami; Rationing; The laws of evening; Egg-face; The way love works; Circling the hondo; Mirror studies

"Like the spare and prescribed movements of a Japanese tea ceremony, the stories in The laws of evening. . . present a deceptively smooth and elegant surface. Underneath this unruffled exterior, however, the smallest nuances convey real depth of feeling." N Y Times Book Rev

Watson, Larry

Orchard; a novel. Random House 2003 241p $24.95

ISBN 0-375-50723-X   LC 2002-35654

The author "introduces us to Henry and Sonya House, a couple who have drifted apart after the death of their 4-year-old son. They own an apple orchard that has been in Henry's family for generations. . . . One day . . . Sonja is approached by Ned Weaver, a local artist with a reputation for sleeping with his models, who asks her to pose for him. She agrees . . . . Weaver becomes obsessed with Sonja, and Henry . . . becomes increasingly jealous until he confronts Weaver." N Y Times Book Rev

Watson's novel is "an uncompromising, perfectly calibrated double portrait of two couples in rural Wisconsin in the 1950s. . . . Sentences and chapters unfurl with a sense of inevitability, and the narrative possesses an uncommon integrity." Publ Wkly

Weber, Katharine

The little women. Farrar, Straus & Giroux 2003 240p $22

ISBN 0-374-18959-5   LC 2003-44062

In a story narrated by 16-year-old Joanna, the modern-day Little Women of the title "grow up in New York City in cozy upper-middle-class bliss, their perfect family the envy of all. But their smug contentment is shattered when they discover their mother's affair; their father's blasé reaction is almost worse. In protest, Joanna and Amy move in with Meg and her roommate, Teddy Bell, at their off-campus apartment near Yale University. . . . Comments from Meg and Amy pepper the text, contesting the structure of Joanna's story and arguing with her about her perspective and her version of reality." Publ Wkly

"In places, the readers' and author's notes do cause the pace to drag. But fortunately, the story of three teenage girls making a go of living in a New Haven apartment with a cute male roommate is lively, interesting and funny enough to carry one over the sluggish bits. . . . Novels with spurious critical apparatus don't often wear it lightly, but Weber's use of the form is both easy and playful." N Y Times Book Rev

Weis, Margaret, 1948-

Mistress of dragons. TOR Bks. 2003 381p $25.95

ISBN 0-7653-0468-6   LC 2003-42618

"A Tom Doherty Associates book"

When the Amazonian order of priestesses, who have kept dragons from interfering with humans, is violated

Weis, Margaret, 1948-—*Continued*

by men, a wild and magical conflict ensues, revealing a secret lineage and dark truth about the Parliament of Dragons

"Full of intrigue, magic, and violence, this first book of Dragonvald—a projected trilogy chronicling the battle to preserve the uneasy relationship between dragons and humans—launches the project powerfully. Weis has brilliantly conceived a world viable for both dragons and humans." Booklist

Weisberger, Lauren, 1977-

The Devil wears Prada. Doubleday 2003 360p $21.95

ISBN 0-385-50926-X   LC 2003-40937

"Here we meet Andrea Sachs, a recent Ivy League graduate hoping to break into the magazine business . . . . She accepts an entry level position at Runway as personal assistant to the editor, Miranda Priestly (rumored to be based on Vogue's Anna Wintour). However, her new job has nothing to do with writing or editing, and everything to do with predicting and fulfilling every outrageous whim her prima donna boss might have. While the job makes incredible demands on Sachs' personal life, the perks are undeniable: rubbing elbows with celebrities, being outfitted in designer clothes, and jetting off to Paris for fashion shows." Booklist

"This fast-paced black comedy has enough dirt to please any fashionista but should serve as fair warning for every girl who dreams of working at a fashion magazine." Libr J

Welsh, Irvine

Porno. Norton 2002 483p $24.95

ISBN 0-393-05723-2   LC 2002-26362

Sequel to: Trainspotting (1994)

"Things are looking up for Simon David Williamson ('Sick Boy'), who has inherited a pub in his native Edinburgh. He's also ready to break into the movies, specifically that branch identified as the 'adult entertainment industry'. . . . The big issue is whether Simon will meet the psychotic Begbie, to whom he mails unsolicited gay porn in jail." Libr J

This novel "signals, if not a return to form, then at least a return to enthusiastic formlessness—to something like the raw, jagged energy of old." N Y Times Book Rev

Welsh, Louise

The cutting room. Canongate 2002 294p $24

ISBN 1-8419-5280-X   LC 2002-437974

"Gay auctioneer Rilke agrees to pack up and sell off an enormous quantity of high-quality goods in an inordinately short amount of time, no questions asked. . . . While clearing out the attic, he discovers a horrfying packet of snuff pornography. Depite his own proclivities for promiscuous, anonymous sex, he is haunted by the woman portrayed in the photographs and determined to discover whether the events depicted actually happened." Booklist

"A remarkable first novel. Like all the best exponents of the genre, Louise Welsh sets up her template and then manipulates it, using the glamour of crime to examine more humdrum kinds of suffering and loss. She piles on atmosphere to produce a Glasgow that is predictably dark and yet still plausible." N Y Times Book Rev

West, Bing *See* West, Francis J., 1940-

West, F. J. *See* West, Francis J., 1940-

West, Francis J., 1940-

The Pepperdogs; a novel; [by] Bing West. Simon & Schuster 2003 369p $25

ISBN 0-7432-3589-4   LC 2002-40860

"Capt. Mark Lang commands the 'Pepperdogs,' an elite four-man Marine reconnassiance team that must rescue an officer who has been wounded and kidnapped by a band of brutal and murderous Serbs. As the 'Dogs' make their grueling trek through the rugged Balkan terrain, the action is fast-paced . . . . The emerging technology of close-in and small-unit warfare that West describes is almost as fascinating as the chase. . . . On a different level, there is political action as the incident becomes public via the Internet, and both sides argue just who are the war criminals." Libr J

Westerfeld, Scott

The risen empire. TOR Bks. 2003 304p $24.95

ISBN 0-7653-0555-0   LC 2002-42952

"A Tom Doherty Associates book"

"In an interstellar empire of 80 human worlds, ruled by an emperor who lets selected humans cheat death, tensions between most humans and the resurrected elite, aka the Risen, are increasing. The Rix, a cult of cyborgs who worship compound AI minds, hunger to liberate the empire's worlds from mere human control. When a Rix raiding party captures the emperor's sister, Capt. Laurent Zai of the Imperial Navy must save her." Publ Wkly

"Westerfeld's speculations about the rise and fall of civilizations are appealingly quirky . . . and his action scenes have a breathless realism that does not gloss over the bloody nature of combat. Perhaps most important, his moral calculus never lapses into Q.E.D. As the narrative jumps from intimate glimpses of the Empire to the Rix Cult and back again, we grow less and less clear about whom we are rooting for." N Y Times Book Rev

Westlake, Donald E.

For works written by this author under other names see Stark, Richard

Money for nothing. Mysterious Press 2003 294p $24.95

ISBN 0-89296-787-0   LC 2002-35888

"New York advertising executive Josh Redmont finds himself in the middle of an espionage drama, cast as the hero but utterly unprepared for the role. Seven years earlier, Redmont began receiving $1,000 checks, issued by 'United States Agent'; after trying unsuccessfully to track down the source of the checks, Redmont began depositing them and has been doing so ever since. His 'found money,' however, comes with very big strings, as Josh learns when he is approached by an unassuming-looking man who announces, 'I am from United States Agent. You are now active.'" Booklist

"Although Westlake has written funnier books and his characters could use more dimension, 'Money for Nothing' has all of his trademarks: an ample supply of silliness and suspense wrapped up in a wacky plot." N Y Times Book Rev

Westward; a fictional history of the American West: 28 original stories celebrating the 50th anniversary of the Western Writers of America; edited by Dale L. Walker. Forge 2003 432p $25.95

ISBN 0-7653-0451-1   LC 2002-45481

"A Tom Doherty Assiates book"

Analyzed in Short story index

Contents: First horse, by Coldsmith, D.; Encounter on Horse-Killed Creek, by Gulick, B.; York's story, by Walker, D. L.; Melodies the song dogs sing, by Blevins, W.; Gabe and the doctor, by House, R. C.; A man alone, by Breen, J. V.; Jonas Crag, by Jakes, J.; Inquest in Zion, by Blum, I. B.; Dead Man's Hollow, by Reasoner, J.; The hundred day men, by Black M.;Leaving Paradise, by Carroll, L.; Miss Libbie tells all, by Salzer, S. K.; How I happened to put on the blue, by Carney, O.; The stand, by Braun, M.; The square reporter, by Wheeler, R. S.; Betrayal, by Sandifer, L.; Thirty rangers, by Smith, C.; The whispering, by Graebner, J. E.; The fevers, by Eckhardt, C. F.; I killed King Fisher, by Froh, R.; Noah, by Mehok, E. L.; The big die-up, by Smith, T. D.; Do the dark dance, by Knight, A. W.; Letters to the stove, by Long, E.; East breeze, by Aadland, D.; Big Tim Magoon and the wild west, by Estleman, L. D.; The true facts about the death of Wes Hardin, by Crider, B.

"The collection reveals both the vitality and the diversity of the western genre as well as the enduring appeal of the short story." Booklist

White, Kate

A body to die for. Warner Bks. 2003 294p $23.95

ISBN 0-446-53148-0   LC 2003-41081

"Depressed by her nonexistent love life, Bailey, a freelance true-crime writer for 'Gloss' magazine, leaves Manhattan for some R&R at the Cedar Inn and Spa in Warren, Mass., owned and run by an old friend of her mother's. Her first night there, however, she stumbles on the corpse of one of the inn's female therapists—wrapped in silver Mylar paper. [The therapist's] murder, on top of the accidental death of a male client some months earlier, could spell doom for the inn, unless Bailey can get to the bottom of things." Publ Wkly

"Once again, White's background as editor-in-chief of 'Cosmopolitan' shines through in her snappy dialog, tight plotting, and insider humor. . . . A breezy beach read for mystery fans." Libr J

White, Robin A.

Typhoon; [by] Robin White. Putnam 2003 388p il map $24.95

ISBN 0-399-14935-X   LC 2002-31835

"'Baikal', the last of Russia's giant Typhoon-class submarines . . . . is supposed to be off to the scrap yard at American expense, but corrupt Russian admirals have illegally sold her to China. When the American sub 'Portland' is ordered to [prevent delivery], its aggressive captain, James Vann, becomes obsessed with destroying the 'Baikal', commanded by his old nemesis, Alexander Markov. At the same time, the presence of Lt. Rose Scavullo, the first woman to serve on a U.S. submarine, is a major and divisive distraction . . . . As the ships

duel in the Arctic Ocean, war threatens to break out between the United States and China." Libr J

"The international cat-and-mouse game becomes a contest between American technology and Russian cunning. The setting and stirring pace will remind readers of Clancy's 'The Hunt for Red October'. Though the exhaustive technical details may stymie some readers, enthusiasts of naval warfare will delight in them." Publ Wkly

White, Stephen Walsh

The best revenge; [by] Stephen White. Delacorte Press 2003 353p $24.95

ISBN 0-385-33619-5   LC 2002-67593

FBI agent Kelda James's "latest triumph is the discovery of DNA evidence that ostendibly exonerates death-row inmate Tome Clone, convicted of murdering his girlfriend 13 years prior. Curiosity leads Kelda to pick up the released prisoner herself, and the two ot them . . . develop a curious closeness. Kelda recommends esteemed Boulder psychotherapist Dr. Alan Gregory (star of numerous White novels) . . . to Tom to help sort out potential outside-life issues, but this only serves to make matters even stranger, for client confidentiality bars Alan from discussing the two with each other or with his best buddy, a local detective. Not everyone is convinced the DNA evidence proves Tom's innocence, and some other evil force looms in an effort to exact revenge." Booklist

Wiggins, Marianne

Evidence of things unseen; a novel. Simon & Schuster 2003 383p $25

ISBN 0-684-86969-1   LC 2003-45611

"Born in Kitty Hawk, where the Wright brothers first rose towards the sun, Ray Foster, or 'Fos,' . . . is fascinated by radiance. A portrait photographer who deals with the dynamics of light, Fos . . . keeps a lump of phosphorous glowing in a fish tank by his bedside. . . . After signing on as an official photographer for the Tennessee Valley Authority—hence becoming complicit in kicking countless farmers off their ancestral lands to make way for hydroelectric dams—Fos assumes a similar recordkeeping role at the Oak Ridge Laboratory in Tennessee, one of three research sites for the Manhattan project." Economist

"Wiggins fits her lyrical prose to a distinctly rural, Southern cadence, easily blending the vernacular with luminous imagery, adding bits of poetry, passages explaining scientific phenomena, interpolations about the Scopes trial and even references to Moby-Dick, which serves as a leitmotif." Publ Wkly

Wilcox, James

Heavenly days; a novel. Viking 2003 199p $23.95

ISBN 0-670-03247-6   LC 2003-50164

A novel set in the small Louisiana town of Tula Springs. "Lou Jones, moving through her fifties at too rapid a pace, is unhappy: her husband lost his job and moved out of their $300,000 'Cajun cabin' and is now living in his parents' house. Plus, Lou, who minds everyone's business except her own, has a doctorate in music but makes more money working as the receptionist for a fundamentalist health club than she could ever earn at

Wilcox, James—*Continued*

the state college. Wilcox adds in some dizzying subplots involving Lou's oldest friend, a scandal at the college, a group of militant lesbians, and marital infidelity." Booklist

Wilson, F. Paul (Francis Paul)

The haunted air; a Repairman Jack novel. Forge 2002 415p $24.95

ISBN 0-312-87868-0   LC 2002-72059

"A Tom Doherty Associates book"

This Repairman Jack novel "teams the righteous urban mercenary with his strangest bedfellows yet: a pair of sham spirit mediums who openly operate their occult con game out of a brownstone in Queens. . . . Jack takes the case of brothers Lyle and Charlie Kenton, who've been threatened by other Big Apple pseudo-psychics for horning in on the lucrative seance scene. No sooner has Jack begun . . . than real ghosts begin popping up along with a secret cult of ritual child murderers. . . . Above all, the novel enhances the enigma of Jack, a hero who commands respect despite his curmudgeonly disdain for contemporary culture, his morally ambiguous work-for-hire ethic and his unsettling appeal to the vigilante in every reader." Publ Wkly

Wilson, Francis Paul *See* Wilson, F. Paul (Francis Paul)

Wilson, Jonathan, 1950-

A Palestine affair. Pantheon Bks. 2003 257p $23

ISBN 0-375-42209-9   LC 2002-35499

"It is 1924 and the Zionist movement is beginning to gain momentum. Tensions run high between Jews and Palestinians and between Zionist and Orthodox Jews, and none of the groups quite trust the British, who have a mandate to rule the area. To this intrigue Wilson . . . has added . . . murder and gun-running—as well as the introspective themes of a middle-aged artist whose career and marriage are on the down slope, his wife's own search for an identity, and her lover's coming to terms with his." Booklist

"Wilson has devised a story that tautens the sinuous strands of this period into a lethal knot. The strengths of his novel are the tension and pace of its plot, and its ability to suggest the falling barometer of a storm that will break fully only after another quarter century." N Y Times Book Rev

Wilson, Robert, 1957-

The blind man of Seville. Harcourt 2003 434p $26

ISBN 0-15-100835-3   LC 2002-68495

"Javier Falcón, chief homicide detective in Seville, has a ghastly murder to solve, one that inexplicably strikes into the depths of his being. When two similar murders follow, Falcón finds himself facing a midlife crisis as he penetrates his own past to find connections between the victims and his recently deceased father, a famous painter who lived a life of hidden depravity." Libr J

"Wilson . . . is able to hold reader interest at an almost unbearable pitch of excitement throughout this shocker with exquisite plot pacing and intriguing character revelations." Booklist

Wilson, Robert Charles, 1953-

Blind Lake. TOR Bks. 2003 399p $24.95

ISBN 0-7653-0262-4   LC 2003-47345

"A Tom Doherty Associates book"

"When the research facility at Blind Lake, MN, is placed under military blockade and quarantine, the scientists and workers . . . can only connect their enforced isolation with their research on a newly discovered form of alien life on a distant planet. Journalist Chris Carmody, trapped in Blind Lake, finds his life transformed by his chance encounter with researcher Marguerite Hauser and her troubled daughter, Tessa, a young girl whose unusual mind may hold the key to unraveling the alien mystery." Libr J

"No one knows better than Wilson how to manipulate the language of science to suggest the essential unknowability of the universe. . . . The drama at Blind Like gradually expands to encompass humans and aliens in entirely unforeseen ways." N Y Times Book Rev

Winspear, Jacqueline, 1955-

Maisie Dobbs; a novel. Soho Press 2003 294p $24

ISBN 1-56947-330-7   LC 2002-44656

In this novel "set in WWI-era England, humble housemaid Maisie Dobbs climbs . . . up Britain's social ladder, becoming in turn a university student, a wartime nurse and ultimately a private investigator. . . . Her first sleuthing case, which begins as a simple marital infidelity investigation, leads to a trail of war-wounded soldiers lured to a remote convalescent home in Kent from which no one seems to emerge alive." Publ Wkly

"For a clever and resourceful young woman who has just set herself up in business as a private investigator, Maisie seems a bit too sober and much too sad. Romantic readers sensing a story-within-a-story won't be disappointed. But first, they must prepare to be astonished at the sensitivity and wisdom with which Maisie resolves her first professional assignment." N Y Times Book Rev

Wolitzer, Meg, 1959-

The wife; a novel. Scribner 2003 219p $23

ISBN 0-684-86940-3   LC 2002-36660

"Joan Castleman is en route to Finland to watch her husband, the renowned author Joe Castleman, win the Helsinki Prize when she decides to leave him. What follows is Joan's fascinating recollection of their marriage, his career, and her fading dreams. Telling her story in alternating segments, she starts in the 1950s with the beginning of the couple's professor-student relationship and continues through to the present, their 40 years of marriage stacking up unspoken regrets." Libr J

"Wolitzer's crisp pacing and dry wit carry us headlong into a devastating message about the price of love and fame." Publ Wkly

Wood, James

The book against God. Farrar, Straus & Giroux 2003 257p $23

ISBN 0-374-11538-9   LC 2002-42600

"Tom Bunting begins his narrative with a survey of his miserable bed-sit in London. He is in exile from the wonderful flat in Islington he used to share with his wife, Jane . . . who earned the rent from her work as a

Wood, James—*Continued*

pianist. Penniless and hopelessly given to lying, Tom has also been neglecting his dissertation to scribble little impious aperçus in various notebooks. This he rather grandly calls his 'Book against God'—a sort of anti-Pensées. The book—and in a sense his whole wretched life—is a muffled rebellion against his father, a charming, learned, blissfully married vicar in North England." Publ Wkly

"Much of the novel follows a vaguely allegorical schema designed to force the characters and all that they ostentatiously symbolize (faith, doubt, art, etc.) into a culminating conflict. Among the many reasons you don't necessarily mind havinge your arm twisted in this way is the fact that, first, Wood writes like a dream, and second, the novel is often wildly funny." N Y Times Book Rev

Woods, Stuart

Dirty work. Putnam 2003 322p $25.95

ISBN 0-399-14982-1   LC 2002-32975

"Suave cop-turned-lawyer Stone Barrington is asked to hire someone to take photos of Lawrence Fortescue, the husband of a wealthy socialite, with a woman who is presumably his mistress. Stone hires the nephew of an old friend, who proves to be grossly incompetent when he falls through the skylight onto the man he's supposed to be photographing. Fortescu ends up dead, the supposed mistress disappears, and the photographer is charged with manslaughter. As Stone digs deeper, he discovers that Fortescue wasn't killed by the photographer's fall, but by an injection of poison. Enter Carpenter, aka Felicity Devonshire, Stone's contact in British intelligence. Carpenter suspects the woman involved with Fortescue is actually . . . a trained assassin with a grudge." Booklist

Y

Yancey, Richard

A burning in Homeland. Simon & Schuster 2003 341p $25

ISBN 0-7432-3013-2   LC 2002-70833

"In the summer of 1960 the small town of Homeland, FL, waits for the return of Halley Martin, who served 20 years for a brutal, public murder. Illiterate, teenaged Halley worshiped beautiful Mavis and killed to avenge her honor; she's now the wife of Pastor Ned Jeffries, once Halley's prison chaplain. Seven-year-old Shiny Parker is an uneasy witness to the unfolding events. His family has recently taken in Mavis and her precocious ten-year-old daughter, Sharon-Rose, after the pastor was badly burned in the fire that destroyed their home. The past and the present are revealed through Halley's, Mavis's, and Shiny's narratives and letters." Libr J

"Like most melodramas, 'A Burning in Homeland' must balance two competing goals: it seeks to reassure readers with a familiar story and at the same time catch them off guard by pricking at their fears. Richard Yancey's novel is contemporary enough to name those fears—male violence and female sexuality— and old-fashioned enough to include plenty of iconic scenes." N Y Times Book Rev

Yarbro, Chelsea Quinn, 1942-

Night blooming. Aspect 2002 429p map $24.95

ISBN 0-446-52981-8   LC 2002-16876

"Yarbro's vampire hero Saint-Germain continues his wanderings through history, this time in the late eighth century. The great French king Karl-lo-Magne summons Saint-Germain, here known as Hiernom Rakoczy, to his court. On the way, Rakoczy and his entourage meet Gynethe Mehaut, a young albino afflicted with a stigmata and awaiting news of her fate at a convent. . . . Volunteering to accompany [Gynethe] to the papal court in Rome, Rakoczy soon finds himself haunting his old haunts and falling in love with his charge. But Gynethe . . . is in great danger from those who feel threatened by her, and all Rakoczy's efforts may not be enough to save her." Booklist

"Richly rewarding for longtime readers, the novel also provides a good entry point for new recruits with its subtly supplied back story." Publ Wkly

Ye Zhaoyan, 1957-

Nanjing 1937; a love story; translated with an introduction by Michael Berry. Columbia Univ. Press 2002 355p (Weatherhead books on Asia) $24.95

ISBN 0-231-12754-5   LC 2002-24156

Original Chinese edition, 2001

This novel is "an unlikely love story set against the grim and chaotic backdrop of the infamous Rape of Nanjing in 1937. When inveterate playboy and indifferent professor Ding Wenyu falls unexpectedly in love, the object of his affection is, unfortunately, the bride at the wedding he is attending. Although he ardently and imprudently pursues Ren Yuyuan, a woman 20 years his junior, she ignores his attentions until her husband, a fighter pilot in the Chinese air force, is reportedly killed in action. As the Japanese invasion progresses and Nanjing is threatened, Wenyu and Yuyuan embark upon a love affair destined to end in tragedy." Booklist

"Ye paints a rich tableau of prewar Chinese politics and social mores. The contrast between the advance of the Japanese and Ding's slow seduction of Ren is both poignant and . . . ironic." Publ Wkly

Z

Zabytko, Irene

When Luba leaves home; a profile in stories. Algonquin Bks. 2003 230p $22.95

ISBN 1-56512-332-8   LC 2002-38525

"A Shannon Ravenel book"

Analyzed in Short story index

Contents: Steve's bar; My black valiant; The celebirty; Saint Sonya; The last boat; Obligation; Pani Ryhotska in love; Lavender soap; The prodigal son enters heaven; John Mars, All-American

"Occasionally awkward, but often shining with quiet grace, these 10 interconnected stories by Zabytko. . . follow the childhood-to-young-adulthood trajectory of Luba Vovkovych, who lives with her Ukrainian immigrant parents in Chicago in the 1900s." Publ Wkly

TITLE AND SUBJECT INDEX

This index to the books listed in part 1 includes title and subject entries, arranged in one alphabet. Full information for each book is given in part 1 under the main entry, which is usually the author.

Title entries. Novels are listed under title. Analytical entries are made for novels published in omnibus editions and for novelettes. Such entries carry *In* or *also in* designations and usually include the page numbers in the book where the item is to be found.

Subject entries. Subject headings are printed in capital letters. The listing of a work under a subject indicates that a major portion of the work is about that subject.

BANK ROBBERS
Abrahams, P. Their wildest dreams
Connelly, J. Crumbtown

BANKS
Browne, M. Eye of the abyss
BARBAROSSA *See* Frederick I, Holy Roman Emperor, ca. 1123-1190
The **barbed-wire** kiss. Stroby, W.
Bare bones. Reichs, K. J.
BARRISTERS *See* Law and lawyers
BARS *See* Hotels, taverns, etc.
Baudolino. Eco, U.
The **bay** of love and sorrows. Richards, D. A.
Bay of souls. Stone, R.
A **bed** in heaven. Loo, T. de
The **beginning** of calamities. House, T.
Behindlings. Barker, N.
BEIDERBECKE, BIX, 1903-1931
Turner, F. W. 1929
BELGIAN CONGO *See* Zaire

BEREAVEMENT
Bellows, N. On this day
Dorrestein, R. Without mercy
Maynard, J. The usual rules
McGhee, A. Was it beautiful?
Moloney, S. The dwelling
BERLIN (GERMANY) *See* Germany—Berlin
Berrybender narratives [series]
McMurtry, L. By sorrow's river
McMurtry, L. The wandering hill
Berserker's star. Saberhagen, F.
Best friends. Berger, T.
The **best** revenge. White, S. W.
BEVERLY HILLS (CALIF.) *See* California—Beverly Hills

BIGAMY
Haigh, J. Mrs. Kimble
BIGOTRY *See* Prejudices
BIOGRAPHERS *See* Authors

BIOLOGISTS
Crichton, M. Prey

BIONICS
Westerfeld, S. The risen empire

BIOTECHNOLOGY
Cook, R. Seizure
BIRD WOMAN *See* Sacagawea, b. 1786

BIRDS
See also Parrots
BIRMINGHAM (ALA.) *See* Alabama—Birmingham

BISEXUALITY
See also Homosexuality
BLACK HUMOR *See* Humor; Satire
Black maps. Spiegelman, P.
Black powder, white smoke. Estleman, L. D.
BLACK SERVANTS *See* African American servants
BLACK SOLDIERS *See* African American soldiers
Blacklist. Paretsky, S.

BLACKMAIL
See also Extortion
Ellis, D. Life sentence
Richards, D. A. The bay of love and sorrows
Riordan, R. Cold Springs

BLACKS
See also African Americans
Nunez, E. Grace
Blackwood Farm. Rice, A.
BLESSED VIRGIN MARY, SAINT *See* Mary, Blessed Virgin, Saint

BLIND
Grøndahl, J. C. Lucca
Blind Lake. Wilson, R. C.
The **blind** man of Seville. Wilson, R.

BLOCK ISLAND (R.I.)
Smith, M.-A. T. She's not there

Blood canticle. Rice, A.
Bloody moonlight. Brown, F.
In Brown, F. Hunter and hunted p309-457
Blow fly. Cornwell, P. D.
The **Blue** Moon Circus. Raleigh, M.
The **Bobby** Gold stories. Bourdain, A.
The **body** in the lighthouse. Page, K. H.
A **body** to die for. White, K.

BOHEMIANS

United States
See Czechs—United States
BOMBING MISSIONS *See* World War, 1939-1945—Aerial operations

BOMBS
See also Atomic bomb
BONAPARTE, NAPOLEON *See* Napoleon I, Emperor of the French, 1769-1821
The **bone** vault. Fairstein, L.
The **book** against God. Wood, J.

BOOK OF KELLS
Gill, B. Death in Dublin
The **book** of salt. Truong, M. T. D.
The **book** of the heathen. Edric, R.

BOOKS
See also Books and reading; Manuscripts

BOOKS AND READING
Fforde, J. Thursday Next in Lost in a good book
Tolstafà, T. The slynx
BOSTON (MASS.) *See* Massachusetts—Boston

BOTANISTS
Vanderbes, J. Easter Island

BOTSWANA
Rush, N. Mortals
BOW AND ARROW *See* Archery
A **box** of matches. Baker, N.
The **boy** on the bus. Schupack, D.

BOYS
See also Adolescence; Youth
Adam, C. Love and country
Ammaniti, N. I'm not scared
Emmons, C. His mother's son
Haddon, M. The curious incident of the dog in the night-time
House, T. The beginning of calamities
Lansdale, J. R. A fine dark line
Lethem, J. The fortress of solitude
Bradbury stories. Bradbury, R.
Breakout. Stark, R.
The **breathtaker.** Blanchard, A.
The **Briar** king. Keyes, J. G.
Brick lane. Ali, M.
The **Bridge** of Sighs. Steinhauer, O.

BRIGANDS AND ROBBERS
See also Outlaws; Robbery

BRITISH

Africa
Gordimer, N. Mission statement
France
Cornwell, B. Vagabond
Italy
Craig, A. Love in idleness
Japan
Hazzard, S. The great fire
Malaysia
Carey, P. My life as a fake
Palestine
Wilson, J. A Palestine affair
Russia
Read, P. P. Alice in exile
Switzerland
Pye, M. The pieces from Berlin
United States
Iyer, P. Abandon

CATHOLICS *See* Catholic faith
The **cave**. Saramago, J.

CELEBRITIES
  Sherrill, M. My last movie star
Celt and pepper. McInerny, R. M.
The **center** of everything. Moriarty, L.
CENTRAL INTELLIGENCE AGENCY (U.S.) *See* United
  States. Central Intelligence Agency
CEREMONIES *See* Rites and ceremonies
Changing planes. Le Guin, U. K.

CHEROKEE INDIANS
  House, S. A parchment of leaves
CHICAGO (ILL.) *See* Illinois—Chicago
CHILD AND PARENT *See* Parent and child
Child of my heart. McDermott, A.
CHILDHOOD *See* Boys; Girls

CHILDREN
  See also Adolescence; Boys; Foster children; Girls; Missing children; Orphans

Adoption
See Adoption
CHILDREN, ADOPTED *See* Adoption
CHILDREN, AUTISTIC *See* Autistic children
CHILDREN, SICK *See* Sick children
CHILDREN AS SLAVES *See* Slavery
Children of the storm. Peters, E.

CHINA
  White, R. A. Typhoon

19th century
García, C. Monkey hunting

20th century
García, C. Monkey hunting
Ye Zhaoyan. Nanjing 1937

CHINESE

Cuba
García, C. Monkey hunting

New Zealand
Tremain, R. The color

United States
Raban, J. Waxwings

CHIVALRY
  See also Middle Ages
CHRIST *See* Jesus Christ

CHRISTIANITY
  See also Catholic faith; names of Christian churches or
  sects
  Brown, D. The Da Vinci code

CHURCH SCHOOLS
  House, T. The beginning of calamities
CIA *See* United States. Central Intelligence Agency

CIRCUS
  Davis, A. Wonder when you'll miss me
  Raleigh, M. The Blue Moon Circus
  Siegel, L. Love and other games of chance

CITIES AND TOWNS
  See also Imaginary cities
CIVIL RIGHTS DEMONSTRATIONS *See* African Ameri-
  cans—Civil rights

CIVIL WAR

England
See England—17th century

Spain
See Spain—Civil War, 1936-1939

United States
See United States—Civil War, 1861-1865
Claire and present danger. Roberts, G.

CLAIRVOYANCE
  Hoffman, A. The probable future

Clara. Galloway, J.
The **clarinet** polka. Maillard, K.

CLARK, WILLIAM, 1770-1838
  Hall, B. I should be extremely happy in your company

CLASS DISTINCTION
  See also Social classes
  Yancey, R. A burning in Homeland

CLERGY
  See also Women clergy
  Guterson, D. Our Lady of the Forest
  Wood, J. The book against God
  Yancey, R. A burning in Homeland

CLERGY, CATHOLIC *See* Catholic priests
Close to home. Robinson, P.
CODE DECIPHERING *See* Cryptography
Coffin knows the answer. Butler, G.
Cold pursuit. Parker, T. J.
Cold Springs. Riordan, R.

COLLECTIVE SETTLEMENTS
  Boyle, T. C. Drop City

COLLEGE LIFE
  See also College students; Teachers

COLLEGE STUDENTS
  Vida, V. And now you can go
  Weber, K. The little women
  Wood, J. The book against God

COLLEGE TEACHERS *See* Teachers
COLONIALISM *See* Imperialism
COLONIES, ARTIST *See* Artist colonies
The **color**. Tremain, R.

COLUMNISTS *See* Journalists
COMING OF AGE STORIES *See* Adolescence; Youth
The **commissariat** of enlightenment. Kalfus, K.
COMMUNES *See* Collective settlements

COMMUNISM
  See also Totalitarianism

COMPANIONS
  Marías, J. The man of feeling
The **company** you keep. Gordon, N.
Compliments of a fiend. Brown, F.
  In Brown, F. Hunter and hunted p459-620

COMPOSERS
  Galloway, J. Clara

COMPUTER PROGRAMMING *See* Programming (Computers)
COMPUTER SIMULATION *See* Virtual reality

COMPUTERS
  See also Programming (Computers)
  Iles, G. The footprints of God
  Ullman, E. The bug

CON MEN *See* Swindlers and swindling

CONDUCTORS (MUSIC)
  Ford, R. The student conductor

CONFEDERATE AGENTS *See* Spies

CONFLICT OF GENERATIONS
  Hadley, T. Everything will be all right
  Meloy, M. Liars and saints

CONGO (DEMOCRATIC REPUBLIC) *See* Zaire

CONGREGATIONAL CHURCHES
  Basch, R. The passion of Reverend Nash
The **conjure** woman. Chesnutt, C. W.
  In Chesnutt, C. W. Stories, novels & essays p1-96

CONNECTICUT
  Basch, R. The passion of Reverend Nash
  O'Nan, S. The night country
  Rice, L. The secret hour

New Haven
Weber, K. The little women

CONSCIENCE
  See also Guilt

CONSPIRACIES
  Bahal, A. Bunker 13

DEATH—*Continued*

Johnson, S. The sailmaker's daughter
Maynard, J. The usual rules
McGhee, A. Was it beautiful?
Morgan, R. K. Altered carbon
Morrison, T. Love
Steel, D. Johnny Angel
Death in Dublin. Gill, B.
Death of a nationalist. Pawel, R.
Death of a village. Beaton, M. C.
Death trap. Henry, S.
December heat. García-Roza, L. A.
The **deed.** Blanchard, K.

DEFECTORS

Ford, R. The student conductor
Judd, A. Legacy
The **delicate** storm. Blunt, G.

DEMONOLOGY

See also Satanism
Shirley, J. Demons
Demons. Shirley, J.

DEPARTMENT STORES

Trigiani, A. Lucia, Lucia
Derailed. Siegel, J.
The **deserter.** Langton, J.

DESTRUCTION OF THE JEWS *See* Holocaust, Jewish (1933-1945)

DETECTIVE AND MYSTERY STORIES *See* Mystery and detective stories

DETECTIVES

Archer, Owen. See stories by Robb, C. M.
Arnold, Jessie. See stories by Henry, S.
Banks, Chief Inspector Alan. See stories by Robinson, P.
Bernier, Alex. See stories by Saulnier, B.
Bosch, Harry. See stories by Connelly, M.
Bracewell, Nicholas. See stories by Marston, E.
Brennan, Temperance. See stories by Reichs, K. J.
Brinker, Roscoe. See stories by Mitchell, J. C.
Brunetti, Guido. See stories by Leon, D.
Cardinal, John. See stories by Blunt, G.
Carella, Lieutenant Steve. See stories by McBain, E.
Chee, Sargeant Jim. See stories by Hillerman, T.
Chin, Lydia. See stories by Rozan, S. J.
Coffin, John. See stories by Butler, G.
Cole, Elvis. See stories by Crais, R.
Darling, Annie. See stories by Hart, C. G.
Davenport, Lucas. See stories by Sandford, J.
Deal, John. See stories by Standiford, L.
Decker, Peter. See stories by Kellerman, F.
Delorme, Lise. See stories by Blunt, G.
Diamond, Peter. See stories by Lovesey, P.
Dobbs, Maisie. See stories by Winspear, J.
Dowling, Father. See stories by McInerny, R. M.
Du Pré, Gabriel. See stories by Bowen, P.
Fairchild, Faith. See stories by Page, K. H.
Gunther, Joe. See stories by Mayor, A.
Hunter, Am. See stories by Brown, F.
Hunter, Ed. See stories by Brown, F.
Jackson, J. W. See stories by Craig, P. R.
John the Eunuch. See stories by Reed, M.
Jones, Fearless. See stories by Mosley, W.
Kelly, Homer. See stories by Langton, J.
Kerney, Kevin. See stories by McGarrity, M.
Knight, Phillip. See stories by McInerny, R. M.
Knight, Roger. See stories by McInerny, R. M.
Langdon, Skip. See stories by Smith, J.
Lazarus, Rina. See stories by Kellerman, F.
Leaphorn, Lieutenant Joe. See stories by Hillerman, T.
Lieberman, Abe. See stories by Kaminsky, S. M.
Liu Hulan. See stories by See, L.
Macbeth, Hamish. See stories by Beaton, M. C.
March, John. See stories by Spiegelman, P.
McGarr, Chief Inspector Peter. See stories by Gill, B.
Minton, Paris. See stories by Mosley, W.
Montalbano, Inspector Salvo. See stories by Camilleri, A.
Pascale, Lily. See stories by Thomas, S.
Peabody, Amelia. See stories by Peters, E.
Pepper, Amanda. See stories by Roberts, G.
Pickett, Joe. See stories by Box, C. J.
Pigeon, Anna. See stories by Barr, N.
Pitt, Inspector. See stories by Perry, A.

Plum, Stephanie. See stories by Evanovich, J.
Quinn, Terry. See stories by Pelecanos, G. P.
Qwilleran, Jim. See stories by Braun, L. J.
Rane, Harry. See stories by Stroby, W.
Rawlins, Easy. See stories by Mosley, W.
Reacher, Jack. See stories by Child, L.
Rebus, Inspector. See stories by Rankin, I.
Repairman Jack. See stories by Wilson, F. P.
Rhymes, Lincoln. See stories by Deaver, J.
Robicheaux, Dave. See stories by Burke, J. L.
Scarpetta, Kay. See stories by Cornwell, P. D.
Seddon, Carole. See stories by Brett, S.
Sewell, Hitchcock. See stories by Cockey, T.
Slider, Inspector Bill. See stories by Harrod-Eagles, C.
Smith, Bill. See stories by Rozan, S. J.
Smith, Mac. See stories by Truman, M.
Spenser. See stories by Parker, R. B.
St. George, Sweeney. See stories by Taylor, S. S.
Strange, Derek. See stories by Pelecanos, G. P.
Taylor, Jack. See stories by Bruen, K.
Thorn. See stories by Hall, J. W.
Walker, Amos. See stories by Estleman, L. D.
Wallander, Kurt. See stories by Mankell, H.
Warshawski, V. I. See stories by Paretsky, S.
Weggins, Bailey. See stories by White, K.
Wine, Moses. See stories by Simon, R. L.

DETECTIVES, PRIVATE

Pronzini, B. Spook

DETROIT (MICH.) *See* Michigan—Detroit
The **Devil** wears Prada. Weisberger, L.

DEVIL WORSHIP *See* Satanism

DIARIES (STORIES ABOUT)

Higgins, J. Bad company

DIARIES (STORIES IN DIARY FORM)

See also Letters (Stories in letter form)
Boyd, W. Any human heart
Palahniuk, C. Diary
Diary. Palahniuk, C.

DICTATORS

See also Totalitarianism

DIRECTORS, MOTION PICTURE *See* Motion picture producers and directors
Director's cut. Simon, R. L.
Dirty work. Woods, S.

DISAPPEARANCES *See* Missing persons

DISASTERS

See also Floods

DISEASES

See also AIDS (Disease); Alzheimer's disease

DISNEY WORLD (FLA.) *See* Walt Disney World (Fla.)
DISNEYWORLD (FLA.) *See* Walt Disney World (Fla.)
The **distant** echo. McDermid, V.

DISTRICT OF COLUMBIA *See* Washington (D.C.)

DIVORCE

See also Divorced persons; Marriage problems

DIVORCED PERSONS

Abrahams, P. Their wildest dreams
Adam, C. Love and country
Grøndahl, J. C. Lucca
Muller, M. Cyanide Wells
Smiley, J. Good faith

DIVORCÉES *See* Divorced persons

DIVORCÉS *See* Divorced persons

DOCTORS *See* Physicians; Women physicians

DOCUMENTS *See* Manuscripts

DOGS

Brown, L. The rabbit factory
Haddon, M. The curious incident of the dog in the night-time
Parkhurst, C. The dogs of Babel
Sparks, N. The guardian
The **dogs** of Babel. Parkhurst, C.
Dogs of Riga. Mankell, H.

DOMESTIC RELATIONS *See* Family life
Domino. King, R.

DON JUAN (LEGENDARY CHARACTER)

Millhauser, S. An adventure of Don Juan

INTROSPECTIVE NOVELS *See* Psychological novels

INVENTIONS
Hautman, P. Doohickey

INVENTORS
Gilling, T. The adventures of Miles and Isabel
Invisible gardens. Shigekuni, J.

IPHIGENIA (GREEK MYTHOLOGY)
Unsworth, B. The songs of the kings

IRELAND
19th century
O'Connor, J. Star of the Sea
20th century
Llywelyn, M. 1949
Farm life
See Farm life—Ireland
Rural life
Hardie, K. A winter marriage

IRISH
United States
Edwards, L. Oscar Wilde discovers America
Walsh, M. And all the saints

IRISH AMERICANS
Greeley, A. M. Second spring
McDermott, A. Child of my heart

ISEUT (LEGENDARY CHARACTER)
Millhauser, S. The king in the tree

ISLAM
Houellebecq, M. Platform
Iyer, P. Abandon

ISLANDS
See also names of individual islands and groups of islands
Ashley, R. Someplace like this
Gunesekera, R. Heaven's edge
O'Hagan, A. Personality
Palahniuk, C. Diary

ISLANDS OF THE PACIFIC
Spencer, J. The pilots
Isn't it romantic? Hansen, R.

ISRAEL
See also Zionism
Miller, R. Welcome to Heavenly Heights

ISRAELITES *See* Jews

ITALIAN AMERICANS
Trigiani, A. Lucia, Lucia

ITALIANS
England
O'Hagan, A. Personality

ITALY
See also Pompeii (Ancient city)
Milan
King, R. Domino
Tuscany
Ammaniti, N. I'm not scared
Craig, A. Love in idleness
Venice
Alison, J. The marriage of the sea

J

The **Janson** directive. Ludlum, R.

JAPAN
1945-
Hazzard, S. The great fire
Ōe, K. Somersault

Tokyo
Perdue, L. Slatewiper

JAPANESE
China
Ye Zhaoyan. Nanjing 1937

JAZZ MUSIC
Turner, F. W. 1929

JEALOUSY
Watson, L. Orchard
Jennifer Government. Barry, M.

JESUS CHRIST
Wangerin, W. Saint Julian

JEWEL ROBBERIES *See* Robbery

JEWELRY
Parks, S.-L. Getting mother's body

JEWISH-ARAB RELATIONS
Wilson, J. A Palestine affair

JEWISH HOLOCAUST (1933-1945) *See* Holocaust, Jewish (1933-1945)

JEWISH REFUGEES
See also Holocaust survivors

JEWS
See also Antisemitism; Jewish-Arab relations
Persecutions
See also Holocaust, Jewish (1933-1945)
Denmark
Follett, K. Hornet flight
England
Brookner, A. Making things better
Germany
Browne, M. Eye of the abyss
Michigan
Baxter, C. Saul and Patsy
Netherlands
Loo, T. de. A bed in heaven
New York (State)
Cantor, J. Great Neck
Russia
Richler, N. Your mouth is lovely
United States
Epstein, J. Fabulous small Jews
Powers, R. The time of our singing
Siegel, L. Love and other games of chance

JOCKEYS
Smith, B. All hat
Johnny Angel. Steel, D.

JOURNALISTS
See also Women journalists
Bahal, A. Bunker 13
Barker, P. Double vision
Grass, G. Crabwalk
Lee, M. The canal house
Sherrill, M. My last movie star
Wilson, R. C. Blind Lake

JOURNALS *See* Diaries (Stories about); Diaries (Stories in diary form)
Joust. Lackey, M.
Jubilee. Dann, J.

JUDAISM
See also Jews; Zionism

JULIAN, THE HOSPITALLER, SAINT
Wangerin, W. Saint Julian

JURY DUTY *See* Trials

K

KANSAS
Moriarty, L. The center of everything

Lost light. Connelly, M.

LOUISIANA
    Gear, K. O. People of the owl
    Martin, V. Property
    Wilcox, J. Heavenly days
           New Orleans
    Alison, J. The marriage of the sea

Love. Morrison, T.

LOVE AFFAIRS
    See also Love stories; Marriage problems
    Adam, C. Love and country
    Alison, J. The marriage of the sea
    Berger, T. Best friends
    Blake, J. C. Under the skin
    Blanchard, K. The deed
    Busch, F. A memory of war
    Byatt, A. S. A whistling woman
    Gordimer, N. Mission statement
    Griesemer, J. Signal & noise
    Heller, Z. What was she thinking?
    Johnson, D. L'affaire
    Kempadoo, O. Tide running
    Kim, S. The interpreter
    Lee, M. The canal house
    Lefcourt, P. Eleven Karens
    Lively, P. The photograph
    Llywelyn, M. 1949
    Marías, J. The man of feeling
    Rush, N. Mortals
    Spencer, S. A ship made of paper
    Stone, R. Bay of souls
    Templeton, E. Gordon
    Upadhyay, S. The guru of love
    Watson, L. Orchard
    Weber, K. The little women
    Wilson, J. A Palestine affair
    Wilson, R. C. Blind Lake
    Yancey, R. A burning in Homeland
    Ye Zhaoyan. Nanjing 1937

Love and country. Adam, C.
Love and other games of chance. Siegel, L.
Love in idleness. Craig, A.
Love me. Keillor, G.

LOVE STORIES
    See also Love affairs
    Abu-Jaber, D. Crescent
    Chalmers, R. Who's who in hell
    Chesnutt, C. W. The house behind the cedars
    Cohen, L. H. Heart, you bully, you punk
    Docx, E. The calligrapher
    Ford, R. The student conductor
    Freda, J. The patience of rivers
    Gilling, T. The adventures of Miles and Isabel
    Glendinning, V. Flight
    Gowdy, B. The romantic
    Grøndahl, J. C. Lucca
    Gunesekera, R. Heaven's edge
    Hansen, R. Isn't it romantic?
    Hazzard, S. The great fire
    House, S. A parchment of leaves
    Itani, F. Deafening
    Iyer, P. Abandon
    Koeppen, W. A sad affair
    Lightman, A. P. Reunion
    Ligon, S. Safe in heaven dead
    Lipman, E. The pursuit of Alice Thrift
    Maillard, K. The clarinet polka
    Mawer, S. The fall
    Millhauser, S. An adventure of Don Juan
    Millhauser, S. The king in the tree
    Mitchard, J. Twelve times blessed
    Morrison, T. Love
    Morton, B. A window across the river
    Paul, J. Elsewhere in the land of parrots
    Read, P. P. Alice in exile
    Sparks, N. The guardian

Lovers crossing. Mitchell, J. C.
Lucca. Grøndahl, J. C.
Lucia, Lucia. Trigiani, A.
Lucky girls. Freudenberger, N.

LUMBER INDUSTRY
    See also Loggers

LUMBERJACKS *See* Loggers
LUMBERMEN *See* Loggers

M

MACABRE STORIES *See* Horror stories
MADDEN, OWNEY, 1892-1965
    Walsh, M. And all the saints
MADNESS *See* Mental illness
MADRID (SPAIN) *See* Spain—Madrid
MAFIA
    See also Gangsters.
    Green, N. The angel of Montague Street
    Robinson, S. Callahan's con
MAGAZINES *See* Periodicals
MAGIC
    See also Supernatural phenomena
MAHMUD II, SULTAN OF THE TURKS, 1785-1839
    Wallach, J. Seraglio
Maisie Dobbs. Winspear, J.
Making things better. Brookner, A.
MALAYA
    See also Malaysia
MALAYSIA
    Manicka, R. The rice mother
MALINCHE *See* Marina, ca. 1505-ca. 1530
MALINTZIN *See* Marina, ca. 1505-ca. 1530
The **mammoth** cheese. Holman, S.
MAN, PREHISTORIC *See* Prehistoric man
Man eater. Haywood, G. A.
The **man** of feeling. Marías, J.
MANHATTAN (NEW YORK, N.Y.) *See* New York (N.Y.)—
    Manhattan
MANHUNTS
    See also Adventure
MANORS *See* Houses
MANSIONS *See* Houses
MANUSCRIPTS
    Weber, K. The little women
MAORIS
    Tremain, R. The color
MARIE ANTOINETTE, QUEEN, CONSORT OF LOUIS
    XVI, KING OF FRANCE, 1755-1793
           About
    Thomas, C. Farewell, my queen
MARINA, CA. 1505-CA. 1530
    Falconer, C. Feathered serpent
MARINE CORPS (U.S.) *See* United States. Marine Corps
MARINES (U.S.) *See* United States. Marine Corps
MARRIAGE
    See also Family life; Husband and wife; Interfaith mar-
        riage; Interracial marriage; Marriage problems
    Ali, M. Brick lane
    Baxter, C. Saul and Patsy
    Bragg, M. A son of war
    Erdrich, L. The Master Butchers Singing Club
    Galloway, J. Clara
    Hay, E. Garbo laughs
    Meloy, M. Liars and saints
    Pearson, A. I don't know how she does it
    Shreve, A. All he ever wanted
    Stirling, J. The piper's tune
MARRIAGE, INTERFAITH *See* Interfaith marriage
MARRIAGE, INTERRACIAL *See* Interracial marriage
MARRIAGE COUNSELING *See* Marriage problems
The **marriage** of the sea. Alison, J.
MARRIAGE PROBLEMS
    See also Family life; Interfaith marriage; Love affairs
    Ashley, R. Someplace like this
    Basch, R. The passion of Reverend Nash
    Berger, T. Best friends
    Cumyn, A. Losing it
    Emmons, C. His mother's son

N

NARCOTIC HABIT *See* Drug addiction

NARCOTICS, CONTROL OF *See* Drug traffic

NARCOTICS AGENTS *See* Drug traffic

NATIONAL SOCIALISM
> *See also* Germany—1918-1945
Browne, M. Eye of the abyss
Pottinger, S. The last Nazi
Taibo, P. I. Returning as shadows

NAVAL BATTLES
> *See also* United States—Civil War, 1861-1865—Naval operations
White, R. A. Typhoon
The **navigator** of New York. Johnston, W.

NAZIS *See* National socialism

NAZISM *See* National socialism

NEANDERTHAL RACE
> *See also* Prehistoric man

NEBRASKA
Hansen, R. Isn't it romantic?

NEGROES *See* African Americans

NEIGHBORS
Gowdy, B. The romantic
Mendelson, C. Morningside Heights

NEPAL

Kathmandu
Upadhyay, S. The guru of love

NERVOUS BREAKDOWN
Wilson, R. The blind man of Seville

NEURASTHENIA *See* Nervous breakdown

NEVADA
Crichton, M. Prey

NEW BRUNSWICK *See* Canada—New Brunswick

NEW ENGLAND
Baker, N. A box of matches
Hoffman, A. The probable future

NEW JERSEY
Price, R. Samaritan

NEW MEXICO
Shigekuni, J. Invisible gardens

NEW ORLEANS (LA.) *See* Louisiana—New Orleans

NEW YORK (N.Y.)
Hamill, P. Forever

20th century
Hustvedt, S. What I loved

21st century
Westlake, D. E. Money for nothing

Brooklyn
Cohen, L. H. Heart, you bully, you punk
Green, N. The angel of Montague Street
Lethem, J. The fortress of solitude
Maynard, J. The usual rules
Nunez, E. Grace

Greenwich Village
Trigiani, A. Lucia, Lucia
Wolitzer, M. The wife

Manhattan
Blanchard, K. The deed
Block, L. Small town
Bram, C. Lives of the circus animals
Busch, F. A memory of war
DeLillo, D. Cosmopolis
Dierbeck, L. One pill makes you smaller
Donohue, J. J. Sensei
Fairstein, L. The bone vault
Geary, J. M. Spiral
Grimes, M. Foul matter
Jaffe, R. The room-mating season
Keillor, G. Love me
Kim, S. The interpreter
McElroy, J. Actress in the house

Mendelson, C. Morningside Heights
Morton, B. A window across the river
Robinson, R. Sweetwater
Schwarz, C. All is vanity
Solomon, N. Single wife
Vida, V. And now you can go
Walsh, M. And all the saints
Weber, K. The little women
Weisberger, L. The Devil wears Prada

Queens
Spiegelman, I. Everyone's burning

NEW YORK (STATE)
> *See also* Adirondack Mountains (N.Y.); Long Island (N.Y.)

20th century
Clements, M. Midsummer
Freda, J. The patience of rivers
Spencer, S. A ship made of paper

21st century
Oates, J. C. The tattooed girl
Shriver, L. We need to talk about Kevin

New York City
See New York (N.Y.)

NEW YORKER (PERIODICAL)
Keillor, G. Love me

NEW ZEALAND
Tremain, R. The color

NEW ZEALANDERS

France
Knox, E. Daylight

NEWSPAPER PUBLISHERS *See* Publishers and publishing

NEWSPAPERMEN *See* Journalists

NIECES
Carey, J. The Crossley baby
Night blooming. Yarbro, C. Q.
The **night** country. O'Nan, S.
Night watch. Pratchett, T.
No graves as yet. Perry, A.
No second chance. Coben, H.
Noise. Clement, H.

NORTH CAROLINA
Chesnutt, C. W. The marrow of tradition
Dierbeck, L. One pill makes you smaller
Inman, R. Captain Saturday
Patterson, J. Four blind mice
Sparks, N. The guardian

NORTH DAKOTA
Erdrich, L. The Master Butchers Singing Club
Not guilty. MacDonald, P. J.
Not quite kosher. Kaminsky, S. M.
Not the end of the world. Atkinson, K.

NOTRE DAME UNIVERSITY *See* University of Notre Dame

NOVELETTES
> *See also* Short stories
Gordimer, N. Karma
Gordimer, N. Mission statement
Loo, T. de. A bed in heaven
Martin, S. The pleasure of my company
Millhauser, S. An adventure of Don Juan
Millhauser, S. The king in the tree
Millhauser, S. The king in the tree: three novellas
Millhauser, S. Revenge
Oster, C. My big apartment

NOVELISTS *See* Authors

NOVELLAS *See* Novelettes

NOVELS, UNFINISHED *See* Unfinished novels

NUCLEAR BOMB *See* Atomic bomb

NUCLEAR WARFARE
> *See also* Atomic bomb

NUREYEV, RUDOLF, 1938-1993
McCann, C. Dancer

O

O' artful death. Taylor, S. S.

OBESITY

Psychological aspects
See also Anorexia nervosa

OBSESSIVE-COMPULSIVE DISORDER
Martin, S. The pleasure of my company

OBSTETRICIANS *See* Physicians

OCCULTISM
See also Supernatural phenomena

OCEAN TRAVEL
O'Connor, J. Star of the Sea

OCEANIA *See* Islands of the Pacific
The **October** horse. McCullough, C.
Off the chart. Hall, J. W.
Office of innocence. Keneally, T.

OFFICE WORKERS
Moon, E. The speed of dark

OKLAHOMA
Blanchard, A. The breathtaker

OLD AGE
Brookner, A. Making things better
Hassler, J. The Staggerford flood
Scott, A. Calpurnia
Updike, J. Seek my face
Old flames. Lawton, J.

OLD LADIES *See* Old age

OLD MAIDS *See* Single women

OLD MEN *See* Old age

OLD WOMEN *See* Old age

OLIVEIRA SALAZAR, ANTONIO DE *See* Salazar, Antonio de Oliveira, 1889-1970
On the nature of human romantic interaction. Iagnemma, K.
On this day. Bellows, N.
One pill makes you smaller. Dierbeck, L.
The **only** good thing anyone has ever done. Newman, S.
Only one thing missing. Ruiz, L. M.

ONTARIO *See* Canada—Ontario

OPERA
Marías, J. The man of feeling

OPERATION DESERT STORM *See* Persian Gulf War, 1991
Orchard. Watson, L.

ORPHANS
Johnston, W. The navigator of New York
Newman, S. The only good thing anyone has ever done
Raleigh, M. The Blue Moon Circus
Wallace, D. The Watermelon King
Oryx and Crake. Atwood, M.
Oscar Wilde discovers America. Edwards, L.
The **other** side of silence. Brink, A. P.
Our Lady of the Forest. Guterson, D.

OUTDOOR LIFE
See also Country life; Wilderness survival

OUTER SPACE
See also Space flight

OUTLAWS
Estleman, L. D. Black powder, white smoke
Resnick, M. The return of Santiago

OVERLAND JOURNEYS TO THE PACIFIC
Mosher, H. F. The true account

P

PACIFIC OCEAN

World War, 1939-1945
See World War, 1939-1945—Pacific Ocean

PAINTERS
See also Women painters

PAINTINGS
Lowell, E. Die in plain sight

PAKISTAN

Karachi
Shamsie, K. Kartography

PALESTINE
See also Israel

20th century
Wilson, J. A Palestine affair
A **Palestine** affair. Wilson, J.

PALESTINIAN ARABS
See also Jewish-Arab relations

PAPACY *See* Catholic faith

PAPERS *See* Manuscripts

PARABLES
See also Allegories

PARANOIA
Gibson, W. Pattern recognition
Parasites like us. Johnson, A.
A **parchment** of leaves. House, S.

PARENT AND CHILD
See also Conflict of generations; Fathers and daughters; Fathers and sons; Mothers and daughters; Mothers and sons
Clements, M. Midsummer
Cumyn, A. Losing it
Dorrestein, R. Without mercy
Fromm, P. As cool as I am
Haddon, M. The curious incident of the dog in the night-time
Hustvedt, S. What I loved
McDermott, A. Child of my heart
Meloy, M. Liars and saints
Spencer, S. A ship made of paper
Weber, K. The little women

PARIS (FRANCE) *See* France—Paris

PAROCHIAL SCHOOLS *See* Church schools

PARROTS
Paul, J. Elsewhere in the land of parrots

PARTISANS *See* Guerrillas
The **passion** of Reverend Nash. Basch, R.

PASTORS *See* Clergy

PATHOLOGISTS *See* Physicians
The **patience** of rivers. Freda, J.
Pattern recognition. Gibson, W.

PEDIATRICIANS *See* Physicians

PENNSYLVANIA
Meyer, C. Brown eyes blue
Smiley, J. Good faith

Philadelphia
Griffin, W. E. B. Final justice
Scott, A. Calpurnia
Scottoline, L. Dead ringer
People of the owl. Gear, K. O.
The **Pepperdogs**. West, F. J.

PERFORMERS *See* Entertainers

PERIODICALS
Weisberger, L. The Devil wears Prada

PERSIAN GULF WAR, 1991
Huebner, A. We Pierce

PERSONALITY
Moon, E. The speed of dark
Personality. O'Hagan, A.

PERSONALITY DISORDERS
See also Insane, Criminal and dangerous
Persuader. Child, L.

PHILADELPHIA (PA.) *See* Pennsylvania—Philadelphia

PHILOSOPHICAL NOVELS
Coetzee, J. M. Elizabeth Costello
Eco, U. Baudolino
Grass, G. Crabwalk
Harrar, G. The spinning man
Hazzard, S. The great fire

RUSSIAN REVOLUTION, 1905 *See* Russia—1900-1917
RUSSIAN REVOLUTION, 1917-1921 *See* Russia—1917-1945
RUSSIANS

England

Judd, A. Legacy
Lawton, J. Old flames

S

SACAGAWEA, B. 1786
Glancy, D. Stone heart
Hall, B. I should be extremely happy in your company
SACAJAWEA *See* Sacagawea, b. 1786
A **sad** affair. Koeppen, W.

SADISM
Templeton, E. Gordon
Safe in heaven dead. Ligon, S.
The **sailmaker's** daughter. Johnson, S.

SAINT HELENA
Hansen, B. The monsters of St. Helena
Saint Julian. Wangerin, W.

SAINTS
Wangerin, W. Saint Julian
SALAZAR, ANTONIO DE OLIVEIRA, 1889-1970
Antunes, A. L. The inquisitors' manual
SALVATION
See also Atonement
Samaritan. Price, R.
SAN FRANCISCO (CALIF.) *See* California—San Francisco
San Remo Drive. Epstein, L.

SANTA BARBARA (CALIF.) *See* California—Santa Barbara
SANTA MONICA (CALIF.) *See* California—Santa Monica
SAPPHO
Jong, E. Sappho's leap
Sappho's leap. Jong, E.
SARGENT, JOHN SINGER, 1856-1925
Diliberto, G. I am Madame X

SATANISM
Ruiz, L. M. Only one thing missing
SATIRE
See also Humor
Barker, N. Behindlings
Barry, M. Jennifer Government
Bing, S. You look nice today
Connelly, J. Crumbtown
Fitzhugh, B. Heart seizure
Grimes, M. Foul matter
Holman, S. The mammoth cheese
Inman, R. Captain Saturday
Johnson, A. Parasites like us
Johnson, D. L'affaire
Kafka, F. Amerika
Kalfus, K. The commissariat of enlightenment
Keillor, G. Love me
Lelchuk, A. Ziff
Piazza, T. My cold war
Raban, J. Waxwings
Robbins, T. Villa incognito
Sandlin, T. Honey don't
Tolstaîâ, T. The slynx
Weisberger, L. The Devil wears Prada
Wolitzer, M. The wife

SATURN (PLANET)
Bova, B. Saturn
Saturn. Bova, B.
Saul and Patsy. Baxter, C.
SCHOLARS
See also Intellectuals
SCHOOL TEACHERS *See* Teachers
SCHUMANN, CLARA, 1819-1896
Galloway, J. Clara
SCHUMANN, ROBERT, 1810-1856
Galloway, J. Clara

SCIENCE FICTION
See also Extrasensory perception; Fantasies; Future; Interplanetary wars; Life on other planets; Space colonies; Space flight; Space ships; Time travel
Atwood, M. Oryx and Crake
Barry, M. Jennifer Government
Baxter, S. Evolution
Bova, B. Saturn
Bradbury, R. Bradbury stories
Crichton, M. Prey
Dann, J. Jubilee
Doctorow, C. Down and out in the Magic Kindgom
Drake, D. Grimmer than hell
Kerr, K. Snare
McCaffrey, A. Acorna's rebels
Morgan, R. K. Altered carbon
Patterson, J. The lake house
Resnick, M. The return of Santiago
Ridley, J. Those who walk in darkness
Robinson, S. Callahan's con
Saberhagen, F. Berserker's star
Sagan, N. Idlewild
Silverberg, R. Roma eterna
Simmons, D. Ilium
Steele, A. M. Coyote
Tolstaîâ, T. The slynx
Varley, J. Red thunder
Westerfeld, S. The risen empire
Wilson, R. C. Blind Lake

SCIENTISTS
See also Anthropologists; Biologists; Inventors; Women scientists
Powers, R. The time of our singing
Wiggins, M. Evidence of things unseen

SCOTLAND

20th century
McDermid, V. The distant echo

Rural life
O'Hagan, A. Personality

Edinburgh
O'Neill, A. The lamplighter
Welsh, I. Porno

Glasgow
Stirling, J. The piper's tune
Welsh, L. The cutting room
SCRIPTWRITERS *See* Authors

SCULPTORS
Barker, P. Double vision
SEANCES *See* Spiritualism
SEATTLE (WASH.) *See* Washington (State)—Seattle
SECOND SIGHT *See* Clairvoyance; Extrasensory perception
Second spring. Greeley, A. M.
The **secret.** Hoffman, E.
SECRET AGENTS *See* Secret service; Spies
Secret father. Carroll, J.
The **secret** hour. Rice, L.
The **secret** life of bees. Kidd, S. M.
SECRET SERVICE
See also International intrigue
Lawton, J. Old flames
Ludlum, R. The Janson directive

SECRETARIES
Bing, S. You look nice today

SEDUCTION
Dierbeck, L. One pill makes you smaller
Mawer, S. The fall
Seek my face. Updike, J.
Seizure. Cook, R.
SELF-DEFENSE *See* Martial arts

SELF-SACRIFICE
Wolitzer, M. The wife
SELIM III, SULTAN OF TURKEY, 1761-1808
Wallach, J. Seraglio
SENATE (U.S.) *See* United States. Congress. Senate
Sensei. Donohue, J. J.

SUCCESSION *See* Inheritance and succession
Such sweet thunder. Carter, V. O.
SUFFERING
    See also Good and evil
SUFISM
    Iyer, P. Abandon
SUICIDE
    Due, T. The good house
    MacDonald, P. J. Not guilty
    Palahniuk, C. Diary
    Perry, T. Dead aim
SUMMER
    Clements, M. Midsummer
SUMMER RESORTS
    Craig, A. Love in idleness
    Morrison, T. Love
SUPERNATURAL PHENOMENA
    See also Ghost stories; Horror stories
    Due, T. The good house
    Koontz, D. R. By the light of the moon
    Moloney, S. The dwelling
    Wallace, D. The Watermelon King
SUPERSTITION
    See also Vampires; Voodooism
SURGEONS
    See also Physicians; Women physicians
SURGERY
    See also Transplantation of organs, tissues, etc.
SURREALISM
    Lethem, J. The fortress of solitude
SURVIVAL (AFTER AIRPLANE ACCIDENTS, SHIP-WRECKS, ETC.)
    See also Wilderness survival
SURVIVORS, HOLOCAUST *See* Holocaust survivors
SUSPENSE NOVELS
    See also Adventure; Conspiracies; Horror stories; International intrigue; Kidnapping; Murder stories; Mystery and detective stories; Psychological novels; Secret service; Spies; Terrorism
    Abrahams, P. Their wildest dreams
    Ammaniti, N. I'm not scared
    Bahal, A. Bunker 13
    Barnard, R. The mistress of Alderley
    Blanchard, K. The deed
    Block, L. Small town
    Brown, D. Air Battle Force
    Brown, D. The Da Vinci code
    Browne, M. Eye of the abyss
    Coben, H. No second chance
    Cook, R. Seizure
    Crichton, M. Prey
    Cussler, C. White death
    Deutermann, P. T. Darkside
    Donohue, J. J. Sensei
    Ellis, D. Life sentence
    Fairstein, L. The bone vault
    Fitzhugh, B. Heart seizure
    Follett, K. Hornet flight
    Forsyth, F. Avenger
    French, N. Land of the living
    Geary, J. M. Spiral
    Gerritsen, T. The apprentice
    Gerritsen, T. The sinner
    Griffin, W. E. B. Final justice
    Gruber, M. Tropic of night
    Hambly, B. Days of the dead
    Hardie, K. A winter marriage
    Harrar, G. The spinning man
    Harris, R. Pompeii
    Haywood, G. A. Man eater
    Higgins, J. Bad company
    Hirshberg, G. The Snowman's children
    Hoffman, A. The probable future
    Hospital, J. T. Due preparations for the plague
    Iles, G. The footprints of God
    Judd, A. Legacy
    King, L. R. Keeping watch
    Knox, E. Daylight

    Koontz, D. R. By the light of the moon
    Koontz, D. R. The face
    Lawton, J. Old flames
    Lehane, D. Shutter Island
    Leroy, M. Postcards from Berlin
    Lescroart, J. T. The first law
    Lindsey, D. L. The rules of silence
    Lowell, E. Die in plain sight
    Ludlum, R. The Janson directive
    McDermid, V. The distant echo
    Mewshaw, M. Shelter from the storm
    Mrazek, R. J. Unholy fire
    Muller, M. Cyanide Wells
    O'Shaughnessy, P. Presumption of death
    Parker, T. J. Cold pursuit
    Patterson, J. Four blind mice
    Patterson, J. The lake house
    Patterson, R. N. Balance of power
    Pearl, M. The Dante Club
    Perdue, L. Slatewiper
    Perry, T. Dead aim
    Pottinger, S. The last Nazi
    Preston, D. Still life with crows
    Quick, A. Late for the wedding
    Rice, L. The secret hour
    Ridley, J. Those who walk in darkness
    Riordan, R. Cold Springs
    Ruiz, L. M. Only one thing missing
    Sanchez, T. King Bongo
    Saylor, S. Have you seen Dawn?
    Siegel, J. Derailed
    Siegel, S. Final verdict
    Smith, A. Good morning, killer
    Smith, M.-A. T. She's not there
    Sparks, N. The guardian
    Stark, R. Breakout
    Steinhauer, O. The Bridge of Sighs
    Taibo, P. I. Returning as shadows
    Teran, B. The prince of deadly weapons
    Tracy, P. J. Monkeewrench
    Turow, S. Reversible errors
    Ullman, E. The bug
    Westlake, D. E. Money for nothing
    White, S. W. The best revenge
    Wilson, J. A Palestine affair
    Wilson, R. The blind man of Seville
    Woods, S. Dirty work
Sweetwater. Robinson, R.
SWINDLERS AND SWINDLING
    See also Business—Unscrupulous methods
    Haigh, J. Mrs. Kimble
    Newman, S. The only good thing anyone has ever done
    Siegel, L. Love and other games of chance
    Smiley, J. Good faith
    Smith, B. All hat
SWISS ALPS *See* Alps
SWITZERLAND

            Zurich
    Pye, M. The pieces from Berlin
SYMBOLISM
    See also Allegories

T

TAIWAN
    White, R. A. Typhoon
TALIBAN (AFGHANISTAN)
    Brown, D. Air Battle Force
    Hosseini, K. The kite runner
TANGIER (MOROCCO) *See* Morocco—Tangier
The tattooed girl. Oates, J. C.
TAVERNS *See* Hotels, taverns, etc.
TEACHERS
    See also Tutors
    Baxter, C. Saul and Patsy
    Cohen, L. H. Heart, you bully, you punk
    Cumyn, A. Losing it
    Harrar, G. The spinning man

VIETNAMESE WAR, 1961-1975

Robbins, T. Villa incognito

VIGILANCE COMMITTEES

Franklin, T. Hell at the breech

Villa incognito. Robbins, T.

VINCI, LEONARDO DA *See* Leonardo, da Vinci, 1452-1519

A **vineyard** killing. Craig, P. R.

VIOLENCE

See also Terrorism

Brink, A. P. The other side of silence

Brown, L. The rabbit factory

Chesnutt, C. W. The marrow of tradition

Deb, S. The point of return

Emmons, C. His mother's son

Franklin, T. Hell at the breech

Heinrich, W. The king's evil

Miller, R. Welcome to Heavenly Heights

Naslund, S. J. Four spirits

Oates, J. C. The tattooed girl

Pawel, R. Death of a nationalist

Price, R. Samaritan

Richards, D. A. The bay of love and sorrows

Shamsie, K. Kartography

Shriver, L. We need to talk about Kevin

Spiegelman, I. Everyone's burning

Vera, Y. The stone virgins

Vernon, O. Eden

Wangerin, W. Saint Julian

VIRGIN MARY *See* Mary, Blessed Virgin, Saint

VIRGINIA

Holman, S. The mammoth cheese

19th century

Jones, E. P. The known world

VIRTUAL REALITY

Sagan, N. Idlewild

VIRUSES

Pottinger, S. The last Nazi

VISIONS

See also Dreams

VOLCANOES

Harris, R. Pompeii

VOODOOISM

Due, T. The good house

Stone, R. Bay of souls

VOYAGES AND TRAVELS

See also Adventure; Tourist trade; Travelers

W

Waiting for April. Morris, S.

WALES

Mawer, S. The fall

Rural life

Powell, S. The Mushroom Man

WALT DISNEY WORLD (FLA.)

Doctorow, C. Down and out in the Magic Kindgom

The **wandering** hill. McMurtry, L.

WAR

See also Interplanetary wars; names of individual wars

Forsyth, F. Avenger

Lee, M. The canal house

West, F. J. The Pepperdogs

Ye Zhaoyan. Nanjing 1937

WAR CORRESPONDENTS *See* Journalists

Was it beautiful? McGhee, A.

WASHINGTON (D.C.)

19th century

Mrazek, R. J. Unholy fire

20th century

Patterson, R. N. Balance of power

21st century

Sandlin, T. Honey don't

WASHINGTON (STATE)

Guterson, D. Our Lady of the Forest

Seattle

Raban, J. Waxwings

The **Watermelon** King. Wallace, D.

WATERMELONS

Wallace, D. The Watermelon King

Waxwings. Raban, J.

The **way** to paradise. Vargas Llosa, M.

We need to talk about Kevin. Shriver, L.

We Pierce. Huebner, A.

WEALTH

DeLillo, D. Cosmopolis

Glendinning, V. Flight

Johnson, D. L'affaire

Lindsey, D. L. The rules of silence

Morrison, T. Love

WEATHER UNDERGROUND (ORGANIZATION)

Gordon, N. The company you keep

Weatherhead books on Asia [series]

Ye Zhaoyan. Nanjing 1937

Welcome to Heavenly Heights. Miller, R.

WEST (U.S.) *See* Western States

WEST INDIES

See also Trinidad and Tobago

WEST INDIES REGION *See* Caribbean region

WEST VIRGINIA

Hoffman, W. Wild thorn

Maillard, K. The clarinet polka

WESTERN STATES

Raleigh, M. The Blue Moon Circus

WESTERN STORIES

See also Adventure; Ranch life; Western States

Estleman, L. D. Black powder, white smoke

McMurtry, L. By sorrow's river

McMurtry, L. The wandering hill

Mosher, H. F. The true account

Murphy, G. The Indian lover

Westward

Westward. Entered in Part I under title

WHALES

Moore, C. Fluke, or, I know why the winged whale sings

What I loved. Hustvedt, S.

What was she thinking? Heller, Z.

When Luba leaves home. Zabytko, I.

When the women come out to dance, and other stories. Leonard, E.

Where Europe begins. Tawada, Y.

A **whistling** woman. Byatt, A. S.

White death. Cussler, C.

WHODUNITS *See* Mystery and detective stories

A **whole** world of trouble. Chappell, H.

Who's who in hell. Chalmers, R.

WIDOWERS

Coben, H. No second chance

Lively, P. The photograph

McElroy, J. Actress in the house

Parkhurst, C. The dogs of Babel

Rinehart, S. Built in a day

Saramago, J. The cave

WIDOWS

Barker, P. Double vision

Mawer, S. The fall

Millhauser, S. Revenge

Mitchard, J. Twelve times blessed

Powell, S. The Mushroom Man

Robinson, R. Sweetwater

Ruiz, L. M. Only one thing missing

Sparks, N. The guardian

Updike, J. Seek my face

The **wife**. Wolitzer, M.

WIFE AND HUSBAND *See* Husband and wife

The **wife** of his youth and other stories of the color line. Chesnutt, C. W.
  In Chesnutt, C. W. Stories, novels & essays p97-266
WIFE SWAPPING *See* Marriage problems
Wild thorn. Hoffman, W.
WILDE, OSCAR, 1854-1900
  Edwards, L. Oscar Wilde discovers America
Parodies, imitations, etc.
  Self, W. Dorian
WILDERNESS SURVIVAL
  Riordan, R. Cold Springs
WILLIAM, OF WYKEHAM, BISHOP OF WINCHESTER, 1324-1404
  Robb, C. M. The cross-legged knight
A **window** across the river. Morton, B.
Winter and night. Rozan, S. J.
A **winter** marriage. Hardie, K.
Wintering. Moses, K.
Winterkill. Box, C. J.
WISCONSIN
  Watson, L. Orchard
Farm life
  See Farm life—Wisconsin
WIT *See* Humor
WITCHCRAFT
  See also Voodooism
Without mercy. Dorrestein, R.
WOMEN
  See also Single women
  Ali, M. Brick lane
  Chesnutt, C. W. The house behind the cedars
  Hadley, T. Everything will be all right
  Haigh, J. Mrs. Kimble
  Hoffman, A. The probable future
  King, R. A girl from Zanzibar
  Manicka, R. The rice mother
  Read, P. P. Alice in exile
  Vera, Y. The stone virgins
  Wallach, J. Seraglio
Employment
  Weisberger, L. The Devil wears Prada
  Wilcox, J. Heavenly days
Psychology
  Ashley, R. Someplace like this
  Delinsky, B. Flirting with Pete
  Duisberg, K. W. The good patient
  Emmons, C. His mother's son
  French, N. Land of the living
  Gowdy, B. The romantic
  Hoffman, E. The secret
  Lipman, E. The pursuit of Alice Thrift
  Pearson, A. I don't know how she does it
  Robinson, R. Sweetwater
  Shigekuni, J. Invisible gardens
  Solomon, N. Single wife
  Updike, J. Seek my face
  Vanderbes, J. Easter Island
  Wolitzer, M. The wife
Relation to other women
  Heller, Z. What was she thinking?
  Jaffe, R. The room-mating season
  Schwarz, C. All is vanity
Social conditions
  Brink, A. P. The other side of silence
  Llywelyn, M. 1949
WOMEN ANTHROPOLOGISTS
  Gruber, M. Tropic of night
WOMEN ARTISTS
  Barker, P. Double vision
  Meyer, C. Brown eyes blue
  Palahniuk, C. Diary
WOMEN AUTHORS
  Coetzee, J. M. Elizabeth Costello
  Hay, E. Garbo laughs
  Morton, B. A window across the river

WOMEN CLERGY
  Basch, R. The passion of Reverend Nash
WOMEN EDITORS
  Carey, P. My life as a fake
  Weisberger, L. The Devil wears Prada
WOMEN IN BUSINESS *See* Businesswomen
WOMEN JOURNALISTS
  Updike, J. Seek my face
WOMEN LAWYERS
  O'Shaughnessy, P. Presumption of death
  Pottinger, S. The last Nazi
WOMEN PAINTERS
  Updike, J. Seek my face
WOMEN PHYSICIANS
  Emmons, C. His mother's son
  Lee, M. The canal house
  Lipman, E. The pursuit of Alice Thrift
WOMEN POETS
  Jong, E. Sappho's leap
WOMEN SCIENTISTS
  Perdue, L. Slatewiper
  Vanderbes, J. Easter Island
  Wilson, R. C. Blind Lake
Wonder when you'll miss me. Davis, A.
WORLD WAR, 1914-1918
  Itani, F. Deafening
England
  Perry, A. No graves as yet
WORLD WAR, 1939-1945
  Loo, T. de. A bed in heaven
Aerial operations
  Spencer, J. The pilots
Atrocities
  See also Holocaust, Jewish (1933-1945)
Jews
  See also Holocaust, Jewish (1933-1945)
Underground movements
  Follett, K. Hornet flight
Australia
  Keneally, T. Office of innocence
Denmark
  Follett, K. Hornet flight
England
  Follett, K. Hornet flight
France
  Carter, V. O. Such sweet thunder
Germany
  Grass, G. Crabwalk
  Pye, M. The pieces from Berlin
Pacific Ocean
  Spencer, J. The pilots
Russia
  Gordimer, N. Karma
  Robbins, D. L. The last citadel
WOUNDS AND INJURIES
  Laskowski, T. Every good boy does fine
WRITERS *See* Authors
WYKEHAM, WILLIAM OF *See* William, of Wykeham, Bishop of Winchester, 1324-1404

Y

YORKSHIRE (ENGLAND) *See* England—Yorkshire

You look nice today. Bing, S.
Your mouth is lovely. Richler, N.
YOUTH
> *See also* Adolescence; Boys; Girls

Freda, J. The patience of rivers
Weber, K. The little women

Z

ZAIRE
Edric, R. The book of the heathen

Ziff. Lelchuk, A.
ZIMBABWE
Vera, Y. The stone virgins
ZIONISM
Wilson, J. A Palestine affair
ZURICH (SWITZERLAND) *See* Switzerland—Zurich